An American First

An American First

John T. Flynn and the America First Committee

Michele Flynn Stenehjem

75-37622

ARLINGTON HOUSE·PUBLISHERS
NEW ROCHELLE, NEW YORK

Manufactured in the United States of America

Library of Congress Cataloging in Publication Data

Stenehjem, Michele Flynn.
  An American first.

  Bibliography: p.
  Includes index.
  1. America First Committee. 2. World War, 1939–
1945—United States. 3. United States—Neutrality.
4. Flynn, John Thomas, 1883–1964. I. Title.
D753.S74   322.4   75-37622
ISBN 0-87000-339-9

For Erik, Mother, and Dad,
Who cared enough to make me try

CONTENTS

PREFACE

The America First Committee (AFC) has generally been viewed as an expression of conservative, Midwestern, agrarian isolationism. Yet the committee contained an added dimension. The New York chapter (NYC-AFC), headquarters for the entire Northeastern wing of the America First movement, was decidedly heterogeneous, urbane, and sophisticated in both its composition and its practices. Chaired by economic analyst and journalist John Thomas Flynn, the NYC-AFC included prominent writers, professors, Socialists, and many other philosophical antiwar advocates. The business community in New York, unlike its counterparts in various areas of the Midwest, was particularly reluctant to become involved with the AFC. Previous studies of America First overlook the unique character of the committee's Northeastern flank and thus fail to present a complete picture of the movement to prevent war in 1940 and 1941. Likewise, the only major analysis to date of John Thomas Flynn does not carefully examine the New York journalist's extensive and innovative role as NYC-AFC leader.

The only Ph.D. dissertation written until now on the America First Committee stresses the composition and actions of the organization's Chicago national headquarters and the numerous small chapters within a three-hundred-mile radius of it. This 1952 study, *America First: The Battle Against Interventionism, 1940–41,* by Wayne Cole, deals only sketchily with chapter organization itself, declaring simply that each local unit "was free to wage its own battle against intervention providing it adhered to the general prin-

9

ciples and policies of the America First Committee."[1] Cole also fails to substantiate with concrete data on congressional voting patterns, public opinion polls, and other indicators several of his conclusions regarding committee strength and effectiveness. Four years later Cole added to his work on the AFC by publishing an article entitled "America First and the South, 1940–41."[2] In this piece he explains the almost total failure of the committee to organize in the South on the bases of traditional Southern pride in the military, pro-British sentiment in the region because of Anglo-Saxon stock, political loyalty to the Democratic Party, and the role of defense spending in aiding the South's troubled economy. Like his book, however, Cole's article does not analyze the liberal, progressive roots of non-interventionism in the Northeast.

The only work written to date on John T. Flynn is a doctoral dissertation completed in 1969 by Richard Clark Frey, Jr. Entitled "John T. Flynn and the United States in Crisis, 1928–50," this study covers nearly all of Flynn's productive, adult lifetime.[3] Only one chapter is devoted to the America First experience. No analysis is offered concerning the composition or processes of the NYC-AFC itself, and Flynn's role as chairman is confined to a few highlighted rallies and speaking engagements. Although Frey does note Flynn's wartime frustration at not being able to find a suitable publisher for his articles blaming President Roosevelt for the Japanese attack on Pearl Harbor, the Oregon scholar does not view the America First episode as being seminal in shaping Flynn's subsequent values and beliefs.

The present analysis will offer primarily a careful, detailed consideration of the nature and complexion of the New York chapter of the America First Committee. The chapter's founding, leadership, financial backing, and role in battling the major foreign policy issues of 1941 will be examined. The study will then shift to thematic explorations of the controversial question of anti-Semitism and pro-fascism within the NYC-AFC, and the development of a conspiracy theory of war involvement in the minds of Flynn and some other chapter leaders. Last, the effects of the America First experience on John Flynn's later years, and on the history of the United States, will be scrutinized. The NYC-AFC registered an articulate and reasoned protest not only against the specific policy of war, but also against the general drift toward excessive power and secrecy in the executive branch of the United States government. More than thirty years after the committee disbanded these protests are being accorded by

10

some historians more credibility than they were given in 1940 and 1941.

The chief sources examined in the pursuit of this inquiry were the America First Committee Papers, located in the Hoover Institution on War, Revolution and Peace at Stanford, California, and the John Thomas Flynn Papers, in the University of Oregon Library at Eugene. The Norman Thomas Papers, residing in the New York Public Library in New York City, and the Amos R. E. Pinchot Papers, in the Library of Congress in Washington, D.C., were also consulted. Another useful source was "A Story of America First," a 1942 manuscript prepared by Ruth Sarles, an official of the AFC Washington research bureau.[4] Sarles' own intimate knowledge of the 1940–41 issues and the processes of America First operations, as well as her ability to convey the emotional climate of the period, rendered her work invaluable.

Additional sources consulted were the published books and articles of John T. Flynn and several other participants in the Great Debate of 1941, numerous items in various New York newspapers, the *Congressional Record, Public Opinion Quarterly,* and various secondary sources. Two masters' theses, "The America First Committee: A Study in Recent American Non-Interventionism" by Morris Burns Stanley, and "The Emergence of Anti-Semitism in the America First Committee, 1940–41" by Bart Lanier Stafford III, were consulted, but the conclusions reached in these studies are quite different from those advanced by the author of the current study.[5] Very helpful personal letters were received from Robert D. Stuart, Jr., AFC national executive director; Burton K. Wheeler, former senator and prominent America First supporter; Walter Trohan, close Flynn associate and newspaper correspondent for several years during the 1930s and 1940s; Mrs. Katherine Swim, wife of NYC-AFC treasurer H. Dudley Swim; Peter Cusick, official of the interventionist Fight for Freedom Committee in New York City; Hamilton Fish, Jr., son of the AFC's most vociferous champion in the House of Representatives; Justus D. Doenecke, anti–New Deal historian; and Dr. Wayne S. Cole. Personal interviews were also conducted in Chicago with Robert D. Stuart, Jr.; in New York City with Thomas D. Flynn, John Flynn's son; Rosalie M. Gordon, John Flynn's research assistant of many years; and Robert L. Bliss, ranking NYC-AFC staff member; and by telephone with Page Hufty, America First national committee official.

11

I

Introduction

The idea of America First took form during the spring of 1940, when Adolf Hitler was sending his armies into Denmark, Norway, Belgium, Holland, and France. At that time, American interventionists were organizing the Committee to Defend America by Aiding the Allies (the CDAAA). The phenomenal success of the CDAAA, which established over six hundred local branches within a few months, as well as the prevalent talk by national leaders that the United States must send all possible aid "short of war" to England in order to save itself from becoming Hitler's next victim, concerned a group of law students at Yale University. Many of these students were Reserve Army officers; none was a pacifist. They met regularly to discuss their belief that America was "ambling, unawares, toward a precipice," and they began sending petitions pledging this country to stay out of Europe's conflicts to friends on other Eastern college campuses. When the petitions were hurriedly returned overflowing with names and demands for still more petitions, the Yale men "brushed the amazement from their eyes."[1] They realized that they might have struck a groundswell of popular opinion, and decided to take more definitive steps.

The students were led by Robert Douglas Stuart, Jr., son of the vice president of the Quaker Oats Company. Stuart, a 1937 graduate of Princeton University in the field of government and international relations, was convinced by his studies that "the U.S. had gained nothing and lost a great deal through participation in World War I."[2] He spent the year after his college graduation traveling in Europe, and entered law school in the fall of 1938, hoping to work for the

13

National Labor Relations Board after graduation. Although he did not agree with every aspect of the New Deal's economic program, he was "generally supportive [of it], and my father would have said I was a 'New Dealer.' "[3] Stuart's intense involvement with the America First Committee during the latter half of 1940 and throughout 1941, and then his term as an army artillery major in Europe, interrupted his education. He returned to Yale to complete his law degree in 1946.[4]

During the summer of 1940, Stuart began the actual formation of the America First Committee, which he originally called the Emergency Committee to Defend America First. He attended both the Democratic and the Republican national conventions to enlist the support of prominent national figures. He spoke to persons representing as wide a philosophical swath as progressive Democratic Senator Burton K. Wheeler of Montana and conservative Republican Senator Robert A. Taft of Ohio. Stuart also sent letters to distinguished businessmen throughout the country and held a luncheon for interested leading Chicagoans on July 22. At the same time he obtained a small area of rent-free office space in the Quaker Oats section of the Chicago Board of Trade Building.[5]

In mid-July, as a result of an exchange of letters between Stuart and retired U.S. Army General Robert E. Wood, who was a friend of Stuart's father, Wood accepted the position of temporary chairman of the AFC.[6] Although he considered resigning several times, he remained as chairman until the dissolution of the committee. Sixty-one years old in 1940, Wood had graduated from West Point and had served in the U.S. Army during the Philippine Insurrection. From 1905 to 1915, he had been chief quartermaster and then director of the Panama Canal. Interrupting the business career he had entered upon in 1915, Wood served in World War I and emerged as a brigadier general. He then became acting quartermaster general of the United States from 1918 to 1919. He held several military medals and was a chevalier (knight) in the French Legion of Honor. Vice president of Sears, Roebuck and Company from 1924 to 1928, president from 1929 to 1939, he had been chairman of the board ever since. During the America First experience, Wood also served on the boards of directors of several other large corporations and of the National Association of Manufacturers.[7]

Wood had a record of unblemished integrity in his military and business careers, and John Flynn, chairman of the New York chapter of the America First Committee (NYC-AFC), was convinced that the prestige and stability of Wood's name were "precisely" what the fledgling AFC needed.[8] William Benton, vice president of the University of Chicago and leading AFC spokesman during 1940–41, has revealed that Wood did not want the responsibilities of the committee chairmanship. The old general accepted, however, because of the "idealism and enthusiasm and . . . starry eyes and patriotism" of Stuart and his friends. "How could I turn those nice young men down?" Wood once asked.[9] According to Charles Augustus Lindbergh, famous aviator and AFC national committee member, everyone associated with the America First movement liked Wood. Lindbergh described him as "one of the keenest and ablest men I have ever met—a fine mind and a wonderful character."[10]

Although Wood had approved of several early New Deal reforms, he began with the Undistributed Corporate Profits Tax Bill of 1935 to disapprove of Franklin Roosevelt, and he broke with the President finally in 1940 over foreign policy. Wood definitely was a conservative, as were most of the members of the AFC national committee. Indeed, approximately three-fourths of this body, as well as the entire executive committee, came from the traditionally conservative and isolationist Midwest.[11] One of the most vitriolic attacks ever made against the AFC accused the committee of having an overwhelmingly conservative bias. Samuel Grafton, frequent contributor to the liberal *New Republic,* wrote in that magazine in January 1941 that "it would be hard to find in American life a group more devoted . . . to various versions of yesterday than the roster of the America First Committee. . . . [They] are all men who feel that . . . nothing is wrong with America except its aggravating desire for social reform. . . . Those who fear the future are not anxious to help a neighbor [England] fight for it."[12]

Grafton's criticism was unfair. A strong minority of liberals* and progressives, led by journalist John Thomas Flynn, served to coun-

*The term *liberal* is used here in its Brandeisian sense. John Flynn and many other America Firsters believed that government should regulate business by preventing monopolies and cartels from controlling large sectors of the economy. However, Flynn and his colleagues did not think that the government itself should become a large economic power. This condition would restrict individual freedom, which was the essence of their definition of liberalism. In these views, they supported a school of thought advanced by Woodrow Wilson and his ideological advisor Louis Brandeis. Flynn and his colleagues rejected Franklin D. Roosevelt's brand of liberalism, in which the government entered the economic community as a large employer and customer. This condition, they believed, left no room for individual freedom. For a more detailed explanation of Flynn's view of liberalism, see Chapter 2, especially page 28.

terbalance the conservative tendencies of the AFC national committee. Many America First decisions, especially in the latter half of 1941, were changed or blunted by the vigorous presence of Flynn and other liberals.[13] The New York area generally sent representatives to the national committee who either were not members of the business community or were among the more liberal and progressive segment of the America First movement. Such was the case with ten of the fifteen national committee members from the Northeast. Businessmen in New York were among the hardest America Firsters to recruit.[14]

Ironically, however, Thomas N. McCarter, the first person to join the AFC national committee from the Northeast, was a businessman and a conservative. McCarter was chairman of the boards of directors of the Public Service Corporation of New Jersey, and the Fidelity Trust Company of Newark.[15] Other businessmen from the New York area who eventually served on the AFC national committee were Edward Rickenbacker, World War I flying ace who in 1940–41 was president of Eastern Airlines; Robert Ralph Young, multimillionaire railroad magnate and chairman of the board of directors of the Allegheny Corporation; and Edwin Sibley Webster, Jr., senior partner in the Wall Street investment firm of Kidder, Peabody and Company. Mrs. Ellen French Vanderbilt FitzSimons, Republican national committeewoman from Rhode Island; and Charles Lindbergh, resident of Long Island and Martha's Vineyard during 1940–41, were additional Northeastern conservatives on the national committee.[16]

The strong liberal contingent in the America First Committee resulted from a deliberate attempt to broaden the organization's appeal. Taking the initiative was Kingman Brewster, Jr., editor of the *Yale Daily News,* who contacted his friend Stuart in July 1940. Following a Brewster suggestion, Stuart importuned Progressive Governor Philip La Follette of Wisconsin to join America First. Though La Follette was sympathetic to the AFC's aims, he rejected the invitation. His main reason was that his political coalition in Wisconsin, based as it was on domestic concerns, might disintegrate over foreign policy.[17] However, La Follette did agree to write several of his liberal and progressive friends throughout the nation and urge them to serve. The first persons he contacted in the New York area were Flynn and Oswald Garrison Villard, the famous old "dean of America liberals" and former editor of the *Nation.* Both agreed to serve in August 1940.[18] Others would soon follow the example of Flynn and Villard. Among them were Amos Pinchot, liberal publicist; Chester Bowles, head of the Madison Avenue advertising firm of Benton and Bowles, Inc., but a liberal in his personal and political convictions; and Samuel Hopkins Adams, Academy Award-winning playwright and member of the executive committee of the National Consumers' League. However, the liberal contingent always remained a minority on the AFC national committee, which began with twenty-one members and never grew to more than thirty-five at any time.[19]

The AFC national committee first announced itself in a press release of September 4, 1940. One month later it opened its national advertising campaign with a *New York Times* advertisement titled "PEACE at Home or WAR Abroad? Snap Out of It America! You Can Decide if You Act Now!"[20] With the publication of this advertisement the interventionist-noninterventionist "Great Debate of 1941" officially began. For another month the AFC waged the battle against war solely through radio speeches and additional advertisements, but then it adopted a wholly new approach. It had received so much mail from people across the country asking what they could do specifically to support the antiwar cause that, on November 12, the AFC decided to form local chapters and to seek an active, public membership. At this point Flynn, who had been a nominal member only, decided to take a more active role in the committee.[21]

What was the groundswell of popular opinion that Robert Douglas Stuart and his fellow students had touched? What were the principles and program, expressed by the AFC, that had such a tremendous appeal to grassroots America? The committee began with four simple principles and an equal number of objectives. The principles espoused an "impregnable" national defense for America, a belief that no nation or group of nations could successfully attack a defensively prepared America, a conviction that this nation's democracy and civil liberties could be preserved only by keeping out of the European war, and a view that aid "short of war" to any other nation would weaken national defense at home and threaten to involve the United States, step by step, in war abroad. The objectives were to bring together and to provide national leadership and focus for all Americans of all strata and beliefs who wanted to keep their country out of war (specifically excluding American Nazis, fascists, Communists, and members of the German-American Bund), to urge Americans to keep their heads amid rising war hysteria, and to register noninterventionist opinion with the President and Congress.[22]

On December 9, 1940, a fifth principle was added, which stated

17

that the United States should provide "humanitarian aid" to Britain and to the occupied countries of the continent of Europe within the limits of America's neutrality and with proper safeguards in the distribution of the food and supplies.[23] This principle led the AFC to endorse the efforts of former President Herbert Hoover's National Committee on Food for the Small Democracies. It also brought much criticism from officials of both the United States and the British governments, since a major part of English strategy to defeat Hitler involved blockading and starving his occupied areas.[24]

Two additional principles, dealing with the constitutional issue of which branch of government possessed war-making powers, were incorporated in mid-1941. Many America First leaders had long believed that Roosevelt was waging an undeclared, "back door" war by executive fiat. Amos Pinchot, shortly after the President announced the American occupation of Iceland in July, best expressed the committee's fears when he told Lindbergh: "Allowing a President to get us into conflict on his own hook [that is, to wage an undeclared war] is a monstrous proposition. . . . If we do this we are striding, in one tragic step, into totalitarianism. We are putting ourselves into exactly the position in which the populations of Russia and Germany find themselves."[25] Consequently, the sixth AFC principle urged an official advisory referendum by the people on the question of war and peace.[26] The seventh principle, even more explicit, declared that the Constitution vested the sole war-making power in Congress, and that until that body had voted on the war question, every citizen should write to his representative and senators expressing his views.[27] The committee adopted both in hopes of driving a wedge between Roosevelt and the Congress, and of pushing the legislative branch into asserting itself.

These seven America First principles provided the skeletal framework for thoughtful American noninterventionism of the period. Far from being a mindless, head-in-the-sand isolationism, the noninterventionism of the AFC could be, and was, defended in an articulate and philosophically consistent manner. America Firsters rejected the term *isolationism* as pejorative. Lindbergh liked to say that he favored an "independent destiny" for the United States; most other committee leaders simply called themselves "noninterventionists."[28] John Flynn best explained the AFC's distaste for the isolationist label when he stated: "I prefer [the term] . . . noninterventionist [because] I am against intervening in this war, but I am not against action between the United States and other countries . . . to improve the economic condition of the world."[29]

18

Underlying the committee principles was the conviction that the conflagration in Europe was simply another of that Continent's incessant, jealous quarrels. Barbara MacDonald, head of the AFC National Speakers' Bureau, prepared a portfolio of useful facts to help committee orators prime for questions. In one folder, she pointed out that over the past five hundred years, Spain had been at war sixty-seven percent of the time, England fifty-six percent, France fifty percent, Russia forty-six percent, and Prussia and the German principalities twenty-eight percent. Americans deciding on their relationship to the current war should remember, MacDonald said, that their ancestors had founded this nation partly in order to leave behind Europe's chronic turbulence.[30]

America Firsters believed that England was fighting merely to preserve her overseas empire from Germany, who wished to compete for empire. Edward Reisner, professor of education and NYC-AFC sponsoring committee member, told a Columbia University conference in July 1941 that "that war [in Europe] is not a crusade of the noble and good against the evil forces of this world, but a wicked, useless war entered into as the outcome of . . . selfishness and material ambition."[31] James P. Selvage, a New York advertising executive who occasionally designed copy for the AFC, referred to the war as "a poker game of European power politics."[32] Stuart himself once revealed that his primary motive in founding the committee was his belief that "what turned out to be World War II was simply a renewal of the same nationalistic struggles [that had caused World War I] with the only difference being the new emotional issues . . . [of] anti-Semitism."[33]

At least one influential AFC leader, General Wood, was much impressed by a 1938 book, *Save America First*, by Jerome N. Frank, member and later chairman of the Securities and Exchange Commission.[34] In this book, a rambling treatise advancing solutions for the Great Depression, Frank claimed that England throughout its history deliberately had promoted economic and political anarchy in Europe in order to prevent any strong bloc from emerging to compete for empire. The result of Britain's actions had been a "disintegrating, centrifugal" tendency to promote intra-European wars. These wars, Frank argued, would continue and would solve nothing until the states of Europe learned what the states of America had learned during the period of the Confederation, and formed one federal nation. Therefore, the United States should not be deceived into thinking that one side or the other in these conflicts held liberty, democracy, or progress in its cause. Instead, America should preserve itself and set an example of civilization and liberty for foolhardy Europe.[35]

Charles Lindbergh also agreed with Frank. The aviator was often criticized, especially by members of the Roosevelt Administration, for his forthright statements concerning England's and France's motives in attacking the marauding Hitler in 1939.[36] Lindbergh was convinced that American involvement in World War I, with its guarantee of total victory for the Allies, merely had postponed a fair, realistic, and accommodating arrangement among the powers of Europe. The punitive Versailles treaty allowed the greed and cynicism of the European victors to reign temporarily, and ensured further struggles. "No one," the flier charged, "not even Germany, was more responsible for the conditions that caused this war [World War II] than England and France. . . . If we enter it, we will do no good either to Europe or to ourselves. . . . Europe must straighten out her own family affairs."[37]

The AFC held other uncomplimentary beliefs regarding England. That country was not as desperate for money and matériel as it styled itself, committee leaders asserted. Instead, Britain was taking advantage of a generous but uninformed America. As an ally, the island country was a liability, and the famed Royal Navy was a "luxury, not an indispensability" to American defense.[38] Lindbergh was dismayed to learn in October 1941, from his friend Harold Bixby, director of Pan American Airlines, that the British were competing with Pan American for a commercial concession to a route over Africa. This route had been given to the American company in order that it might ferry military planes under the Lend-Lease plan to the British army in Africa. "Much as they may need the planes for their fighting forces," Lindbergh stated wryly, "the British can still take time out to make a good trade."[39] Barbara MacDonald told AFC speakers in early 1941 to ask their audiences: "How good an ally would Britain be? . . . If we entered the war now . . . and the English fell anyway . . . we might very well suffer what military men call 'defeat in detail,' that is, a defeat far away . . . that seriously impairs our capacity to defend our main position."[40]

In addition to its beliefs concerning England and the basic nature of the European war in 1940–41, the AFC had its own estimates of Hitler's military and economic capabilities. The committee insisted that the German dictator lacked the capacity to invade the geographically isolated United States (as long as this country was prepared defensively), even if he conquered all of Europe and achieved a power base in South America. The nearly impassable jungle and mountain terrain of Central America would prevent a conquest from that direction.[41] A 1941 book by businessman Douglas Miller, entitled *You Can't Do Business with Hitler,* sparked a vigorous public debate when it stated that Germany, if victorious in large areas of Europe, Latin America, and Asia, could ruin the American economy by strangling international trade.[42] The AFC maintained that an "enlarged Germany" would be forced to import even more food and raw materials, and discover even larger export markets for her manufactures, than the current Germany. Therefore, concluded an August 1941 committee pamphlet, "an enlarged Germany . . . would be in no position to dictate the terms on which she would trade."[43]

The discussion of Hitler's possible world economic dominance became a favorite one for AFC speakers. Barbara MacDonald counseled them to point out that only 5 percent of America's national income was derived from export trade. "Therefore," she asserted, "we are very close to a position of saying 'take it or leave it.' " As for imports, MacDonald continued, "we are the greatest raw material market in the world, and Hitler would only be cutting off his nose to spite his face if he successfully withheld raw materials from us." Noting that the United States could manufacture synthetic rubber, and could use silver and aluminum as substitutes for tin if Malaysian raw materials were forbidden, MacDonald concluded that "there is no raw material so indispensable that we need fight outside this hemisphere for it."[44] Amos Pinchot found the entire question of Hitler's possible economic prepotency moot. "To say that we should go to war with another nation," he stated confidently, "because, in the future, that nation may prove a powerful competitor in foreign trade is an absurdity. This country with its vast integrated natural resources, its inventive genius and free competitive industry will be able to overproduce and undersell any country, especially one whose economy is regimented by bureaucrats and held down by the dead hand of the state."[45]

Other beliefs also contributed to the AFC's confidence in the non-interventionist position. The committee, although it did not make a major issue of this point, declared that America was goading an unwilling Japan into war. "In modern history only the United States is inclined toward romantic crusades," an America First pamphlet stated satirically. "Japan is not a romantic nation, she is not going to pull Germany's chestnuts from the fire. . . . Any war with Japan . . . will be . . . of our own forcing."[46] The AFC privately favored the

21

impeachment of Roosevelt because of his alleged breach of peace pledges made in the 1940 presidential campaign. It did not call for this openly because committee leaders feared that such a demand would give the group a partisan appearance.[47]

America Firsters also privately wanted the United States to exert its influence in favor of a negotiated peace in Europe. Total war, they believed, would exhaust the victors and vanquished alike, and thus cause further world economic collapse and bitterness. Committee spokesmen refrained from offering this opinion publicly, however, because they felt it was futile given Roosevelt's strong feelings on the subject, and because they were sure that calls for a negotiated peace would bring an appeasement label to their group.[48] In December 1940 President Roosevelt stated his views clearly: "Is it a negotiated peace if a gang of outlaws surrounds your community and on threat of extermination makes you pay tribute to save your own skins? . . . Nonsense!"[49] Following this pronouncement, most America Firsters realized that only a stalemate in the war could bring an equitable, negotiated peace.

Such, then, was the philosophical "package" that the AFC embodied. A frequent criticism of the movement charged that it only opposed the ideas and goals of others, but had no constructive program of its own. This assessment was generally accurate, although the committee was planning a positive, new program at the time of the Pearl Harbor attack.[50] Nevertheless, the noticeable lack of open, affirmative goals throughout most of the organization's lifetime must be seen as a consequence of the extreme diversity of the membership. Multiformity, above all, characterized the America First Committee. Charles Lindbergh underlined the problem of positive goals for such a heterogeneous group when he said: "We would break up in an instant on almost any other issue [than noninterventionism]."[51] In 1943, when John Flynn was approached by a New York woman, Jessica Forbes, suggesting a revival of the committee, he reaffirmed Lindbergh's judgment. "I think you would find," Flynn told Forbes, "that the people who supported the America First movement . . . hold many differing views on the postwar world."[52]

Indeed, the AFC embraced an ideological spread that stretched from socialists to conservative industrial magnates to the philosophically uncommitted. Socialists and liberals feared that war would destroy the social gains of the past forty years and end democratic attempts to solve America's economic ills. Also they did not want to see America fight to defend what they saw as foreign imperialism. Industrialists predicted that war would create dictatorship and annul the profit system in the United States. Many ordinary citizens in the committee simply did not want to see their sons, husbands, and brothers sent away to fight and die. In addition to these people, the AFC contained extremely practical people who knew that America was dreadfully unprepared militarily, strict constitutionalists who felt that Roosevelt was seizing too much power for the executive branch, and internationalists who feared that full participation in the war would weaken the United States' chances for leadership of the postwar world.[53]

The diversity of the America First movement was seen by at least one of its leaders as one of the group's most constructive accomplishments. Ruth Sarles, official in the AFC Washington research bureau and later committee historian, termed America First "a rebellion against the label ideology that has colored the American scene for the last fifteen years . . . a declaration of individualism against the growing American habit of classification. . . . America First showed that it was possible for individuals and groups of diametrically opposed political, social and economic views to work together" for a common cause.[54] Wood agreed with Sarles, and called the committee "the greatest 'common denominator' mass action the country has ever known."[55]

The America First Committee began among a group of concerned graduate students at Yale University. When these students discovered that their desire to avoid war was shared by many Americans, they contacted prominent national leaders and established a formal vehicle for expressing their views. The national committee that they assembled was primarily conservative, but was supplemented by a strong liberal minority consisting primarily of Northeasterners. The noninterventionist philosophy that the AFC embodied was coherent and logically consistent, and was embraced by the fifteen to twenty million America First members for a wide variety of reasons. Perhaps John Flynn best expressed the spirit of most committee supporters regarding their hybrid group. Denying a charge that the AFC was merely an anti-New Deal "front-group," Flynn affirmed: "I will work with any good American [excluding American Nazis, fascists, Communists, and Bund members], whatever his . . . philosophy, who wants to save this country from war."[56]

23

2

A Philosophy for a Man, and a Beginning for a Chapter

Let me tell you what war will do for us. The flags will fly, the national anthems will ring out, the boys in their new uniforms will march down our bright avenues. . . . Millions of these boys will be taken from their classrooms, their professions, their workbenches. . . . A half million will die. A million may be wounded and a vast, melancholy legion of them will live out long, tortured, frustrated lives in veterans' hospitals. . . .

Every man, woman and child . . . will have to pay the incalculable costs of this mad adventure. . . . Taxes will consume your earnings and cripple your business. . . . A great army of bureaucrats will help to manage every man's affairs. . . . You will spend half your time seeking permits, getting visas, answering questions, making reports and satisfying the thousand and one demands of the supervisors. . . . The gains of labor, the long, painfully acquired right of the worker in his job and his union will be swept away. . . . The apologists for all this will tell you that this is a "new order." But it will be nothing more than the twilight of American democracy. . . .

And when the war is over and the terrible bills come due and the illusions have fallen from our eyes, we will look around for some scapegoats. . . . Amidst these disorders we will have the perfect climate for some promising Hitler on the American model to rise to power with promises of abundance and recovery. The peace, the security, the liberties of a whole generation will be destroyed. And we, who set out once again on a fool's errand to remodel the world . . . will see it [democracy] pass out of our own country.[1]

JOHN T. FLYNN (March 8, 1941)

The views held by John T. Flynn in 1940–41, developed through a long career in journalism and sharpened during the first eight years of Franklin Roosevelt's New Deal, constitute perhaps the most cogent illustration of the liberal aspects of immediate, pre–World War II American noninterventionism. Flynn first expressed his opinion on the "gathering storm" of the late 1930s in his capacity as national chairman of the small, liberal, and pacifistic Keep America Out of War Congress (KAOWC). When this relatively elite and intellectual group failed to generate a popular uprising against war, he became convinced that only a mass movement uniting diverse people on a few basic principles could produce a significant change in American foreign policy. "The America First movement seemed to satisfy [those conditions] . . . and it was for this reason that I was willing to give my time and effort to the committee," he later explained.[2] As Flynn proceeded to organize the "citadel of interventionism," the New York area, he had both to take cognizance of the special conditions and pressures surrounding the war issue in the Northeast, and to attempt to secure the backing of prominent business leaders. When the business community in New York proved too recalcitrant, Flynn shouldered the burden as America First Committee chapter chairman.[3]

John T. Flynn was a man of physical and mental vigor. The AFC executive director Robert D. Stuart once described him as "a person of limitless energy who constantly undertakes more than any one human being can do."[4] Flynn's trim, medium build and his boyishly thick, iron gray hair bespoke his wiry and sprightly animation. Others who knew him best have described most often his quick and colorful wit and his ability as a writer and an economic analyst. He has been called "ruddy . . . volatile . . . strong willed and hot tempered but reasonable and factual in debate . . . an American Hilaire Belloc . . . a brilliant conversationalist and writer . . . the possessor of one of the finest minds I have ever met and a joyous sense of humor."[5] Robert L. Bliss, a high official of the New York Chapter of the America First Committee, recalled admiringly that "you learned something [most often about economics] every time he [Flynn] opened his mouth . . . but he wasn't stuffy. The whole office loved him."[6] Even a virulent opponent in the Great Debate of 1941 recently called Flynn a "decent nice fellow . . . a true isolationist."[7]

Flynn was born on October 25, 1882, in the Washington suburb of Bladensburg, Maryland, to John and Margaret O'Donnell Flynn. The son of an attorney, Flynn was educated first in the public schools of Bladensburg, and later in the parochial schools of New York City. His Irish, Roman Catholic background was used often during 1940–41 by interventionists seeking to discredit him. They called him an "Irish lion-baiter," and an "eternal Hibernian in eruption," and implied that he favored noninterventionism because he was anti-British. Flynn answered these charges by scoffing, "That I may be animated by an interest in my own country is not conceded to me by these critics."[8]

Flynn never attended college, but graduated from Georgetown Law School a few years after the turn of the century. One of his favorite pastimes as a law student was listening to the debates on nearby Capitol Hill. As a member of the audience on January 9, 1900, at the famous Beveridge-Hoar Senate debate on the question of retention of the Philippines, Flynn formed his early and persistent belief that imperialism led to war, and that neither should be pursued as an instrument of national policy.[9] Despite his degree, Flynn never practiced law. He worked as a clerk in his father's office for a short time after graduation, but was always interested in becoming a writer. In 1910 Flynn married Alice Bell and moved to the West Coast. Unable to obtain a journalistic post, however, he returned to New York in 1916 with his wife and two young sons, John Jr. and Thomas.[10]

Flynn began his writing career in 1916 with the *New Haven Register,* and became city editor within a year. He served in that position for two years, and then worked as editor and managing editor of the *New York Globe* from 1920 to 1923. Following the *Globe's* demise in 1923, he turned to freelance writing. Eventually he authored nearly fifteen books on business, economics, and politics, among the most well known of which were *Graft in Business, God's Gold— Story of Rockefeller and His Times, Country Squire in the White House, As We Go Marching, The Roosevelt Myth,* and *The Road Ahead.*[11]

Flynn's widespread notice as a liberal journalist came from a column titled "Other People's Money," which he wrote for the *New Republic* from 1933 until November 1940. For several years he also wrote as a Scripps-Howard syndicated columnist. His series, "Plain Economics," appeared in the *New York World-Telegram,* the *Washington Daily News* and other newspapers. From 1937 to 1941 Flynn served as associate editor of *Collier's* magazine, contributing numerous articles to various journals during this time. He was a member of the New York Press Club. He also served on the staff of the

27

Pecora Commission investigating the stock market in 1933, was economic adviser to the Nye Committee investigating World War I profits in 1934–35, lectured in contemporary economics at the New School for Social Research, New York City, in 1935–36, and from 1935 to 1944 was a Fiorello La Guardia appointee to the New York City Board of Higher Education.[12]

John Flynn never ran for political office, nor did he serve on any political committees, because he wanted to leave himself ideologically free "to throw bricks in any direction I choose."[13] He called himself a liberal all of his life, and he defined liberalism as "not so much a collection of beliefs as a character of the mind. It is not far removed from tolerance—not . . . for men but for ideas." A liberal rebelled against dogma in any form, and his most important quality, said Flynn, had to be "a willingness to examine the ideas of other men and to reexamine his own."[14]

Flynn did not believe in Herbert Hoover's brand of unrestrained capitalism, but he did not believe in socialism either. He wanted a regulated form of capitalism in which the government would enforce fair standards of competition and prevent monopolies, pools, holding companies, and other devices from distorting the market or the stock exchange.

Monopolies and other forms of economic concentration, he was convinced, would ultimately "develop the most complete barrier to new private investment that any dreamer of the capitalist catastrophe could hope for."[15] Flynn did not want the government to solve the monopoly problem by becoming an economic power itself, however. When Samuel Grafton, interventionist contributor to the *New Republic,* charged in early 1941 that Flynn's economic philosophy amounted to nothing more than "an improved version of Teddy Roosevelt's antimonopoly campaign," Flynn was insulted. He termed Grafton's imputation a "nasty little lie."[16] Above all, Flynn desired a society wherein each individual would have as much freedom as possible, and would rise or fall on his own merits, without having avenues of success choked off by business conglomerates. If capitalism were to be preserved, he said in 1931, liberal leaders would have to move beyond the Jeffersonian position, take cognizance of the development of cartels and trusts, and actively work with government to make the economic system behave "as a social economy rather than a racket."[17]

In his later years (post–World War II) Flynn became, in effect, a conservative, although he believed himself to be a liberal betrayed,

28

or a liberal without a party.[18] The change in his lifetime philosophy was inextricably bound up with Franklin Roosevelt's long presidency, and especially with American involvement in World War II. As the New Deal progressed, old definitions and principles seemed to Flynn to become mixed and meaningless propaganda. In 1940, looking back at Roosevelt's 1932 election and the Hundred Days of 1933, Flynn termed the New Deal a "promising adventure," which he had welcomed and had been willing to aid in every possible way in making "realizable reforms." However, he now viewed Roosevelt with "unmixed dismay . . . and a sense of betrayal." The New Deal, he claimed, made a "shocking descent . . . into the most ancient and degrading forms of reaction. . . . I see the standard of liberalism that I have followed all of my life flying over a group of causes which, as a liberal. . . . I have abhorred all of my life."[19] By 1950, Flynn was even more negative. He wrote that the greatest calamity that ever befell the United States occurred in 1880, when Franklin Roosevelt's parents married![20]

What caused this great transformation in Flynn's opinion? He explained in 1940 that several of his friends had warned him against voting for Roosevelt in 1932, but that, at the time, he saw him as the only viable alternative to the national disaster that Herbert Hoover was consummating.[21] Hoover, Flynn believed, had allowed the Great Depression to occur because he failed to restrain greedy monopolies, and especially because he did not regulate the stock market. Then the President compounded his errors by using the Reconstruction Finance Corporation to save large corporations and hopelessly bankrupt railroads, instead of helping small banks and businesses, and the average citizens.[22] On election eve in 1932, Flynn branded Hoover as a "spurious . . . pretended liberal," and stated, "I can hardly wait until tomorrow morning to get to the polls and smite the great Miracle Man."[23]

Flynn's initial support of the New Deal faded quickly. He grew disenchanted, first of all, because he objected to many of the people with whom Roosevelt chose to surround himself. Among the new President's appointments in 1933, Flynn was especially suspicious of William H. Woodin, designated secretary of the treasury. Woodin's name had been uncovered by the Pecora Commission as being on the House of Morgan's list of persons who could buy stocks below market prices. Flynn also was distrustful of the appointment of Dean Acheson, whose law partner was a Wall Street insider, as undersecretary of the treasury. When Earle Bailie, a partner in the firm of J. & W. Seligman and Company, which had been caught selling questionable South American securities, was named as special assistant to Woodin, Flynn's skepticism increased still further. He was shocked and outraged when in 1934 Joseph P. Kennedy, a Wall Street millionaire speculator, was made chairman of the Securities and Exchange Commission. When Kennedy retired from this post in September 1935, however, Flynn praised his fairness.[24]

Several of the New Deal programs, which Flynn believed favored big business, also caused him to deplore Roosevelt's presidency. No measure upset him more than the National Recovery Act of 1933. He saw the NRA codes of competition as the beginning of industrial fascism in America, not because they imposed planning, but because they evolved in practice not unlike the trade associations of the Harding-Coolidge era. In December 1933 Flynn proclaimed that "this New Deal . . . is a fraud. It is nothing else than the scheme which the Chamber of Commerce of the United States has been fighting for for twelve years—the modification of the Sherman Anti-Trust law and turning over the control of industry to the tender mercy of the trade associatons."[25]

Other New Deal measures caused Flynn to feel that the average consumer was not Roosevelt's first concern. He saw the Securities Exchange Act of 1934, which established the Securities and Exchange Commission, and the watered-down version of the war profits bill that passed Congress in the spring of 1935, as toothless compromises with Wall Street.[26] He viewed the Social Security Act of 1935 as laudable in principle, but questionable in practice, because it imposed high rates to build up a huge reserve fund. He became an active member of the American Association for Social Security, and as such, worked for revision of the law.[27]

Throughout 1935–36, Flynn became increasingly critical of Roosevelt's methods of financing New Deal spending projects. He did not oppose government spending as such. In fact, he felt that Roosevelt should spend more than he did on public works projects. However, Flynn believed that government money should come from current revenues, and that these funds should be built up by heavy taxes on those industries and persons that had usurped too large a share of America's income during the past forty years.[28] He opposed the raising of government revenues by deficit spending. He felt that eventually a steadily rising national debt would choke private investment by starving the small investor and causing income to be redistributed from the poor to the rich. He rejected the theory posed by Dr. Alvin Hansen of the Federal Reserve Board that the federal debt never need be paid off, since the interest on this debt went to millions of Americans as annual income in the form of dividends. Flynn pointed out that everyone in the nation was compelled to contribute taxes to pay the interest on the federal debt, but only a relatively small number of wealthy bank and insurance company stockholders received the interest on the debt as income.[29]

A final reason for Flynn's growing distrust of the New Deal during its first eight years concerned Roosevelt's personality. By 1940 Flynn had concluded that the President of the United States was dangerously unfit for his high office. Roosevelt's impulsive and experimental nature, combined with what Flynn felt was an innate militarism, made the journalist extremely apprehensive. Roosevelt, he said, "would put off action or decision on most things until driven to act, but might at any moment, without very much calculation . . . rush into some course or movement."[30] Flynn believed that to Roosevelt a political question was merely a difference of opinion between two men, and that if the men could be induced to compromise and shake hands, the issue could be solved. Consequently, Flynn was positive that the President, by surrounding himself with men representing widely divergent philosophies and by instituting the conceptual conglomerate of the New Deal agencies, displayed only madness and no method.[31]

Flynn adopted from his old friend, Socialist Party leader Norman Thomas, the belief that Roosevelt was "a born militarist." Flynn noted that the President had a propensity, "whenever he had a week or two for jaunting, . . . [to] spend his time on battleships."[32] In 1936 Flynn proclaimed in a radio speech that he could not vote for Roosevelt because he was sure that the President would "do his best to entangle us" in the eventual European war. At the same time, Flynn added that he believed Roosevelt was "engaged in a desperate attempt to break down the democratic system in America." Seven years later, in the midst of war, an embittered Flynn told a friend: "I am sure that was a pretty unconvincing broadcast then. But time has supplied the necessary conviction."[33] Flynn supported Thomas' presidential candidacy in 1936, not out of sympathy for socialism but as a protest against Roosevelt.[34]

After 1936 Flynn became increasingly convinced that Roosevelt was a militarist. The President's "Quarantine the Aggressor" speech in late 1938 was viewed with alarm and despair by the journalist. He warned that Roosevelt needed a huge "miracle industry" to help the

31

nation recover from the Great Depression. Powerful conservatives in Congress and the business community were becoming outspoken in their opposition to the President's spending program, and pumping money into an industry like armaments was the only way for Roosevelt to continue deficit financing and yet satisfy the conservatives. The psychological basis for conservative "devotion to military might" was interesting and complex, Flynn maintained, but he did not examine the motivation in detail. It was sufficient to observe, he asserted, that "militarism is the one great glamorous public-works project" to which conservatives would consent.[35] In order to continue as an effective popular cause, Flynn stated wryly, the "miracle industry" would need to be accompanied by constant war alarms. He reached the grim conclusion, however, that the basic problem with armaments was that "you cannot have war scares and war preparations without having war, or at least making peace a terrific gamble."[36]

When war broke out in Europe in September 1939, Flynn went on the radio to caution Americans that there were two fronts in any war, the economic and the military. He insisted that this nation must not participate on either front, for "if we go into the war on the economic front, we must certainly know . . . that . . . we will end by going to war on the military front."[37] Flynn reached this conclusion from his experience with the Nye committee. He had seen the United States inevitably committed to entering World War I with the very first agreement made by President Wilson to trade, even in nonmilitary goods, with the belligerents. Loans of money for goods had led to loans of ships to deliver those goods, and loans of ships in turn meant the loan of men to man those ships. American men on belligerent ships led to violent international incidents and, eventually, those incidents resulted in war.[38]

Roosevelt's response to the outbreak of the European war deeply disturbed Flynn. When in late 1939 the President signed the bill modifying the Neutrality Act of 1937, in order to allow the sale of munitions to belligerents on a cash-and-carry basis, Flynn was sure that Roosevelt was "coldly planning to create in this country a vast armaments industry" and to justify increased borrowing on the grounds of national defense. "We will have to keep mobilized to oppose every move of the administration to inch us into the crazy thing on the other side," he vowed to noninterventionist Senator Homer Bone of Washington.[39] Flynn termed the President's January 1940 request to Congress for a greatly enlarged defense budget a "deplorable and . . . a gravely upsetting phenomenon. . . . It is the climax of all the preparation he has made of the public mind for the last two years. . . . There has been a systematic infusion of fears into the minds of the people."[40]

The summer of 1940 brought a sharp new series of events distressing to Flynn. Roosevelt, speaking at Charlottesville, Virginia, in early June urged the United States to "go full speed ahead" in producing material resources to defend itself and help the Allies defeat Hitler. Shortly thereafter, he appointed internationalists Henry Stimson and Frank Knox to be secretaries of war and the navy respectively.[41] On June 22 France fell to Hitler's armies and a decided change occurred in American public opinion. Now a much larger proportion of Americans felt that the war in Europe could potentially affect them, that aid to Britain short of war should be increased, and that immediate and drastic expansion of the defense capabilities of the United States should be undertaken.[42] The President responded by supporting the Burke-Wadsworth bill, the first peacetime military conscription bill in American history. Flynn raged: "I am sick of affairs from the crown of my head to the soles of my feet. In all my years of observing public affairs I have never seen anything that was more fraudulent than this manufactured crisis of ours."[43] By August news of the Destroyers-for-Bases agreement with England was in the air and Roosevelt was nominated for a third term as President. A heartsick Flynn could only comment to Norman Thomas that he felt "like a man on whom a building had fallen."[44]

Throughout 1940, in his two regular columns, his various independent articles, and his book *Country Squire in the White House,* Flynn reiterated his view that Roosevelt was collaborating with the conservative, big-business interests of Wall Street to produce economic recovery through war scares. He basically distrusted the President's policies and personality: he believed that Roosevelt's appointees, programs, and methods of financing favored big business, and he was convinced that the President had an unstable, militaristic character. He consistently warned that "the simple truth is . . . that we have a militarist in the White House. . . . And we must be aware of, and weigh these facts about him properly before we can understand what the conflict in Europe is doing as it races through his mind."[45] Consequently, Flynn could not help seeing the war preparations as a hoax to promote economic favors to defense industries, and to provide an amusement for Roosevelt's personal fancy. He commented sarcastically that Wall Street soon would be singing

"Happy Days Are Here Again," and that Americans would be enjoying "the delightful combination of the terror of Hitler and the full pay envelope."[46] The only fear on the national horizon, according to Flynn, was that "peace—the terrible scourge of peace—may descend on us and end this great war industry. If it does it will be one of the greatest economic calamities of our time."[47]

Behind these derisive observations lay Flynn's deepest fears regarding an economy based upon deficit spending and defense industries. He warned that these tendencies would lead to fascism for the United States.[48] Flynn was the most brilliant and consistent spokesman for the third, seemingly obscure, principle espoused by the America First Committee. This principle stated that American democracy and civil liberties could be preserved only by keeping out of the European war.[49] As Barbara MacDonald, director of the AFC Speakers' Bureau, briefly explained this committee tenet: "Experience has taught us that democracy vanishes in wartime. . . . In a long and unpopular war, the sacrifices might well become permanent."[50]

John Flynn's most deeply held belief was that democracy could not be spread by force, and that modern, total warfare would destroy the economic and political liberties of all combatants. The greatest tragedy of American intervention, he predicted, would be that "we who pretend we are going to war to save the freedoms of France and Britain and Greece and Russia will end by losing our own."[51] He was convinced that "if America goes to war, we shall inevitably have fascism in this country."[52] This opinion caused Flynn to become a strict constitutionalist and vigorously to oppose the extension of the power of the executive branch during and after the America First experience.[53]

Flynn examined the rise of fascism in Germany and Italy, and concluded that it had developed in both places as the result of a capitalistic system that collapsed. The people had come to expect that their governments were responsible for providing them with economic abundance and security, and no politician who did not promise these things could achieve power. In order to create abundance, the national leaders had to adopt the expedient of state deficit spending. When conservative opposition to such spending mounted, the leaders turned to militarism as a justification. Militarism then spawned imperialism, because "people cannot be induced to make [sacrifices unless] . . . presented with some national crusade or adventure on the heroic model touching deeply the springs of chauvin-

34

istic pride."[54] Ultimately, dictatorship triumphed as people tired of militaristic adventures, and desperate leaders resorted to force to continue the bogus crusades. For Flynn, dictatorship was a result, not a cause, of fascism.[55]

The parallels with the American economic breakdown of the thirties and with Roosevelt's response to it, at least in Flynn's view of these events, were inescapable. Interventionists in 1940–41, Flynn said, allowed their hatred of Hitler to cloud their perception of the social and economic ills that had produced the German dictator. They enjoyed a "warm, luxurious feeling of piety and righteousness . . . [especially] in the presence of men like myself . . . who can be accused of crawling into our shells like hermit crabs, shutting our eyes to all the agony in the world." However, Flynn maintained, interventionists forgot that Hitler was merely a symptom. While he was deplorable and "easy to hate," the German leader was unimportant as an individual. Fascism, Flynn asserted, was a "parasite disease" that fed upon weakened societies. The Great Depression already had taxed the stamina of American society terribly, and the economic burdens of war would complete this nation's destruction: "War—even a victorious war—will destroy us."[56]

Contrary to popular myth, Flynn never charged that Franklin Roosevelt was a dictator, or that the New Deal was communistic. He did insist that the New Deal was unwittingly promoting fascism because of its alleged deficit-spending–militarism cycle, and that Roosevelt was unknowingly paving the way for a future President to impose dictatorship if he so chose.[57] "The most terrifying aspect of the whole fascist episode," Flynn warned, "is the dark fact that most of its poisons are generated not by evil men or evil peoples, but by quite ordinary men in search of an answer to the baffling problems that beset every society. Nothing could [be] . . . further from the minds of most of them than the final brutish and obscene result."[58]

Flynn had good intellectual company in his views on the coming of fascism and dictatorship to America.[59] Norman Thomas shared Flynn's contention that war would lead to fascism for America, that this process was inevitable, and that neither Roosevelt nor any other well-intentioned citizens would be able to prevent it.[60] Raymond Gram Swing, nationally known radio commentator, described a similar progression in his 1935 book, *Forerunners of American Fascism*. The main difference between Flynn's and Swing's analyses lies in the latter's belief that appeals to racial and religious prejudice, instead of to imperial ventures, would galvanize and maintain

35

popular support.[61] Indeed, Swing so discounted the effects of militarism and war in bringing fascism to America that during 1941 he served as chairman of the strongly interventionist Council for Democracy.

John Flynn also was one of the America First Committee's most vocal and thoughtful spokesmen for its other philosophical commitments to noninterventionism. He had insisted since September 1939 that the European war was just another power struggle in Europe's long history. To view the war as a contest between freedom and oppression, he claimed, was "to miss its meaning altogether."[62] He was thoroughly convinced that "England is not fighting for the four freedoms and is not fighting our battle but is fighting for her empire."[63] For this reason, he often called attention to England's poor treatment of its colonial peoples in India and North Africa, and to the fact that it held approximately thirty thousand political prisoners in Asia. When the British invaded Iran in August 1941, Flynn's opinion was confirmed: "[The English] do not pause at aggression when it serves their purpose. . . . This is a rich opportunity to make a great point of Britain's Indian troubles since the Iranian invasion is a prelude to the battle for her empire there [India]."[64]

Because of his beliefs about the nature of England's fight, and his deep conviction that war could only destroy liberties, Flynn favored a negotiated peace between England and Germany. He admired English literature and government, and believed that any person "honestly concerned" with preserving these contributions to civilization would try to stop the war immediately and salvage at least part of British sovereignty. English leaders and American interventionists who urged the island country to fight its desperate battle to the end, Flynn insisted, were doing both of their countries a grave disservice. The burdens of war would destroy Britain, whether the country won or lost. Throughout 1941 he expected England to fall, but in compliance with America First policy he refrained from calling for a negotiated peace from any committee platform or publication.[65]

Flynn did not believe that England, as many interventionists asserted, was America's first line of defense against Hitler. For one thing, he was philosophically committed to the position, enunciated best by Norman Thomas, that "no nation can depend upon the military forces of another for . . . [its] preservation. It is . . . fantastic . . . to say that a . . . British victory will solve all our problems."[66] For another thing, Flynn was sure that, because of the enormous logistical problems involved in crossing an ocean with an army, landing on a hostile coast, and maintaining supply lines, Hitler could not possibly invade the United States. Roosevelt had noted that Dakar in Africa, which the German dictator conceivably could use as a base, was only five hours by air from Brazil. In an article addressing the invasion question, which the AFC reprinted and distributed widely in its fight against the Lend-Lease bill, Flynn dismissed the President's frightening implication. He pointed out that even if Hitler successfully landed troops in Brazil, the potential invader still would be farther away from the United States than he had been in Germany![67]

Germany's difficulties in attempting to conquer its neighbor, Russia, further convinced Flynn that the whole invasion argument was simply a part of Roosevelt's "mischief." The President, he believed, was trying to scare the American people into an extravagant arms program.[68] Yet Flynn supported the AFC principle that urged an impregnable national defense. He saw that the United States was woefully unprepared militarily, and believed that the country should "provide a defense for [itself] . . . but not a vast military establishment to engage in foreign wars."[69]

After arguing against Hitler as a military threat to this country, Flynn examined the economic question. He concluded that the Nazi economy could never achieve world, or even European, domination. Fascist ideology, bureaucratic organization, and a primitive German plan of trade based on barter, he maintained, would cause the Reich to stagnate economically.[70] The only way Hitler could "beat American business," Flynn argued ironically, "would be if this country were to enter the war and emerge as a fascist state like Germany."[71]

In order to keep America from becoming involved in the upcoming war, John Flynn took several steps aside from offering his opinions in journals and radio speeches. On May 30, 1938, he and several other liberal and intellectual New York noninterventionists founded the Keep America Out of War Congress. Among the promoters were John Haynes Holmes, minister of New York's Park Avenue Community Church; Harry Elmer Barnes, revisionist historian of World War I; Oswald Garrison Villard, former editor of the *Nation*; and Norman Thomas. Actually the idea for an antiwar organization came from Thomas, who had been convinced by a 1937 tour of Europe that war was imminent.[72]

The KAOWC was not a membership organization, but was conceived as a coordinating body to integrate the work of several already existing peace groups.[73] Its principles were more generalized than those of the AFC, because the KAOWC was intended as a long-term "watchdog" organization against all wars and for civil liberties. It was quasi-pacifistic and differed sharply with the AFC on the question of military preparedness. The KAOWC slogan, coined by Thomas at the first meeting, was: "The maximum American cooperation for peace; the maximum isolation from war." Its five-point program advocated strengthening democracy at home by defending civil liberties, and opposed "hysterical and unplanned armaments programs" and military conscription. KAOWC principles further supported a generous relief policy for victims of war and oppression and recommended asylum for political and religious refugees, resisted all forms of United States imperialism in Latin America, and rejected all alliances among nations for the purpose of war but promoted world cooperation in peaceful ventures.[74]

During 1941 there was limited cooperation between the KAOWC and the New York chapter of the America First Committee. Flynn was the main link between the two groups. He became national chairman of the KAOWC shortly after its formation, and remained in that capacity until the summer of 1941. Only after the popular success and practical effectiveness of the NYC-AFC had far surpassed the popularity and usefulness of the KAOWC did he turn away from the latter organization. Thomas remained the leading intellectual spokesman for the KAOWC, and Mary W. Hillyer managed its daily operations. Hillyer, originally from Kansas, had served for many years as a field secretary for the League for Industrial Democracy. She gained national prominence in early 1941 by making four antiwar speeches on national radio networks.[75]

Throughout 1939-40 Flynn used the KAOWC as a platform from which to denounce measures such as the revision of the 1937 Neutrality Act and the Destroyers-for-Bases agreement. He predicted that the altered Neutrality Act would lead to war because British and French buying power would be exhausted within two years, and the United States would then grant credit to these nations and become entangled in Europe's war.[76] He objected to the Destroyers-for-Bases agreement on the dual grounds that it was a step toward war and that the President had usurped too much power. When the agreement was announced Flynn called for Roosevelt's impeachment.[77]

As the presidential election of 1940 drew near, Flynn found himself in a strange position. He had earlier refused a request by Oswald Garrison Villard that he help organize a group of liberal writers in support of Republican candidate Wendell Willkie. Flynn not only fell back on his long-held personal vow never to serve on political committees, but insisted that Willkie's stand on foreign affairs was little different from that of Roosevelt.[78] Yet he believed he had to speak out against the President. On election eve, he went on the radio and in an address sponsored by the American Writers for Willkie lashed out against Roosevelt. He warned of the horrors of war that would follow the President's reelection: "I am so fully convinced that if he is reelected he will take us into this war that I cannot remain silent . . . If you vote for him . . .the blood of your sons will be not merely upon his, but on your own hands.[79] Never once in the talk did Flynn mention Willkie's name. His defense of this unusual position was simple: "I would be against Christ himself if he were running for a third term."[80]

It is not known for whom Flynn voted in 1940, but it is very likely that, as a protest of both major party candidates, he again voted for Thomas. Flynn was deeply distressed with the President's reelection. He attributed the victory to the vast sums of money at Roosevelt's disposal, and to the President's "provocative speeches" and ability to scare the nation into believing that Hitler would invade America if he defeated England.[81]

The problem of living with a powerfully resurgent Roosevelt and restraining him from taking the country into war began to preoccupy Flynn shortly after the election, though he was "in seclusion" completing his book *Men of Wealth* for most of November 1940.[82] He decided that the best way to provide a check on the administration would be to found a vigorous AFC chapter in New York. At committee headquarters in Chicago, Stuart and other national leaders reached the same conclusion.[83]

New York City was regarded by all participants in the Great Debate of 1941 as the "interventionist capital city."[84] Flynn reported that in late 1940 the leading interventionist group, the Committee to Defend America by Aiding the Allies (the CDAAA), was conducting "a veritable reign of terror . . . intimidating and smearing . . . whoever lifted his voice in New York to protest against war."[85] The city's large foreignborn population, its Park Avenue and Long Island upper classes who had traveled in Europe and admired England, and its business community with extensive international ties rendered it inhospitable to noninterventionists. Ironically, its very reputation as a prowar stronghold made New York a crucial and coveted prize for the AFC. Harry Schnibbe, assistant director of organization for the national committee, explained: "If it [the America First movement] were whipped on this strategic Eastern battleground . . . it could have retreated into its own heart [the isolationist Midwest]; but a heart cannot sustain itself. America First would have collapsed and perished. New York was a salient point."[86]

During the fall of 1940 Flynn himself was unwilling to become chairman of a New York AFC chapter. He felt that he could make his greatest contribution to the noninterventionist cause through journalism. More important, he believed that to be effective in New York a committee chapter should be led by powerful and prominent businessmen. Already the city was heavily organized by interventionist and aid-to-Britain groups. These organizations commanded the support of a majority of the influential Northeastern media. To get a fair hearing in the "enemy territory," Flynn reasoned, an NYC-AFC would have to attract strong business interests with large advertising budgets. He knew well the inefficacy of the liberal, intellectual antiwar groups with which he had worked.[87]

In truth, businessmen in New York had been, and continued to be, pressured into an interventionist position by the presence of a large number of Jewish customers in the city and by the fact that many New York offices were the headquarters for national and international companies. One prominent officer of the Guaranty Trust Company of New York told Robert Wood that while he agreed with the AFC's principles, he would not join the committee. Such an action, he went on to explain, "would probably be misunderstood as [being] unsympathetic with the dangers and privations" that the employees of his firm's foreign offices were experiencing.[88] Another New York director of an internationally connected firm stopped contributing to the AFC midway through 1941. He noted that recent publication of his name on a list of committee donors had "brought down criticism from stockholders and . . . the threat of an organized protest at the forthcoming stockholders' meeting."[89] Famous aviator Charles Lindbergh, after lunching one day in August 1941 with a group of eminent New York bankers, observed ruefully: "Like so many businessmen . . . they are all ready to admit that the country is headed toward chaos, but few of them are willing to expose their own positions enough to take part in opposing that which they believe is wrong [intervention]."[90]

As the fall of 1940 wore on, Wood and Stuart began to urge personal friends within the New York business community to assume the NYC-AFC chairmanship. Wood spoke to Robert M. Harriss, wealthy cotton broker with the firm of Harriss and Vose. Harriss refused the post because he was chairman of a Queens County Democrats-for-Willkie group and did not want to jeopardize potential votes by spearheading a controversial cause. Curiously, he gave no reason why he could not accept the NYC-AFC chairmanship after the 1940 election.[91] Stuart approached advertising executive Chester Bowles after telling Lindbergh that he felt Bowles was the perfect nominee for chairman because "he is not thought of as a Tory, he is extremely interested and a dynamo as far as accomplishing things."[92] Bowles not only rejected the position, but requested that the AFC national committee state clearly in its record that he had never been to any policy meetings and never prepared any advertising for or visited the office of either the New York or the Chicago AFC headquarters.[93] He explained to a friend: "Unfortunately, I simply have to pull in my neck . . . advertising is one helluva business . . . you are usually more or less owned by the clients for whom you work."[94]

As the New York businessmen hesitated and procrastinated in accepting the NYC-AFC chairmanship, several people with relatively unknown connections stepped forward and offered to assume the leadership post. Of three such individuals who requested chapter applications from national headquarters during December 1940, two never bothered to complete the forms and the one who actually submitted an application was rejected by the AFC for having insufficient references.[95] A fourth and rather eccentric individual, Marie Luhrs, was turned away because she insisted in repeated letters to Stuart and other Chicago leaders that she favored bribing congressmen into voting for the noninterventionist position. Bribery was the only effective means of combating Roosevelt's "madness," Luhrs claimed. "If you haven't got the money and influence to do this," she contended, "you might as well close up the committee at once."[96]

Two additional potential NYC-AFC leaders would have transformed the committee into a crusade against the New Deal and thus divided the heterogeneous following. An overture from Stanley W. Burke and another from George Eggleston and Douglas Stewart were rejected on the grounds that they could attract only wealthy conservatives to the committee. Burke was a New York investment banker who had been active since 1937 in the National Committee to Uphold Constitutional Government. This committee condemned the New Deal as being socialistic, sought to restore a strong profit system in America, and played a prominent role in the defeat of

Roosevelt's Judicial Reorganization Bill of 1937, his Executive Reorganization Bill of 1938, and his attempts to purge conservatives from the Democratic Party in the congressional primaries of 1938.[97] Following his rejection as committee chairman, Burke did contribute generously to the NYC-AFC, and he served as a member of the chapter's sponsoring committee from July to December 1941. Eggleston and Stewart were the publishers of *Scribner's Commentator,* a magazine known for its laissez-faire economic views and its implicit anti-Semitism.[98] They continually attacked Roosevelt for allegedly promoting "social democracy," or a leveling of all class and economic barriers in America. When Robert D. Stuart refused the two publishers he explained to Lindbergh: "I do not like the tone of . . . [their] political philosophy. They think of everything in terms of a single pattern. . . . I am sure they would bring the Social Democracy business into all of . . . [the committee] work."[99]

The attempt at organizing and leading an America First chapter in New York that was, to Flynn, the most undesirable came from Merwin Kimball Hart. Hart, director of a fiscally conservative private group known as the New York State Economic Council (later named the National Economic Council), was a strong anti-Zionist. Flynn, Bowles, and Sidney Hertzberg, a well-known noninterventionist journalist in New York, strongly advised the AFC national headquarters to veto Hart's autumn 1940 offer to establish a committee chapter in the Northeast. "If Hart's connection becomes known," the three men warned, "the group will find it difficult to operate effectively. . . . Hart himself is the super superpatriotic type. He has been widely accused of fascist leanings . . . and is constantly being 'exposed.' "[100] Stuart, after meeting with Hart personally, concurred in the judgment of Flynn, Bowles, and Hertzberg, and Hart was rejected.[101]

As Flynn surveyed the several attempts at NYC-AFC organization, he became concerned that the entire America First reputation might be tarnished if responsible and competent leadership did not prevail in New York. Harry Schnibbe best expressed Flynn's growing fears by declaring that in the Northeast, "with the enemy on four sides, . . . it would be disastrous to experiment with generals."[102] Still hoping to persuade a prominent businessman to shoulder the NYC-AFC chairmanship, Flynn sponsored a luncheon at Town Hall Club on December 6, 1940. Among those present were Bruce Barton, advertising executive, author, and former Republican congressman from New York City, and H. Dudley Swim, banker with the National Investors Corporation and later treasurer of the NYC-AFC. Former President Herbert Hoover was invited, but he declined on the ground that he preferred to express his noninterventionist views independently. Flynn summarized the luncheon as "very promising." Six days later he held another, much larger luncheon at which General Wood spoke.[103]

Soon after the luncheons Flynn thought that he had found the perfect man to assume the chairmanship. Colonel Allen Pope, president of the First Boston Corporation of New York, had attended both gatherings and seemed very enthusiastic. Pope's high degree of respectability and financial power, in Flynn's view, could give the fledgling chapter the same kind of strength that Wood provided in Chicago.[104] After a good deal of pressure from Flynn, Pope agreed to serve on the conditions that three officers of large New York banks be on the committee, and that a prominent businessman serve as executive secretary and be responsible for the daily affairs of managing the group. Flynn confidently assented to Pope's terms. The chapter's sponsors already included three bank presidents: W. H. Bennett of Emigrant Savings, Harvey Gibson of Manufacturers' Trust, and F. Abbott Goodhue of the Bank of Manhattan. Additionally, Edwin Sibley Webster, Jr., senior partner in the Wall Street investment firm of Kidder, Peabody and Company, had heard of Flynn's plans from a mutual friend and volunteered to act as secretary.[105]

These initial successes elated Flynn, but he was soon disappointed. During the holiday season of 1940 people began to recant their commitments to him. Bennett became ill and took a long vacation in the South, and the board of directors of the Bank of Manhattan ruled that the controversial nature of the America First movement might offend some of the bank's depositors and refused to let Goodhue serve. When Pope heard of these changes he refused to become chairman. Although Pope denied business pressure, Flynn was unconvinced. "One by one," he fulminated later, "most of those who had agreed to serve had to notify me that they were unable to do so for the same or similar reasons."[106]

Only Edwin Webster remained firm in his active noninterventionist commitment. A forty-year-old bachelor, Webster was well liked by most of the national AFC leadership, and in January 1941 a discouraged Wood termed him "an answer to [our] prayers."[107] Stuart viewed Webster as "an able and energetic individual . . . [who] is certainly enthused," and the committee founder was personally convinced that the investment banker would be the real "sparkplug" of the NYC-AFC, surpassing even Flynn in ability and devotion.[108] Lindbergh also was very favorably impressed with Webster, and the two remained friends for many years after the America First experience. When they first met in January 1941 Lindbergh described the banker as "the type of man who will carry this country through this crisis—if it is to get through." He saw his new friend as an excellent example of the "dormant" but potentially boundless leadership resources of the United States: Webster belonged to a category of men "who will step forward to leadership when times become so chaotic that they can no longer continue to absorb themselves in their . . . [own] affairs."[109] At least some NYC-AFC leaders had a differing view of Webster, however. Ranking staff member Robert L. Bliss later described the banker as "difficult . . . emotionally unbalanced . . . [and] used to getting his own way." By late 1941 Flynn was also disenchanted with Webster, and the two men ended their association with a bitter feud.[110]

In January 1941, however, Flynn was enthusiastic about Webster, but he was so impatient with the refusals of other businessmen that he abruptly decided himself to accept the NYC-AFC chairmanship. He declared to Stuart: "I have been greatly annoyed by the shocking timidity of business leaders here. . . . In any case, we shall wait no longer on these timid souls."[111] America First national committee leaders were pleased with Flynn's decision. "The Chicago directors realized," Schnibbe later affirmed, "that when they got John Flynn . . . they had the best."[112] In later years, Flynn never regretted preempting the businessmen in New York, but he did recite his first objection to becoming chairman himself—that his relative absence from the journalistic field during the Great Debate of 1941 left the noninterventionist position with a lack of articulate testimony. "The thought struck me," he confided to Lindbergh shortly after the Pearl Harbor attack, "that ten or fifteen years from now when writers sit down to put together the sorry story of these times, our side of this controversy will be rather poorly represented."[113]

As the NYC-AFC "struggled out of its swaddling clothes" in January 1941, Flynn and Webster seemed to be the ideal working complements. Flynn, the liberal journalist, was also a pragmatist. He joined forces with the conservative Webster in order to forge the strongest possible barrier against intervention. Flynn had moved during his long career from approval to apprehension of Franklin Roosevelt and the New Deal. He had used the small, intellectual

44

KAOWC as a platform from which to denounce the President, but Roosevelt was now powerfully entrenched as the nation's first third-term chief executive. Flynn saw the America First Committee, and especially a strong New York chapter, as the best way to curb the drift to war, and he knew that he needed a prominent businessman to broaden the appeal of the antiwar movement in the Northeast. The accuracy of Flynn's practical new realization was graphically illustrated when one merchant told Wood that many members of the New York business community found it hard to respond to the journalist: "According to businessmen, he [Flynn] is always against everything and the force of his broadcasts is therefore minimized." When Webster and Flynn came together, each was able to exercise his own unique talents. The conservative handled the details of managing the NYC-AFC's hectic Manhattan headquarters, and undertook several high-level fundraising campaigns. The liberal supervised publicity and made the more substantive, intellectual policy decisions.[114] For their first task in 1941 the two men had to concentrate on compiling a prominent sponsoring committee, securing financial contributors, and organizing a staff.

3

Anatomy and Methods of the NYC-AFC

As the New York chapter of the America First Committee took shape in the early weeks of 1941, many prominent and diverse individuals became associated with it. Liberals and conservatives both were essential to the total effectiveness and appeal of the organization. Although generous donors came forth and the chapter was the richest in the nation, there was never enough money. Staff turnover was high, and the committee was unable to expand into the small towns and rural areas of the Northeast. Nevertheless, the chapter was the largest and most highly organized one in the America First movement.[1] The various branches of the New York organization were controlled as tightly as possible from Flynn's central Manhattan headquarters: the NYC-AFC was not operated as a democracy.[2] Flynn also maintained a close and active involvement with the multifarious publicity efforts of the chapter.

Aside from Edwin Webster and himself, as executive secretary and chairman respectively, Flynn secured the services of H. Dudley Swim as treasurer, and Amos R. E. Pinchot and Adelaide Hooker Marquand as the additional members of the NYC-AFC executive committee. Flynn believed that a small executive committee was most practical because it could be called together quickly and could work efficiently.[3] The executive committee met approximately every two weeks and passed judgment on publicity measures, rally plans, and other means of implementing national committee policy in New York. Flynn generally took the initiative in executive committee proposals and dominated the group.[4]

Next to Flynn, Amos Pinchot was the most influential member of the NYC-AFC executive committee. Sixty-eight years old during the America First experience, he was the younger brother of Gifford Pinchot, former President Theodore Roosevelt's chief conservationist. Amos, a veteran of the Spanish-American War, was admitted to the bar in 1900. He disliked the everyday practice of law, however, and after one year as deputy assistant district attorney in New York, he ceased to take legal cases unless they involved a cause that particularly interested him. Instead, he spent his life managing the wealthy estates of his immediate family, and dabbling in various liberal crusades. He wrote several articles and portions of two books, and liked to refer to himself as a liberal publicist.[5] Pinchot defined liberalism as a compromise between "the dignified but glacial immobility of the conservative and the dogmatic appeal of his light-footed brother of the left-wing."[6]

Pinchot's early beliefs about government, economy, and war were very similar to those of Flynn. Pinchot stated in 1914 that a "reckless and thoughtless commercialism" had taken hold of the United States. He insisted that government should regulate railroads, natural resources, and other monopolies as a means of restoring competitive industrial conditions and of assuring an equal chance for each individual. He wanted government not to level social and economic classes, but simply to "level opportunity. . . . Then we will have what is better than equality, for equality is unnatural."[7] He broke with his former idol, Theodore Roosevelt, during 1912–14, when the Bull Moose Progressive candidate began to rely for advice on George Perkins, a Morgan partner and a director of United States Steel Corporation. In 1916 Pinchot labeled Roosevelt the "bellhop of Wall Street."[8] During World War I the publicist sympathized with the Allies but did not want the United States to enter the war. This nation's defense was not threatened, he said, and commercial interests agitated for and finally provoked American military involvement. Pinchot served as chairman of the Union Against Militarism (predecessor of the American Civil Liberties Union), and he organized and directed a committee that advocated an eighty-percent profits tax to enable the country to avoid deficit war financing.[9]

Pinchot and Flynn also held analogous views of the initial New Deal and the war scare in 1940–41. Though Pinchot had reservations about Franklin Roosevelt in 1932, he voted for him, believing he would be more vigorous than Herbert Hoover in purging the

American economy of monopolies and restoring purely competitive capitalism. He stated wryly shortly before the election: "I long ago gave up hope of being able to vote for a presidential candidate cut precisely to my pattern."[10] Pinchot turned quickly against the New Deal with the advent of the National Recovery Administration. He regarded the NRA as "pure regimentation" that would strengthen trusts and oppressive trade associations.[11] By 1938 he had concluded that the President was impulsive, excessively pragmatic, and dangerously unfit. "He has no compass to guide him," Pinchot charged, "except a consuming desire for power."[12] Two years later Pinchot was extremely depressed over what he termed the President's "war salesmanship." Roosevelt was using the war scare, he asserted, to "hide the tragic breakdown of an Administration which . . . has failed to lift the depression . . . and to serve as an excuse for breaking the anti-third term tradition and expanding the already immense powers of the President to the point of dictatorship."[13]

Nonetheless, Pinchot and Flynn differed in their ultimate assessments of the New Deal. While Flynn regarded the Roosevelt Administration as proto-fascistic, Pinchot veered sharply to the right and asserted that the President was party to an international plot "bent on delivering the United States to socialism."[14] By early 1937 Pinchot had come to fear big government more than he had once feared big business, and he allied himself with conservatives to fight for the profit system in America. At this time, he and two conservative publishers, Frank Gannett and Edward A. Rumely, formed the National Committee to Uphold Constitutional Government. This group favored a strict and literal interpretation of the Constitution, and was influential in defeating the Judicial Reorganization Bill of 1937, and the Executive Reorganization Bill and Roosevelt's attempted purge of conservative Democrats in 1938.[15]

By 1941 Pinchot was convinced that the President was actively collaborating with Communists in a plan to use war to impose collectivism on the United States. Roosevelt envisioned himself, Pinchot maintained, as the future omnipotent "President of a United States of the World," and was pragmatically courting international Communist support.[16] He warned AFC executive director Robert D. Stuart explicitly that "war (which is what Roosevelt wants) . . . [will] impoverish our people and create revolution (which is what Roosevelt wants)."[17] Pinchot completely distrusted the President's advisers, whom he called the "rusophile [sic] liberals . . . at Washington."[18] Roosevelt and his advisers, Pinchot insisted, had

49

"no desire to see the capitalist system and free enterprise survive
.... [They believe] that the establishment of a cooperative common-
wealth is the way out."[19]

Pinchot regarded the America First movement as the last hope for
the United States to continue as a reasonably free society and to
remain at peace. He worked hard for the committee, and defended it
staunchly. When an interventionist friend suggested that Pinchot
had allowed his hatred of Roosevelt to "subconsciously distort" his
judgment on the war issue, he was insulted. "Your letter," Pinchot
replied angrily, "is . . . a rather typical example of the arguments
being addressed against America First members. . . . Your letter is
not an appeal to reason . . . [but] a lot of name-calling and silly
charges."[20] Pinchot embraced the committee, he explained to another friend, because it sternly rejected the "frothy yet deadly megalo-
maniacal dream . . . that America should go over the world and
dominate it, fight its wars, write its peace . . . reform all the peoples
of the world . . . guarantee them a millennium of justice and happi-
ness, world without end, amen! . . . No nation has ever [done
this] . . . without losing its own integrity, its power, and its usefulness to its own people and everyone else."[21]

The conservatism and extreme antipathy for government regula-
tion of the economy that Pinchot adopted in his later years were
characteristic of Webster and Swim all of their lives. Both were
investment bankers: Webster was a senior partner in the Wall Street
firm of Kidder, Peabody and Company, and Swim was an official of
the National Investors Corporation. Both men believed that Roosevelt wanted a collectivist economy, and therefore they opposed all
that the President advocated. Very early in 1941 Webster urged that
the AFC establish itself as a permanent organization to serve as a
watchdog for the principles of strict constitutionalism. "What we
are seeking to do, it seems to me," he insisted to Stuart, "is to give
America back to the Americans since Roosevelt has taken it away
from them."[22] Swim recommended that the committee adopt the
slogan "Stop Hitlerism in America" and make a point of referring to
the Nazis as German New Dealers and to the Japanese as Asiatic
New Dealers. These measures, he said, would have strong appeal to
"conservatives who have been torn between war impulses and a
dislike for Roosevelt . . . [for they would see that] we [America
Firsters] are clearly carrying the flag for America."[23]

Swim was more prolific in his suggestions for attracting business
support to the AFC than was Webster. The chapter treasurer also

advocated that the committee run a series of advertisements in the *Wall Street Journal.* These messages could be designed, he counseled, to show businessmen ways in which expansion of American firms allegedly was being blocked by the British, to "take the part of business in this ridiculous priorities fiasco . . . [and to] attack the uneconomic characteristics of the Excess Profits Tax."[24] With a ready eye for a profitable business deal, Swim further urged that no "open credits" be advanced to England, but that credit for arms purchased by Britain in this country be arranged to represent either payment for American purchase of English real estate in this hemisphere or loans against British-owned American securities.[25]

While Webster and Swim represented the conservative faction of the NYC-AFC executive committee and Pinchot served as the transition or "swing" figure, Flynn's liberal position was bolstered by Adelaide Hooker Marquand, the second wife of Pulitzer Prize-winning novelist John Phillips Marquand. She began her work with the chapter as an office volunteer. When Flynn noticed her great organizational ability, he quickly promoted her to a decision-making post.[26] Very little is known of Adelaide Marquand's beliefs with the exception of the fact that she deeply admired Flynn and consistently took his part in most matters of America First policy.[27] In late November 1941 she was replaced on the chapter executive committee by author Doris Fielding Reid, daughter of distinguished Johns Hopkins University geologist Harry Fielding Reid. Described as "level-headed, soothing . . . brimful of ideas," Doris Reid also staunchly supported Flynn's positions.[28]

In addition to a balanced and efficient executive committee, Flynn realized, the NYC-AFC needed a "dress" committee of prominent sponsors. Harry Schnibbe, assistant director of organization for the national AFC, said that the selection of an eminent and credible sponsoring committee was "the most vulnerable spot" in assuring America First acceptability in New York.[29] Flynn chose carefully. Among those who agreed to serve were Archibald and Theodore Roosevelt, Jr., sons of former President Theodore Roosevelt; Samuel Hopkins Adams, Academy Award-winning playwright; and William S. Thomas, son of Socialist Party leader Norman Thomas. The chapter sponsoring committee had a moderate turnover rate and, in general, reflected an increasingly liberal composition as 1941 progressed.[30]

The liberal side of the NYC-AFC was further enhanced by many prominent New Yorkers who were associated with the committee in

51

an unofficial, advisory capacity. Most of these individuals were old friends and colleagues of Flynn from the Keep America Out of War Congress or the field of journalism. Many of them had been asked to become NYC-AFC members, but refused because of religious or intellectual objections to America First's advocacy of an impregnable national defense. These people often spoke from AFC platforms in the New York area, signed aggregate open letters sent by the committee to Washington, and provided Flynn with research or research contacts.

The most involved of these associates was Norman Thomas, who refused to join the AFC in late 1940 because he believed the committee's program "constitutes armaments economics."[31] The Socialist leader did not oppose World War II on grounds of absolute pacifism, but he did believe that pacifists "may be the prophets and pioneers of the ultimate protest against war which will save the world."[32] He was a member of the American Civil Liberties Union's Committee on Conscientious Objectors, and when an NYC-AFC staff member proudly announced that the committee had persuaded a pacifist to accept military service, Thomas commented wryly: "This is what I should expect America First to try to do. . . . I have always felt that America First was . . . too prone to militarism and imperialism to meet my convictions." He then added that, in spite of its faults, the AFC did "some very useful work."[33] Repeatedly during 1941 Flynn, Stuart, and America First national chairman Robert E. Wood importuned Thomas to become a member of either the New York chapter or the national committee, but the Socialist leader insisted that he could "serve our common cause best by parallel and friendly action."[34]

In spite of his unwillingness to embrace the America First movement officially, Thomas shared most of Flynn's convictions regarding the nature of the war in Europe and Roosevelt's motives for intervention. "Age-old European power conflicts plus new imperialist struggles for oil, coal, spheres of influence and investment, and markets for exclusive trade," Thomas charged, were the true roots of the Anglo-German contest. In view of their records of repression in India and Morocco, England and France could not honestly claim that they were fighting for democracy.[35] Thomas did not believe that Hitler could invade the United States successfully, and so he urged America to "keep out of war, make its own democracy work, use its influence at the right time for the right sort of peace offensive, and stand ready for that degree of economic cooperation which would make for the stabilizing and improving of a world at peace."[36]

Any attempt by this country to spread democracy by the sword, Thomas insisted, would be foolhardy. "Even victory," he declared, "would be accompanied, not by the achievement of noble purposes . . . but by an American or Anglo-American imperialism which would perpetuate armaments, and for which fascism at home in this generation must be the inevitable accompaniment." He was convinced that "it isn't Hitler the man, but Hitlerism that is the disease. . . . Hitlerism isn't born of the devil; it is born of a bad system. . . . The triumph of American Hitlerism . . . would be the probable consequence of our entry into total war far more probably than under any other circumstances."[37] Roosevelt, in gambling with intervention, was displaying his innate militarism and his love of "power for power's sake." The President was dangerous because he believed that the United States could "play God to the world."[38]

Thomas worked in many ways to prevent American participation in the European war. He entered the presidential campaign of 1940 in hopes of obtaining a strong protest vote against "war, conscription and other follies." Roosevelt and Republican candidate Wendell Willkie were essentially identical, he charged, and both were beholden to "Wall Street and other interventionists who would stake everything on the preservation of the British Empire."[39] The Socialist candidate was very disappointed with his party's poor showing at the polls, but he continued his antiwar efforts through the KAOWC.[40] He also testified against the Lend-Lease Bill before both the House and Senate Foreign Relations Committees, and against the Draft Extension Bill before the Senate Military Affairs Committee. In at least one of these cases he requested and received aid in preparing his remarks from the AFC Washington research bureau. Further, he spoke at two large NYC-AFC rallies, undertook two college speaking tours financed and arranged by America First, and signed several committee letters to Congress.[41]

Another distinguished Northeastern liberal who cooperated with the NYC-AFC in an unofficial capacity was advertising executive Chester Bowles. Bowles was "sorely torn" over the intervention question, especially because he was "a strong believer in the Democratic Party—and . . . particularly . . . in everything that [Franklin] Roosevelt has stood for, with the exception of his foreign policy." In late 1940 Bowles decided in favor of the noninterventionist position because he believed that United States' foremost national responsibility lay in fulfilling the New Deal's promises "for a more abundant life for the average American." He also was convinced that the Allied countries were fighting mainly to protect their colonial empires, and that the United States' rejection of the League of Nations in 1920 indicated that "the American people were not yet ready to participate effectively in world affairs."[42]

In addition to Thomas and Bowles, other noted Northeastern liberals also aided the New York America First Committee as advisers and associates. Among these were KAOWC leaders Harry Elmer Barnes, John Haynes Holmes, Harry Emerson Fosdick, and Oswald Garrison Villard. Democratic Senator David I. Walsh of Massachusetts, famous historian Charles A. Beard, economist and muckraker Stuart Chase, and author Sinclair Lewis, also acted in concert with the committee. Lewis' most recent book, *It Can't Happen Here*, outlined the possible coming of fascism to America. Although they were not Northeasterners, Democratic Senators Burton K. Wheeler of Montana and Gerald P. Nye of North Dakota were close personal friends of Flynn and worked closely with the NYC-AFC.[43]

If the liberal wing of the NYC-AFC was strengthened by outsiders associated with the organization, so was the conservative side aided by its friends. The most eminent of these was former President Herbert Hoover, who lived at the Waldorf-Astoria Hotel in New York City throughout most of 1940–41. Hoover opposed intervention because he felt Roosevelt was proceeding in an unconstitutional manner against the will of Congress, and because he feared the postwar threat of world communism if the United States assisted Stalin in fighting Hitler. Hoover also was convinced that participation in the war would "establish further centralization of authority amounting to practical dictatorship in the United States. . . . After the war . . . forces pressing for continued economic dictatorship would be stronger than ever."[44] The former President made quietly successful financial appeals to several wealthy New Yorkers on behalf of the AFC, but he declined to speak at any of its rallies. Personal speaking experiences, he explained, would require him to engage in distasteful emotional appeals.[45] At least some NYC-AFC supporters believed Hoover a liability and were pleased at his refusals to identify closely and publicly with the movement. Norman Thomas and famous aviator Charles Lindbergh were two who felt this way. Lindbergh reported after addressing a committee rally in September 1941 that the "least popular portion" of his speech consisted of a quotation from Hoover.[46]

In addition to Hoover, other notable Northeastern conservatives aided the NYC-AFC in various ways. Most prominent among these were Lindbergh, *New York Daily News* publisher Joseph Medill

Patterson, Republican Senators Robert A. Taft of Ohio and Charles Tobey of New Hampshire, and Republican Representative Hamilton Fish of Garrison, New York.[47]

In addition to these auxiliary supporters of the NYC-AFC who gave their time in speaking or in making other appeals, other prominent New Yorkers were associated with the committee as financial donors. The most substantial donor was Edwin Webster, who gave slightly over five thousand dollars to the chapter and nearly half that amount to the national committee.[48] The brothers Lunsford and Henry Smith Richardson, who chaired the board and the executive committee, respectively, of Vick Chemical Company, were the second most generous contributors. Together they gave nearly as much as did Webster to the NYC-AFC, as well as twenty-two thousand dollars to the national committee.[49] The America First experience created a bond of friendship between the Richardson brothers and Charles Lindbergh that lasted many years. In December 1940, when the three men were first introduced by General Wood, the aviator was elated. "The Richardsons," he confided in his diary, "are . . . unusually able men, with . . . sincerity and determination. . . . Meeting them made me feel that we are at last getting the right kind of men on our side of the war issue. Up to the present time there has been too large a percentage of cranks and people with strange ideas."[50]

Nevertheless, the majority of NYC-AFC money did not come from wealthy donors. Approximately three-fourths of the chapter's revenue was contributed by very average, or even poor, people.[51] Roughly seventy-five percent of the chapter's members (nearly two hundred thousand people in all) were too poor to give anything at all, and so the movement cannot be accused of being financed or composed of elitists. As Ruth Sarles, official of the AFC Washington research bureau and later committee historian, has said: "It is a tale of 'little people' who alone were without power, who worked together to the end that their deep conviction against war would reach the ears of the men in power."[52]

The efforts of the small and large donors made the New York organization the richest AFC chapter in the country. It was almost four times as well off as the second-place one, the Chicago chapter, and almost half as wealthy as the national committee itself.[53] Because of its relative affluence, the NYC-AFC was classified as self-sustaining and was asked to contribute to the chronically struggling national committee treasury. At the time of the movement's dissolution, the chapter also paid several thousand dollars to cover the debts of many other Northeastern America First units.[54]

In spite of its comparative wealth, the NYC-AFC never had adequate funds. Indeed, the movement's continual poverty and the makeshift operations that resulted were described best by William Benton, vice president of the University of Chicago and leading AFC spokesman during 1940–41, when he said: "There are very few things in the twentieth century of American politics that got more noise for less money than the AFC."[55] Flynn and the entire executive committee, as well as hundreds of volunteers, served without pay.[56] Office conditions at central Manhattan headquarters were described by Lindbergh as "overcrowded and poorly lighted ... hot and without enough ventilation. Flynn and Webster have a small office together with no outside windows." Lindbergh added, however, that the NYC-AFC staff and volunteers carried on their work "enthusiastically.... The thing I like most about this work is the loyalty and spirit I find."[57] Another observer has given a similar picture of the dedication in spite of the poor working conditions in the chapter headquarters: "The office at 515 Madison Avenue ... was a bedlam. Volunteers stayed till the early morning hours energized by a hot revivalist fever. Mothers stayed away from their homes, and family life was disrupted in [the] ... crusade for peace."[58]

Along with the executive committee and the many volunteers, the NYC-AFC retained a small paid staff. Salaries began well below the level that most chapter employees could earn in other endeavors, and as 1941 progressed and the committee threw itself into vigorous and expensive publicity campaigns, pay was lowered still further.[59] For this reason, staff turnover was high. Those employees who did remain were typically young (under thirty-five years of age), college-educated with a background in journalism or publicity, and extremely idealistic regarding the America First cause. Two such staff members were Robert L. Bliss and Joseph Boldt. AFC national organization director in Chicago for six months, Bliss came to the New York chapter in June 1941 to serve as a special assistant for publicity. He was a young Cornell graduate who had worked for the J. Walter Thompson advertising agency and later quit his job with New York's *PM* newspaper because of that publication's increasingly interventionist stand.[60] He once stated that work with the AFC was a moral imperative to him, and that he "let all personal affairs and business contacts 'go by the boards' in the interest of America First."[61]

Eastern regional field representative for the national committee was Joseph Boldt. A thirty-year-old reporter who had worked in the editorial library of the *New York Times,* Boldt held a master's degree in American history from Rutgers University. His thesis was on the American peace movement from 1914 to 1917.[62] As one of six field representatives for the AFC, Boldt organized new chapters throughout the Northeast, checked on various chapter leaders and policies, and acted as a general troubleshooter in area disputes. He maintained an office in the NYC-AFC Manhattan headquarters, and worked in conjunction with Flynn in supervising the New York chapter's branches.[63] In March 1941, even though his wife was expecting a child, Boldt accepted a fifty-percent salary cut. "I have never regarded my work for the AFC as merely a job," he explained. "I am doing this because I believe . . . it is the only thing worth doing at the present time. I want to see it all the way through."[64]

The NYC-AFC staff and volunteers handled the daily work load of answering correspondence, arranging rallies and other publicity techniques, and enrolling new members, while Flynn maintained tight personal control over policy decisions.[65] He supervised the selection of branch officials and made them directly responsible to him for carrying out AFC programs. The charters of errant or defiant chapters were revoked. Flynn dealt with the media himself, and closed the chapter financial office to all save a few high committee officials. Further, he and Pinchot, and later Marquand and Webster, served as the NYC-AFC's only active liaisons with the national committee.[66] Flynn feared that subversive, profascist, and anti-Semitic groups in New York would gain an influence over AFC policy if he did not maintain careful vigilance.[67] (In some areas—Queens and the Bronx, for instance—such elements did gain a foothold in America First chapters and then openly refused to work with Flynn.)[68]

Additional reasons for Flynn's dictatorial methods of operating the NYC-AFC concerned the pace and size of the movement. Issues arose so quickly in the Great Debate and the chapter sprawled over such a vast network of people and areas, he explained, that a democratically run organization would not be able to function.[69]

All AFC chapters in New Jersey, Connecticut, Long Island, Westchester County, and the five boroughs of New York City technically were under the jurisdiction of Flynn's Manhattan headquarters. Within the larger Northeastern chapters, distinct local neighborhood "units" also existed. By the end of 1941, the NYC-AFC controlled eighty-four chapters and units, and operated twenty-eight storefront offices. In addition to the branches which it managed directly, the NYC-AFC exercised an indirect, supervisory influence over the America First chapters in Massachusetts, Vermont, Maine, Pennsylvania, and Buffalo, New York (the only AFC chapter in upstate New York).[70]

In the Northeast the America First movement was almost exclusively urban-based: there were no counterparts to the countywide or "area" chapters of the rural regions of the strongly isolationist Midwest. Only the heterogeneous and tolerant atmosphere of the larger Northeastern cities permitted a cause that was not popular with all segments of the population of the region to flourish at all. Several church and pacifistic groups dominated the antiwar movement in the small towns of the Northeast. These liberal groups had no mass appeal, but they did occupy the attention of those local leaders who might otherwise have formed America First chapters. When several upstate New York and New England cities seemed on the verge of starting chapters in September 1941, a disastrous and controversial AFC speech delivered by Charles Lindbergh at Des Moines, Iowa, caused them to back away.[71]

NYC-AFC chapters were general membership units: there was no specialized division into interest groups. Flynn tried to organize a special Jewish division in the early fall of 1941, in order to counteract mounting charges of anti-Semitism against the committee, but this branch never materialized.[72] A concurrent attempt to form Northeastern college units also failed because most administrators and faculty members were strongly interventionist, and defiant student protest movements were not common in the America First era. Only Stuart's own group at Yale University persisted with a strong AFC chapter.[73] In November Flynn and Bliss established contact with Thomas W. Myles, a prominent black Republican political worker in Harlem, with an eye to establishing a separate "colored" AFC organization. The proposed black division was to be "based on broader racial problems than just the America First point of view . . . . War jeopardizes their [blacks'] social gains" in all fields. Mindful of probable conservative opposition to such a liberally oriented black organization, Flynn planned the group as a somewhat clandestine NYC-AFC subsidiary. There would be "no . . . indication to the public that we [the NYC-AFC] are sponsoring it."[74] Because of the Pearl Harbor attack, however, plans for the division were aborted. Suggestions for separate NYC-AFC squads of high school students, clergymen, blue-collar workers, and veterans were also considered and rejected in favor of overall unity.[75]

The only group of American citizens (aside from native Nazis, Communists, and Bundists) barred from committee membership was United States servicemen on active duty. This AFC policy was instituted in August 1941, after a particularly bitter incident between committee spokesman Burton K. Wheeler and Secretary of War Henry L. Stimson. The senator had mailed under his congressional frank one million AFC postcards to a cross section of Americans compiled from his own mailing lists and those of the Democratic national committee. When approximately four of these cards reached servicemen in training camps, Stimson accused Wheeler of "treason or near treason" in attempting to impair the discipline and morale of the armed forces.[76] Although the mailings to servicemen were accidental, and Stimson apologized a few days later, AFC national headquarters directed all of its chapters to scrutinize their lists and remove the names of men on active duty. As the NYC-AFC central office explained to one young draftee, the policy did "not mean that we subscribe to the view that a man who enters the armed forces gives up his rights to free speech and petition . . . [but] we should do nothing which might be seized upon as a pretext for undermining public confidence in America First."[77] Nevertheless, three months later when the commander of Lowry Field in Denver, Colorado, placed all AFC literature and meetings out of bounds to the men on his base, Flynn and several other committee leaders protested the order vigorously.[78]

Aside from closely supervising the various branches of the NYC-AFC, Flynn maintained a dominant role in the committee's publicity efforts. He advocated steady and utilitarian publicity methods, and eschewed singular, flamboyant projects. He delivered an average of one public speech or radio address every five days throughout 1941, and wrote or edited nearly all of the chapter's literature.[79] (This required considerable effort, as the NYC-AFC produced more original literature than any other America First chapter.)[80] Foremost among Flynn's publicity projects was a series of pamphlets, dealing with the war situation and the American economy, that he prepared for distribution by the national committee. He also contributed the daily copy for the AFC portion of a *New York Daily News* feature titled "The Battle Page." This page presented the interventionist and noninterventionist positions on various points of debate throughout 1941, and Flynn termed the outlet a "tremendous instrumentality for the [America First] Committee."[81] Furthermore, he designed several advertisements that opposed specific Roosevelt measures, as well as a series of ads depicting the horror of war in physical terms and in terms of the destruction of American civil liberties and economic freedom. One such ad, reprinted by the AFC in newspapers nationwide, posed the frightening thought: "War is the Breeder of Isms. The Last War Brought: Communism to Russia, Fascism to Italy, Nazism to Germany. What Will Another War Bring to America?"[82]

Independent NYC-AFC publications were supervised closely by Flynn. In May 1941 he began a weekly chapter newspaper entitled the *AFC Bulletin.* It was legally separate from the incorporated NYC-AFC, being operated by Flynn from his own personal funds. He started it in order to provide the committee with a running, current source of literature concerning local meetings and rallies, as well as clear statements of noninterventionist positions on the issues. He kept the newspaper separate primarily to prevent the post office, which delivered it to subscribers, from gaining legal access to America First membership files. An additional reason was his desire to keep the publication away from all jurisdiction or influence of Webster and Swim, whom Flynn had come to distrust. By the end of 1941, the *AFC Bulletin* boasted subscribers from committee chapters as far away as Arizona.[83] Another small antiwar weekly, *Uncensored,* was published by the NYC-AFC. This liberal sheet had been founded by the KAOWC, but was adopted by the New York America First chapter early in 1941. Its purpose, Flynn explained, was "to call attention to the activities of all kinds of persons designed to involve the United States in the European war."[84] In September 1941 the NYC-AFC published the book *We Testify,* a compilation of statements defending the noninterventionist position by public figures including Flynn, Pinchot, Lindbergh, Thomas, Hoover, and others.[85]

Prominent NYC-AFC leaders and associates contributed to the chapter's publicity effort in various other ways. Lindbergh, Pinchot, and Thomas published several journal articles and delivered numerous public speeches.[86] Hoover offered six radio speeches in which he independently espoused the noninterventionist cause. Even Chester Bowles published an article, in which, without mentioning the AFC, he argued against American intervention in the European conflict because it would weaken this country's power to aid international understanding and collaboration after the peace treaty. He looked forward to a strong postwar international federation, and concluded: "The trouble with the Isolationists is their belief that we can afford to ignore the world and build our civilization behind a barricade of armaments. The trouble with the Interventionists is their belief that we can establish world democracy with the sword."[87]

Less famous NYC-AFC supporters aided the chapter's publicity drive in many ways. One New Yorker, Reidy Reid, wrote a song entitled "America First, Last and Always," which was adopted by the AFC national committee as the movement's official song.[88] Professors Edward Reisner of Columbia University and William Orton of Smith College, as well as Oswald Garrison Villard, addressed a series of foreign policy forums that Flynn arranged at New York's Town Hall in the autumn of 1941. This lecture series was intended to bring dispassionate scholarship to a time of extreme controversy, but the speakers did not pretend to be neutral on the intervention issue. Orton told his audience: "The war party has completely failed, after two years' trying, to convince the country of the necessity of America's active entry . . . into the European War, so now it is falling back upon a fake slogan of 'unity.' "[89] Several young NYC-AFC volunteers also gave their time and talents as "street speakers." They held impromptu sessions from stepladders on Manhattan streetcorners from Greenwich Village to 111th Street every weeknight from April until September. They were quite successful and popular, and sometimes gathered huge crowds and even converted persistent and annoying hecklers to their cause.[90]

The NYC-AFC participated in innumerable other publicity-generating devices. Window-display contests among the chapter branches, pins, buttons, auto-bumper stickers, posters, and billboards were utilized. Flynn's favorite sign, a huge one painted atop the La Resista Corset Company in Bridgeport, Connecticut, read: "Stand Up for America First!"[91]

Cartoons were supplied in syndicated form by John T. McCutcheon, an artist with the *Chicago Tribune.* McCutcheon's most popular caricatures in New York were variations on a theme that depicted World War II as a seductive young woman and Uncle Sam as a blind old man flirting with her while she prepared his coffin.[92] The NYC-AFC also cooperated in promoting and showing locally two short national committee films, *Which Way, America?* and *We Will Stay Out of War.*[93]

Prevalent committee slogans included: "The Path to War Is a False Path to Freedom"; "Let's Keep Democracy at Home, Not Lose It Abroad"; "A Telegram a Day Keeps War Away"; and "This Is a Park Avenue War." After Roosevelt denounced Lindbergh as a "copperhead" (defeatist) in April 1941, NYC-AFC members defended the aviator with the slogan "Show Your Mettle!" In August, however, the chapter rebelled against a national committee slogan that proclaimed "National Defense at Any Expense but Keep Our Boys at Home." Flynn believed that the committee should launch an attack against the great financial waste perpetrated by the cost-plus method of defense contracting. If such an assault were undertaken, he reasoned, this slogan would be incongruous.[94]

Aside from the various publicity projects, Flynn emphasized only one other tactic in the battle against intervention. He constantly urged America Firsters to telegraph and write Roosevelt and members of Congress to express objection to the President's several foreign policy bills and actions. Flynn believed that Roosevelt, as a politician, could be diverted from his warlike policies only if he were shown by public opinion that he would have to take the consequences for his actions "on his chin. . . . That chin is extremely sensitive to public opinion."[95] Secondly, Flynn was convinced that a barrage of noninterventionist letters to Congress would embolden that body into asserting its constitutional rights before growing presidential usurpation of power. He distributed widely a 1940 article by NYC-AFC supporter and former Republican congressman Bruce Barton, entitled "How to Write Your Congressman," and he urged the various NYC-AFC branches to hold contests on the volume of mail sent to Washington.[96]

Despite the ongoing publicity and mail efforts, the NYC-AFC membership grew restive and advocated more glamorous public relations techniques. Many noninterventionists wrote to Flynn complaining that the committee had too few positive and aggressive goals, and saying that the constant role of opposing Roosevelt's initiatives gave the movement the image of being "down with everything."[97] Wrote one woman: "I am almost crazy. . . . Something very violent and vigorous has to be done."[98] New York America Firsters inundated the chapter offices with suggestions for special projects that would galvanize interest in the cause and seize the offensive from the President. The Five Towns, Long Island, chapter conducted a special project called "Your Books for Your Boys," in which volumes on self-taught mechanics and other subjects of interest to young draftees were sent to army and navy training camps. The undertaking was meant to enhance the good name of the America First movement.[99] Several chapters in Connecticut and Massachusetts also ran booths at county and state fairs during 1941, and plans for a large display at the New York State Fair were well under way when the NYC-AFC was refused space at the last minute.[100]

To assuage the membership's pleas, Flynn acquiesced in a few dramatic measures. Most notable among the gala events were the six giant rallies held by the entire NYC-AFC organization. The largest of these, held in Madison Square Garden in October 1941, attracted nearly fifty thousand people. While Flynn at first agreed that the huge meetings were useful in promoting chapter growth, he increasingly favored quieter and more sophisticated endeavors.[101] However, he did allow the New York chapter to participate in the nationwide America First campaign to persuade Congress to require a national advisory referendum before passing a war declaration. Nevertheless, he confided to Norman Thomas that he did not have much faith in the referendum idea: "The trouble is that war declarations . . . are . . . formal affairs. The whole [propaganda] job of getting a democratic country into war is done long before the referendum is held."[102] During the summer of 1941 Flynn became immersed in a special investigation of principal spokesmen and backers of the American interventionist movement, and in a series of special public opinion polls funded by the NYC-AFC.[103] He also agreed verbally and secretly to direct America First branch and chapter chairmen in the Northeast to undertake a clandestine program of writing letters to England. The letters would urge British subjects to demand that their government negotiate a peace settlement with Germany. Because of the extreme criticism that this endeavor, had it become public, would have brought to the AFC, no written records were kept to indicate whether the plan actually was implemented.[104]

By far the most often suggested idea of New York America Firsters for a glamorous event was that of a massive march on Washington. Joseph Boldt told Stuart in May that on the Eastern seaboard the idea of a march was so popular that "people are virtually ready to rise spontaneously and go."[105] Kathryn Holmes, head of the NYC-AFC branch at 111 Broadway, Manhattan, explained: "Perhaps it is the idea of 'ACTION'—whatever it is—nothing we hear discussed has more appeal."[106] Flynn thoroughly opposed the idea. Spectacular projects, he believed, were not nearly as effective in the long run as simple, steady, utilitarian publicity methods. A large mass of people in already overcrowded Washington might easily become disorderly and bring discredit to the America First movement. He counseled

Henry Christ, chairman of the Queens AFC chapter and a persistent advocate of the march, that the poorest America First organizations in the country were those with "small but excitable memberships who clamor constantly for dramatic action like impeachment of FDR, marches, motorcades, etc.; actions which get no results whatever and frequently lead to the most unfortunate incidents."[107]

In addition to the idea of a march on Washington, several other special projects were proposed that Flynn vetoed. Among the suggestions were a "peace train" whereby a different local NYC-AFC unit would send a trainload of people to lobby in Congress every week, a "Bundles for America" charity that would parody the "Bundles for Britain" activities of the interventionists, a systematic letter-writing campaign to Northeastern newspapers by chapter staff members using pseudonyms, and a "peace petition" crusade already begun by John Haynes Holmes and the KAOWC.[108]

In prohibiting each of these special undertakings, Flynn voiced his belief that the NYC-AFC's energies would be needlessly drawn away from more constructive and concrete endeavors. The America First movement, he knew, had urgent and difficult business in countering each of the rapid foreign policy initiatives of the Roosevelt Administration, and in simply holding itself together. The committee in New York was a heterogeneous blend of liberals and conservatives. It was beset by financial worries, fears of subversives, and many other problems attendant upon rapid growth. Flynn kept tight personal control of the sprawling chapter, both administratively and in terms of the committee's primary publicity functions. Ever the pragmatist, Flynn realized the importance of firm direction and coordinated efforts in the quick succession of battles over issues in the Great Debate of 1941.

4

Lend-Lease:
A Test of Strength

The first important test of strength and viability for America First's New York chapter as an agent of the noninterventionist cause came quickly, in the battle over President Roosevelt's Lend-Lease bill. This struggle brought the chapter to life, provided a temporary *raison d'être*, and then almost killed the young organization. The NYC-AFC employed an essentially defensive, rearguard strategy as it fought to establish itself, as well as to overcome the President's popularity in the minds of Northeastern citizens and congressmen. When the Lend-Lease bill became law in mid-March 1941, the entire America First movement entered a period of intense gloom. Nevertheless, it quickly rebounded with a series of successful public relations overtures, and it was able to enter the spring in an optimistic fighting mood.

The Lend-Lease drama began while the NYC-AFC was in its earliest formative stage. On December 8, 1940, Prime Minister Winston Churchill of England wrote to Roosevelt and warned him that Britain's ability to pay cash for arms purchased in the United States, as required by the Neutrality Act of 1939, was almost exhausted.[1] When the President introduced Churchill's letter in a cabinet meeting on December 19, Secretary of War Henry Stimson urged an immediate plunge into the European war. Roosevelt, however, chose to proceed more slowly.[2] Ten days later, he made his famous "arsenal of democracy" statement in a fireside chat to the American people. At that time he carefully and explicitly laid the foundation for the basic position he would hold throughout 1941; America's fate, he asserted, was tied inextricably to that of England. "If Great Britain goes down," the President warned, "the Axis powers will control the continents of Europe, Asia, Africa, Australia, and the high seas—and they will be in a position to bring enormous military and naval resources against this hemisphere. It is no exaggeration to say that all of us in the Americas would be living at the point of a gun . . . with explosive bullets, economic as well as military."[3]

The Lend-Lease bill itself, formally proposed by Roosevelt to Congress on January 6, 1941, was promoted as a measure for peace. The bill authorized the President to sell, lease, lend, or transfer the title of any defense article to any country whose defense he deemed vital to that of the United States.[4] In his December 29 talk, Roosevelt maintained that the sole purpose of his national policy was "to keep war away from our country and . . . our people."[5] His proposal to Congress was bolstered by the famous garden hose analogy. He likened the loan of armaments to England in wartime to the loan of a garden hose to a neighbor whose house was burning. Common sense in preventing the neighbor's fire from spreading to our house, the President asserted, should dictate the bill's passage.[6] He also allegedly vowed in private that he wanted the bill passed only in order to enable England "to negotiate a better peace than she could otherwise obtain — 'a sixty-percent peace instead of a forty-percent peace.' " He had no intention, reportedly, of using the bill to push the United States into war.[7] In addition to Roosevelt's peaceful avowals, Stimson termed the Lend-Lease bill "about the last call to lunch to carry out by nonviolent efforts the defense of our country."[8]

In spite of reassurances that the bill was meant to promote peace, the America First Committee was unconvinced. It was sure that Lend-Lease would lead to dictatorship and war. The proposal threatened the constitutional guarantee of liberty through separation of powers, the committee maintained, by conferring enormous power on the President in the areas of war-making and defense appropriations. By virtually extending credit to belligerent England, the AFC warned, Lend-Lease would start the same inevitable progression to war that had ensnared President Wilson in 1916-17, and could raise the national debt so high that severe economic controls and possibly totalitarianism would be necessary after the war. For these reasons, America First literature and spokesmen consistently referred to the measure as "the war-dictatorship bill." The official national committee statement charged: "The tragic irony of this bill is that it seeks to protect democracy by abandoning democracy."[9] John Flynn assailed Lend-Lease as "an outright act of war ... undeclared war."[10] Additional AFC objections to the bill were based on the beliefs that England was not truly broke but that clever British propagandists were foisting the measure on a generous but gullible United States, and that America's navy would be spread over too wide an area to ensure adequate defense at home.[11]

The strong antipathy of many New York noninterventionists toward Lend-Lease erupted into rapid activity almost immediately after the President proposed the bill to Congress. Flynn, hearing of Roosevelt's speech, hastily agreed to accept the NYC-AFC chairmanship.[12] Countless area citizens, after hearing a radio rebuttal to the President by former Progressive Governor of Wisconsin Philip La Follette, wrote enthusiastic letters expressing their desire to join the antiwar crusade.[13] La Follette, in his address entitled "The Doctrine of Fear," castigated Roosevelt for having no faith that the United States could "stand on her own feet . . . [for] whimpering constantly that Hitler . . . can lick us whenever he gets around to it . . . that we must hide in the shadows of the British Empire . . . [and] thumb a ride on the British fleet." The Progressive also mocked the President's garden-hose analogy, taunting that "no man of good sense would burn his own house to the ground because his neighbor's fire *might* spread to his house."[14] Within ten days of the two speeches, NYC-AFC executive secretary Edwin Webster, Jr., reported that "enthusiasm around New York [for the AFC] is building up," and Eastern regional field representative Joseph Boldt confirmed that "offers to help are coming in fast."[15] A few days later Louis Timmerman, a wealthy business friend of Webster, donated rent-free offices to the NYC-AFC for the duration of the Lend-Lease fight.[16] By January 29, a visitor from Chicago headquarters was able to relay excitedly to national chairman Robert E. Wood that the NYC-AFC was "a real going concern."[17]

With office and organizational procedures barely established, Flynn threw himself into the Lend-Lease contest, and he and the New York chapter made significant and unique contributions to the overall America First fight. NYC-AFC executive committee member Amos Pinchot, famous aviator Charles Lindbergh, Socialist leader Norman Thomas and historian Charles Beard all testified against the bill at the congressional committee hearings. Beard castigated Lend-Lease by claiming that it would "subject all labor energies and all wealth of the United States to the President's personal orders issued at his discretion."[18] Most significant, however, was Flynn's presen-

67

tation to the Senate Foreign Relations Committee of a set of figures disputing Secretary of the Treasury Henry Morgenthau's testimony. Morgenthau had refused to be drawn into a debate on the merits of the bill but, using figures supplied by the British government arranged in tables by himself, added considerable strength to the Lend-Lease cause by telling the Senate committee: "The British just haven't got the dollars to finance their purchases in this country." Flynn, employing Morgenthau's own figures dealing with the estimated expenditures and receipts for the British Empire during the fiscal year of January 1, 1941–January 1, 1942, reached a very different conclusion. He estimated Britain's deficit to be only approximately one-half of a billion dollars, whereas Morgenthau had adjudged a figure of three times that amount.[19]

Flynn further attacked Morgenthau's conclusion regarding other types of British assets. He asserted that the English government possessed, outside the United States, enormous investments that could be converted readily to dollars. Morgenthau had told the Senate committee that these investments were virtually worthless, since they would have to be sold first in the foreign nations in which they were held, and that it would be impossible to exchange these foreign currencies for dollars. Flynn concluded that the English financial picture was not bleak or desperate at all. Britain was attempting to make it appear so, he charged, in order to draw the credulous United States closer to war participation. He also castigated Morgenthau harshly, calling the secretary an accomplice of the British propagandists. The whole tenor of Morgenthau's remarks, Flynn maintained, left no doubt that "the Secretary was completely under the dominion of a desire not to throw light on this subject . . .but to make as strong a case as possible for the British Empire."[20]

Flynn then argued, in an NYC-AFC pamphlet entitled "The Effect of the Lend-Lease Bill on the American Merchant Marine," that England was attempting to deceive the United States with regard to shipping capabilities. He asserted that Britain had many ships that could be pressed into military service but that currently were engaged in commercial trading in neutral zones. Yet England was asking for the loan or lease of American vessels at a time when the United States was dependent on other nations for transport of all but one-fourth of its foreign trade. Flynn concluded that Britain could have but two motives for such a course: an unwillingness to suffer undue financial hardship during the war, and a desire to create a crucial American stake in an English victory.[21]

Flynn launched numerous other efforts against the Lend-Lease bill. He designed the NYC-AFC's first advertisement, entitled "Is It to Be War?" for publication in the *New York Times* of January 28, 1941. Further Flynn contributions included an open letter to Roosevelt that eventually was signed by thirty-eight prominent New Yorkers, a vivid pamphlet called "War, What Is It?" and numerous public speeches and debates.[22] He sarcastically told the Keep America Out of War Congress that because of the vast defense industries the bill would support, Lend-Lease should be renamed "An Act to Promote the Welfare and End Poverty and Economic Insecurity in the United States."[23] Together with Montana Senator Burton K. Wheeler, Flynn debated two pro–Lend-Lease spokesmen, Oklahoma Senator Josh Lee and *Louisville Courier* editor Herbert Agar, on "American Forum of the Air." During this broadcast, Wheeler made the most famous statement of the entire Lend-Lease controversy. Referring satirically to the Agricultural Adjustment Act's early program, he called Lend-Lease "the New Deal's triple-A foreign policy; it will plow under every fourth American boy!"[24] Shortly afterward, Roosevelt angrily termed Wheeler's comment "the most untruthful . . . most dastardly . . . rottenest thing that has been said in public life in my generation!"[25]

Amos Pinchot entered the Lend-Lease fray with the first of his well-known open letters to the President. Emphasizing the enormous grants of executive power contained in the bill, Pinchot contended that the British Parliament, even though Britain was under immediate and deadly attack by Hitler, would never grant such sweeping power to Churchill. If the British Prime Minister even dared to ask for such power, Pinchot maintained, he would be "compelled to leave the House of Commons through aisles of jeering and indignant men." Pinchot concluded by insisting that Lend-Lease was an "unnecessary, un-American, and thoroughly vicious measure [that will] . . . drive this nation into a foreign war."[26]

The NYC-AFC held the first of its six large rallies, jointly with the KAOWC, to protest the Lend-Lease bill. Senators Wheeler and Nye, as well as Norman Thomas, Flynn, and liberal New York journalist Dorothy Dunbar Bromley, addressed the February 20 gathering, and all speakers stressed the theme of strict constitutionalism. Wheeler colorfully paraphrased Roosevelt's 1935 comment made when the Supreme Court struck down the National Recovery Act, by stating that the Lend-Lease bill ignored "the Constitution as something out of the horse and buggy days!"[27]

Despite their energetic fight, NYC-AFC leaders were discouraged throughout the Lend-Lease battle. *New York Daily News* publisher Joseph Patterson confided to Wood his belief that even the bill's defeat "would not greatly impede our drift to war. It seems to be our dark destiny."[28] In early January Lindbergh privately admitted that he thought noninterventionists were losing ground: "The pall of war seems to hang over us. More and more people are simply giving in to it. Many say we are as good as in already."[29] Six weeks later, as the Lend-Lease bill neared passage, he was so depressed over the likelihood of war that "life and spark were gone" from his favorite pastimes.[30] Flynn, after a February trip to Washington to examine the Lend-Lease bill's chances, reported that there was no hope of defeating it. The AFC's course, he counseled, should be directed at drawing out the hearings as long as possible in order to gain time to educate the public to the measure's warlike potentiality, work for some modifying amendments, and then concentrate in the home districts of a few undecided congressmen in hope of making the vote as close as possible.[31]

The fears of New York's leading noninterventionists that war was very near and that Lend-Lease was unbeatable were reinforced by several events which occurred inside the country. While the House Foreign Affairs Committee was conducting its hearings on the bill, Roosevelt lifted the "moral embargo" on the export of airplanes and airplane equipment to the Soviet Union, in order to help that country resist a possible German invasion.[32] On January 29 the Scripps-Howard newspaper chain revealed that the War Department had just ordered four and one-half million medical tags of the type used to identify men killed or wounded in action.[33] Republican Wendell Willkie, only three months after losing the 1940 presidential election to Roosevelt, told the Senate Foreign Relations Committee hearings on Lend-Lease that his former opposition to the President's foreign policy had been "just a bit of campaign oratory."[34] Both the Roosevelt Administration and the English were so confident of the bill's passage that in early February British ambassador Lord Halifax discussed its timetable of passage through Congress with Walter George and Sol Bloom, respective chairmen of the Senate and House Foreign Affairs Committees. As a result of these conversations, AFC executive director Robert D. Stuart sent a telegram to Roosevelt protesting Halifax's "improper attempt to influence the legislative process of the United States."[35]

The major public opinion polls of the day revealed that a majority of the American people also supported the Lend-Lease bill, but that many voters were either uninterested or confused. A January Gallup poll taken on the substance of the bill but without the name attached showed an approval rate of sixty-eight percent. Throughout the remaining period until the measure became law on March 11, the approval rate on the specific Lend-Lease proposal itself hovered between fifty-four and fifty-eight percent. However, the disapproval rate never rose above twenty-seven percent, and only thirty-one percent of the people believed that the bill's passage would result in sending an American army to fight abroad.[36] A mid-February Gallup poll indicated that if the measure passed, fifty-six percent of the American people would prefer to see its sweeping grants of executive power restricted to a limited time period, and not given for the duration of the European war.[37]

The opinion expressed in this last poll was translated into law when an amendment limiting the original grant of power to two years was added to the Lend-Lease Act. Additional amendments stated that nothing in the measure should be construed to allow American naval convoying of arms, to authorize United States ships to violate the Neutrality Act by entering combat zones, or to change existing law relating to the use of this nation's armed forces outside the western hemisphere. These last three clauses, known as the no-convoy, neutrality, and no-AEF (American Expeditionary Force) amendments, were often regarded as meaningless as far as legal effect was concerned. They did not specifically prohibit the President from doing anything that other laws did not already disallow. However, they did constitute what Ruth Sarles, official in the AFC Washington research bureau and later committee historian, termed "an expression of congressional intention in response to public demand." At the time they were passed, Sarles contended, "they were so understood . . . by both proponents and opponents of the bill."[38]

The passage of Lend-Lease plunged the entire AFC into a deep gloom and nearly ruined the fledgling New York chapter. As Ruth Sarles later described the situation, America Firsters entered a "blue funk," and even General Wood considered resigning.[39] The NYC-AFC lost its rent-free office space, since the businessman who had donated it felt that the noninterventionist cause was finished. The wealthy Richardson brothers of Vick Chemical Company, whose financial support was crucial to both the New York chapter and the AFC national committee, wrote Wood to say that they were not sure they wanted to contribute further. They now believed that national

71

unity was needed to carry out the Lend-Lease policy.[40] University of Chicago vice president and leading America First spokesman William Benton, a friend of the Richardsons, reported that the brothers were under extreme social pressure from several of their prominent friends who felt that the antiwar position was now so impractical that it was foolish to "even discuss the subject."[41] Webster and Boldt both confirmed the fact that fundraising was nearly impossible in New York, as most people were sure that the AFC would soon disband.[42]

The badly wounded committee received a near fatal blow two days after Lend-Lease became law. Herbert Agar, speaking at Boston University, vindicated America First's deepest fears concerning the new statute. A strong interventionist, Agar asserted that there had been too much "lying" by the supporters of Lend-Lease in Congress and in the press. "Senator Wheeler," the militant editor proclaimed, "has denounced the measure as not a bill to keep America out of war but a bill to enable the President to fight an undeclared war on Germany. That is precisely what it is!"[43]

The AFC national committee met in mid-March to consider its precarious situation in light of the Lend-Lease Act. Dissolution of America First was a real possibility. Flynn, Pinchot, and others, however, strongly favored persevering. They reasoned that many congressmen and a large segment of the public misunderstood the true intentions of the new statute. A massive public relations offensive that would explain to the country the law's dangers, as well as the overall noninterventionist philosophy, was needed. "To whatever extent we fail to prove our point . . . at this time," Joseph Boldt had contended shortly before the bill passed, "it will not be because the principle on which we urge our point is [wrong] . . . but because we have not yet succeeded in dispelling the mists of confusion skillfully spread by the Administration."[44] Webster agreed: "Our job is obviously . . . to educate the public."[45] After hearing similar arguments during a long and emotional meeting, the national committee voted unanimously to continue the antiwar crusade with "redoubled vigor."[46]

The initial post–Lend-Lease public relations campaign sponsored by the AFC was a flurry of speaking tours by committee leaders. Flynn moved quickly. He began his tour with a radio address the night after the national committee resolved to fight on. He delivered a sweepingly optimistic speech that credited the America First movement with securing the Lend-Lease Act's amendments, and depicted these clauses as crucial noninterventionist bulwarks. "We therefore have been able to stop the march to war for the moment," he boasted. "The Administration was all set to railroad it through. But the AFC and the KAOWC went out before the American people and told them what was afoot in Washington."[47] Boldt used Flynn's address as a vehicle to inspire the sagging morale of America First chapters throughout the Northeast. The New York chapter chairman, Boldt maintained, had served "powerful and moving . . . notice that the AFC has just begun to fight." The Eastern field representative also insisted that committee efforts had made the Lend-Lease Act "a far less dangerous measure than it otherwise would have been."[48] Shortly thereafter, Lindbergh, Philip La Follette, Senators Wheeler and Nye, Congressman Hamilton Fish, and several other America Firsters left on cross-country speaking tours.[49]

A principal theme stressed by AFC orators on their spring tours was the message that steps "short of war" would surely lead to war. Flynn was convinced that Roosevelt well understood the 1916–17 American progression to war, and that he was attempting to repeat the process. There were "three fatal steps," the New York chapter chairman derisively told a Springfield, Massachusetts, America First rally: "Aid 'short of war,' then war 'short of men,' and finally men short of lives and America short of democracy . . . and peace."[50] When, in a late March address, the President expressed an American determination to use "all our resources" to help defeat Hitler, and referred to the passage of Lend-Lease as an indication that the "plain people" of the country had affirmed that determination, Flynn was incensed.[51] Roosevelt's statement seemed to Flynn to be a giant conceptual leap from the specific, expressed powers and intentions of the bill. He was sure that the President and his supporters, whom Flynn consistently termed "the War Party," were trying to use the new statute as a pretext to "make the American people believe that we are [already] in the war. . . . But we can say with relief that we are not . . . and that any attempt to make the people believe so is a deception."[52]

The idea that Roosevelt was cunningly easing the United States into war through a series of tricky steps proved to be a motif in AFC thinking throughout 1941. In October Flynn tabulated the President's initiatives of the year and concluded that Roosevelt had pursued a "step-by-step plan of painting black things white . . . [of] fooling . . . and deceiving the American people by steps 'short of war.' "[53] At least one historian has averred that America First's emphasis on describing all administration moves, however disguised, as deliberate attempts to embroil this nation in the European war was a distortion of the Great Debate.[54] Nevertheless, in the AFC view there was only one 1941 issue, that of peace or war, and it was a distortion to confuse this one issue with discussions of bills and actions that were designed, in Flynn's words, as "trickery [and] subterfuge to befuddle the public mind."[55]

A second major theme of the America First spring speaking tours concerned the President's 1940 campaign peace promises. Committee spokesmen, convinced that these pledges had been meaningless expedients to Roosevelt, determined to echo them until they became a great embarrassment to the President. One campaign vow in particular, delivered by Roosevelt to the fathers and mothers of Boston less than two weeks before the election, was emphasized: "I give you one more assurance. I have said this before, but I shall say it again and again and again. Your boys are not going to be sent into any foreign wars."[56] Flynn recorded several of the President's peace pledges and played them to enthusiastically jeering crowds at AFC rallies across the country. The New York chapter chairman would always quip that Roosevelt "sounds just like Lindbergh!" (or Wood or Stuart or the local America First chapter chairman). The speakers' bureaus of the NYC-AFC and the national committee also compiled lists of antiwar pledges made in earlier years by interventionist senators, representatives, cabinet officers, and prominent local officials. These vows were then recited at the appropriate home areas along the America First speaking route.[57]

The NYC-AFC leader most upset by Roosevelt's broken pledges was Amos Pinchot. He joked in May that the President had been indulging in a six-month orgy of "promise-eating," and that White House chefs were kept busy inventing palatable new ways to serve digestible promises. Roosevelt successfully consumed promises "fried, broiled, fricasseed, and *a la mode*," but he loved "*a la king*" promises the best, Pinchot laughed.[58] Despite his kidding, however, Pinchot was deeply worried about the promise-eating. The idea of electing a man on the basis of his personality, rather than on a set of specific principles, was, to him, "unadulterated Hitlerism" and a denial of the underlying concept of democracy.[59] Lack of accountability by the nation's chief executive, he believed, was simply the first of many American liberties that would become casualties of war: "Thus already," he asserted to Lindbergh, "under the shadow of war . . . Berlin is converting Washington to its doctrines."[60] Pinchot extended his concern with broken pledges to Roosevelt's cabinet officers and spokesmen. He harshly castigated Secretary of the Navy Frank Knox for a warlike June speech. The address, Pinchot charged, "said in effect to the world. . . . 'We, the Roosevelt Administration, hereby [announce that] . . . when we make a promise, it should not be taken more seriously than the promises of the dictators.' "[61]

Apparently the America First barrage of attacks on the promise-eaters was effective. Lindbergh confided in late May that he believed that the American people were beginning to realize that "a Roosevelt promise is not to be relied upon, and that what he says one month is often the reverse of what he says the next."[62] Eleanor Roosevelt was concerned enough about the AFC charges to respond to them. In early November 1941 she wrote to the *New York Daily News,* the leading noninterventionist newspaper in New York, to say that she felt her husband was justified in breaking his 1940 pledges. She explained that America Firsters failed to acknowledge that the President had added the phrase "except in case of attack" to his promises, and that threats to United States interests in any part of the world could be construed as indirect "attacks." Such "attacks" released Roosevelt from the moral bind of his vows. Joseph Patterson scoffed at the First Lady's logic as "a devious and specious explanation which does not explain."[63]

The AFC speaking tours, with their sharp assaults on the President's "short of war" policy and on his broken campaign pledges, had a measurable effect also on Roosevelt himself. The Lend-Lease bill had passed by a comfortable margin in both houses of Congress (260–165 in the House, and 60–31 in the Senate), and the President was surprised to see the America First forces rallying and gaining strength so quickly. In a March 29 Jackson Day address he urged national unity and attacked the noninterventionists by naming them "unwitting" helpers of nazism who attempted to "exploit" the natural love of the American people for peace. He charged pointedly: "They have preached, 'peace-peace,' in the same way the Devil can speciously quote Scripture."[64] A few months later, when Roosevelt was told in a conference with congressional leaders that it would be impossible to pass a bill authorizing an American Expeditionary Force at that time, he reportedly "blew up, castigating [the AFC] . . . for sending speakers into every community causing 'disunity.' "[65]

America First leaders in New York and elsewhere were delighted with the high-level response drawn by their speaking tours. Large

and enthusiastic crowds at rallies across the country also contributed to a buoyant committee optimism within two months after the
immediate post–Lend-Lease despair. Lindbergh reported after addressing a successful Minneapolis rally in early May that "if this
country is run by people, we will not enter this war."[66] Flynn happi-
ly relayed to Wood his impression that, in the Northeast, people
were "beginning to learn that the problem before them is no longer
aiding Britain short of war, but of actual warfare, and this has had a
sobering effect."[67] Stuart exuberantly noted that "in a word the tours
are terrific. . . . This thing is snowballing to beat hell."[68] He was
emboldened to approach the Richardson brothers for new donations, and won them back to the America First cause by telling them
that the tours indicated "things are definitely swinging our way."[69]

Only one cloud seemed to besmirch the AFC horizon during the
committee's halcyon spring days. The Gallup and Roper polls, the
two major public opinion sounders of the day, seemed inconclusive,
paradoxical, and impossibly mercurial to Stuart. On one occasion he
pondered lodging a formal complaint with Dr. George Gallup to
protest an "iffy and hypothetical question that no scientist seeking
accurate information would possibly tolerate."[70] In late April he
lamented to advertising executive Chester Bowles that the "biased
wording of the questions themselves" made the Gallup poll the
AFC's "worst enemy."[71] Many other America Firsters also believed
that the principal polls were deliberately "loaded against us in this
fight." Flynn explained: "The trouble with the Gallup poll is that
the man who asks the question gets into long discussions with the
person questioned and can easily shape the answers to suit
himself."[72]

The AFC's conviction that the Gallup poll in particular was heavily biased against the noninterventionist cause was further strengthened by a study conducted by Dr. Ross Stagner, associate professor
of psychology at Dartmouth College. The committee commissioned
Stagner, a noninterventionist, to examine all of the Gallup poll questions regarding intervention against Germany from April 1937 to
February 1941. In fifty-nine questions, Stagner found fifty-five cases
of "dubious practice," such as the introduction of prestige-bearing
names or terms, the presence of an unjustified assumption in the
statement of the question, or the suggestion of a positive answer. Of
the questions involving dubious practice, more than four-fifths, he
decided, were biased in favor of a prowar answer.[73]

Whether or not the AFC's view that the major public opinion polls were partial was justified, it is true that overall poll results were more helpful to the interventionist than to the antiwar cause. When Americans were asked whether they would vote to go in or stay out of war in Europe, provided that they had to vote at the very moment they were being questioned, an overwhelming majority (seventy-nine to eighty-five percent) replied that they would vote to stay out. This result held constant from October 1940 until a few days before the Pearl Harbor attack.[74] However, when people were asked to disregard what they hoped would be the case, and then to decide whether they thought the United States would enter the war sometime before the conflict ended, the number answering in the affirmative rose from fifty-nine percent in December 1940 to eighty-five percent by May 1941. There the percentage hovered until the Pearl Harbor attack.[75] More significantly, in a choice of whether it was more important for this country to stay out of the war or to help England and assure the defeat of Germany, public opinion had changed from an even division in November 1940 to a majority of sixty-eight percent in favor of the latter alternative by December 1941. In answer to the blunt query, posed in May 1941, of whether they would rather see Britain surrender to Germany than have the United States enter the war, sixty-two percent of the American people answered no.[76]

In other words, the major 1941 public opinion polls indicated that most Americans wished to avoid war if they could, but that most felt that participation in the conflict was inevitable and that war was preferable to a German victory. These results upset Lindbergh profoundly. He mused in his diary that the polls gave cause to doubt the basic intelligence and character of the American people. In wanting Britain to win but in not wanting to "pay the price of war," he warned, many people were "indulging in a type of wishful thinking that must lead us, sooner or later, to an impossible position." He asserted that if he had truly believed that the war in Europe was "our war," he would have personally entered the fighting long ago.[77]

Like Lindbergh, most other noninterventionists were dissatisfied with the Gallup and Roper poll results. Both sides in the Great Debate misread, misquoted, and exaggerated polls to bolster their respective causes. Interventionists often cited the high percentages of people in favor of war without mentioning the specific conditions that were incorporated into the poll questions. For example, an April Gallup poll revealed that forty-one percent of the American people favored naval convoys, while an additional thirty percent approved of them if it appeared certain that Britain would be defeated without the aid of such convoys.[78] Leading spokesmen of the prowar committees then proclaimed simply that seventy-one percent of the people favored convoys![79] America Firsters, including Flynn, erred by insisting that the only consistent, and therefore the only valid, reading was the one that indicated that at any given moment seventy-nine to eighty-five percent of the people would vote to stay out of the European war. Throughout 1941, spokesmen announced this poll at almost every AFC meeting in the country, and noninterventionists often made the incorrect conceptual leap to say that it meant that the vast majority of Americans "were against" entering the war.[80] Ruth Sarles confidently described this index as "the rock bottom reluctance of the American people to go to war . . . [and] the strength of America First."[81]

In order to bolster still further the contention that their favorite poll indicated an American unwillingness to go to war, America Firsters sponsored a number of their own polls in the spring and summer of 1941. The AFC polls posed the same basic query as did the committee's pet Gallup index. In the most prominent America First national committee poll in the New York area, all of the registered voters in Hamilton Fish's congressional district were contacted. The district covered Orange, Dutchess, and Putnam counties. Ninety percent of those responding checked the second space on ballots reading: "The United States should: go into the war_____, stay out of the war_____."[82] Flynn donated NYC-AFC funding and staff assistance to a *New York Daily News* poll that checked the opinion of a randomly chosen ten percent of New York State's voters. Seventy percent of those responding to the newspaper poll answered no to the question: "Shall the United States enter the war to help Britain defeat Hitler?"[83] These poll results helped to boost the expansive spring confidence of the AFC still further. Stuart told Joseph Patterson that the Fish and *Daily News* polls and a similar poll by the noninterventionist *Chicago Tribune* were the three "mainstays" of the committee.[84]

Other Northeastern polls were sponsored by America First. Committee funds were often channeled, sometimes secretly, into other organizations that directly supervised the polls. Using a grant from the NYC-AFC, William T. Leonard, chairman of the Brooklyn committee chapter, polled thirty-five thousand Catholic clergymen nationwide. Leonard conducted the poll through a personal subsidiary known as the Catholic Laymen's Committee for Peace, and found that ninety percent of the clergymen responding did not favor the United States' entering a shooting war outside the Western Hemisphere.[85] A *Yale Daily News* poll funded by the AFC discovered that sixty-one percent of the students on Northeastern college campuses thought America should not enter the European war.[86] A reading undertaken by the New York professional polling firm of Samuel Gill and financed by the committee received a seventy-five-percent negative response to the question of whether the United States should enter the war as an active belligerent in June 1941.[87] Finally, a local newspaper poll underwritten by the Springfield, Massachusetts, AFC chapter uncovered an amazing ninety-eight percent of those responding opposed to a plunge into the war.[88]

The extensive polling and poll-watching done by the NYC-AFC and the national committee, as well as the nationwide speaking tours, contributed to a buoyant America First assurance in the spring of 1941. The hard but futile fight over Lend-Lease had left the committee temporarily faltering and gloomy. However, the deep conviction that the public and Congress understood neither the true menace of the controversial law nor the overall noninterventionist philosophy gave America Firsters hope even during their deepest despair. Bold public relations ventures were proposed and tried throughout the spring, and a surge of AFC confidence resulted. By early summer, Flynn felt so dauntless that he evaluated the Lend-Lease bill's passage as "a modified and diluted victory . . . for the war forces . . . . More importantly, it marked the emergence of the NYC-AFC as a force to be reckoned with."[89] The New York America First chapter was strong and ready for its next major battle: the struggle over the use of the United States Navy to convoy the Lend-Lease goods to England.

5

Summer of 1941:
A Time of False Optimism

The Lend-Lease Act virtually repealed the "cash" portion of the 1939 Neutrality Law's "cash-and-carry" provisions. After March 1941 the "carry" part of the two-year-old statute became the major focus in the Great Debate. As one historian succinctly stated: "Lend-Lease materials would not help Britain . . . if German submarines sent them to the bottom of the ocean. The Roosevelt Administration considered, proposed, and implemented various actions to assure delivery of the goods."[1] The first important sequel to the Lend-Lease fight was a furious battle over the use of the United States Navy to convoy war matériel to England. After Adolf Hitler's June invasion of the Soviet Union, the extension of Lend-Lease aid to Russia also became a point of contention. To interventionists, "delivery of the goods" was a logical concomitant of the Lend-Lease Act itself. To leaders of the New York chapter of the America First Committee and other noninterventionists, convoys and the extension of aid to Russia were new and treacherous steps on the path to war.

As America Firsters fought these measures, their ebullient spring optimism grew. Although their spirits reached a brief low in mid-July following the American occupation of Iceland, the important struggle over the Draft Extension bill of 1941 revived noninterventionist confidence. In general, the period from late April through August was one of strength and assurance for the NYC-AFC. Membership figures soared, several Northeastern congressmen seemed to respond to chapter pressure, and even President Roosevelt appeared aware of, and worried by, committee successes. NYC-AFC executive committee member Amos Pinchot was so optimistic during this time that he boasted: "The situation has reached a phase which can only be described as a race on the part of Mr. Roosevelt to provoke war before the peace sentiment of the country can [fully] organize and impress its will."[2]

The development of the convoy question as the major issue in the spring of 1941 did not surprise America Firsters. Noninterventionists had raised the subject months before, and convoys constituted an integral part of the discussion over Lend-Lease. North Dakota Senator Gerald Nye, in his February speech to the NYC-AFC rally, predicted convoying as a direct result of the Lend-Lease bill. He warned that armed convoys would provoke shooting incidents, and then asked: "When that happens, who is foolish enough to believe that the Congress and the country isn't going to be ready to go the rest of the way in an all-out war?"[3] Persistent pressure from the noninterventionist bloc in Congress obtained a no-convoy amendment to the Lend-Lease Act, and even secured a significant change in the wording of the statute's principal section.[4] Instead of the original authorization for the President to "transfer" war matériel to foreign nations, the law as finally passed allowed the chief executive to "transfer title of" armaments to others. The antiwar forces had feared that "transfer" might be construed to mean actual transportation of the goods.

This lack of authorization for convoys in Lend-Lease was stressed heavily by leading advocates of the early 1941 law. Strong anticonvoy statements made during the debate over Lend-Lease, however, later proved embarrassing to some national leaders. In early March interventionist Georgia Senator Walter George declared firmly that he would remain opposed to convoying "until and unless the point shall come when I shall be willing to vote for war; because in my judgment convoying would lead us into actual war."[5] Roosevelt affirmed in a January news conference that convoys would almost certainly result in shooting incidents, and that shooting came "awfully close to war."[6] Noninterventionists seized upon this statement and paraphrased the President's words with the slogan: "Convoys mean shooting and shooting means war." This motto, an apt distillation of AFC beliefs regarding a step-by-step progression to war, became the committee's chief battle cry during all convoy debates.

So troublesome was Roosevelt's statement regarding convoys that it became difficult for him to raise the issue in the spring. In addition to the constraint put on his own words, the President reportedly felt that public opinion was not ready to accept convoys. This observation was voiced in early April by Joseph Alsop and Robert Kintner, two pro-Roosevelt columnists generally believed to have reliable sources inside the administration.[7] As a result, a formal convoy proposal was never submitted to Congress, and the issue did not come to a vote. However, throughout April and May, the subject was discussed almost daily in one or both houses of Congress.[8]

The convoy issue became predominant in the Great Debate in a rather circuitous manner in the weeks following the passage of Lend-Lease. On March 18 the Committee to Defend America by Aiding the Allies (CDAAA), the leading interventionist group, openly called for convoys. The CDAAA declaration was a salient warning to John Flynn and other leading America Firsters, because they regarded the interventionist committee as an administration "front" group.[9] Consequently, in early April noninterventionist Senators Charles Tobey of New Hampshire and Gerald Nye of North Dakota both introduced specific anticonvoy resolutions into Congress. These resolutions were referred to the Senate Foreign Relations Committee, which voted not to hold hearings or to report them out of committee. Tobey later reintroduced his measure as an amendment to an unrelated bill, and his proposal, known simply as "the anticonvoy resolution," became a cardinal rallying point for the AFC.[10]

Roosevelt finally seized the convoy initiative on April 25, but he proceeded in a strangely roundabout manner. He announced the indefinite expansion of neutrality patrols. Patrols had been carried out since the outbreak of war in 1939 but had been strictly coastal and nominal in nature. The President's new announcement left little doubt, in the minds of noninterventionists and interventionists alike, that some form of convoying had been instituted by executive fiat.[11] The NYC-AFC publication *Uncensored* charged that "the substitution of 'patrols' for 'convoys' " was a perfect example of Roosevelt's "deviousness." The principal characteristic of the President's foreign policy, the weekly newspaper asserted, was a "side-stepping of phrases and proposals which the people had come to understand and to oppose as leading to war . . . not by avoiding the issues really, but by avoiding the issues as the people understood them."[12] Socialist leader Norman Thomas was also enraged by the apparent obliqueness of Roosevelt's new patrol system, and he worried about the angry reaction of the American people if they should later learn that they had been deceived. In a letter to the President he warned, "To put us into the war crabwise, by the use of convoys and similar devices, will be almost fatal to the morale which so desperate a struggle will require."[13]

After Roosevelt's announcement of the extension of patrols, the national debate over the convoy question became pronounced. As with the Lend-Lease issue, the NYC-AFC made many significant and unique contributions to the anticonvoy fight. Public speeches, debates, and open letters were utilized, and America Firsters constantly stressed the view that convoys would lead to war and that Roosevelt was provoking war by instituting them without the consent of Congress. Congressman Hamilton Fish of New York asserted that "the signal bell ringing in the engine room of an American naval vessel to start the first convoy would be equivalent to a declaration of an undeclared war by the President. . . . If President Roosevelt [orders convoys without congressional authorization] . . . he and he alone will be responsible to God and country."[14] In a radio debate with Dr. Reinhold Niebuhr, noted theologian and chairman of the interventionist Union for Democratic Action, Flynn charged that in talking of convoys, "we are talking about war; grim, stark, shooting war."[15] Pinchot derisively maintained that any member of Congress voting for convoys as a safe measure "short of war" should be required to ride aboard the naval vessels.[16]

The NYC-AFC's most important contribution to the anticonvoy struggle, however, came in the form of two large rallies. Held in late April and late May, these rallies featured as speakers Charles Lindbergh, Senators Burton K. Wheeler of Montana and David I. Walsh of Massachusetts, Norman Thomas, Flynn, and novelist Kathleen Norris. The two meetings were well attended, drawing nearly forty thousand people each. Lindbergh described the crowd at the April rally as "courteous, good-humored and . . . one hundred percent with us. . . . I think it is due to pent-up emotion and a feeling of frustration—a feeling that we are being pushed into war regardless of how the people feel about it."[17] Flynn termed the meeting simply "the greatest of its kind ever held in New York," and Janet Fairbank, daughter of an AFC national committee member from Illinois, characterized the May rally as "one of the best" she had attended anywhere.[18]

The great success of the NYC-AFC's two anticonvoy assemblies raised the prestige of the America First movement everywhere. National executive director Robert Stuart asserted that in New York "a new wave of hope . . . spread through the city as a result" of the rallies.[19] NYC-AFC membership soared: two thousand new members signed during the April rally alone, and ten thousand more registered at chapter headquarters within the next four days.[20] AFC national chairman Robert E. Wood used the New York meetings as the basis for a massive fundraising appeal to wealthy potential donors across the country, and the entire committee gained a memorable new slogan from one of Wheeler's statements to the May rally. "The greatest eventual glory comes not from wars won or lost but from wars prevented," the Senator declared.[21] Stuart was so excited by the success of the two New York meetings that he brashly proclaimed that only public opinion, inspired by the AFC, was "holding the fort against convoys. . . . What we do during the next sixty days will decide the issue of peace or war."[22]

The America First successes in New York deeply worried interventionists, and the committee's opponents struck back forcefully. Flynn's resignation as a member of the New York City Board of Higher Education was demanded by Joseph Goldstein, a former city judge.[23] More significantly, however, Roosevelt lashed out at Lindbergh and termed the flier a defeatist and a "copperhead."[24] At the April rally, the aviator had maintained that England was losing the war against Germany, and that the last desperate British strategy was to share "the fiasco of this war."[25] After learning of the President's contumely, Lindbergh resigned his commission in the Army Air Corps. "If I take this insult from Roosevelt, more, and worse, will probably be forthcoming. . . . [Also] I would lose something in my own character."[26] NYC-AFC leaders supported Lindberg's decision. Pinchot felt that the presidential attack had strengthened the noninterventionist cause, both because Lindbergh was a popular hero and because the incident could be viewed as an example of the dangers of war or a wartime atmosphere to freedom of speech.[27]

Secretary of War Henry Stimson tried to counter the NYC-AFC spring successes in a manner different from Roosevelt's. In a straightforward ideological confrontation, Stimson declared in a May radio address that he favored active naval assistance to Britain because any other course, in his opinion, would render the Lend-Lease Act impotent. He also flatly asserted, for the first time in public, his belief that war was inevitable.[28] Cordell Hull and Frank Knox, secretaries of state and the navy respectively, also delivered provocative speeches within a few weeks of Stimson. New York

America Firsters saw these speeches as Rooseveltian "trial balloons," and they responded quickly.[29] Within three days, former President Herbert Hoover delivered a radio address to refute Stimson's talk, and wealthy Vick Chemical executive H. Smith Richardson sent Wood a substantial new contribution. Richardson explained that the recent speeches by cabinet members "raised an entirely new question: that of . . . going to war."[30]

The most pointed attack on Stimson, however, came from Amos Pinchot, who was in a unique position because he, his older brother Gifford, and Stimson had been friends for fifty years. Amos Pinchot's disillusionment with Stimson began during the Gifford Pinchot–Richard A. Ballinger conservation controversy of 1909–10. Stimson agreed to become Gifford's legal counsel, later withdrew, and then advised Gifford to retain a lawyer who later dissatisfied both the brothers. The alienation was completed during World War I, when Amos Pinchot was asked to resign from New York's prestigious Boone and Crockett Club because his antiwar views were at variance with the beliefs of the rest of the members. Stimson, Pinchot's sponsor and a leader of the ruling clique of the club, made no effort to defend Pinchot or to give him a chance to defend himself. In 1932, the publicist described Stimson as "by no means a bad sort of person . . . but a typical victim of that careerism which captures promising young college graduates and draws them into the dreary paths . . . of machine business and machine politics . . . where they gradually lose sense of . . . values." Amos charged that Stimson, during his term as Hoover's secretary of state, was instrumental in "delivering this country to a materialism as sordid as any that exists in the world."[31] In May 1941 Pinchot was able to counter Stimson's warlike speech in an exceptional manner by referring to their old friendship in an open letter. Pinchot told the secretary that he was surprised and disappointed at his current militant stand.[32]

The specific degree of noninterventionist success in countering the spring cabinet speeches is hard to measure, but the NYC-AFC was convinced that it had done very well. Only one problem clouded the committee horizon: an upcoming presidential address was expected to be "a very belligerent talk." In the view of most America Firsters, Roosevelt would either proclaim that outright convoying had begun, or call for a declaration of war.[33] Ruth Sarles, official in the AFC Washington research bureau and later committee historian, said that perhaps no other address since the outbreak of war in Europe was so anxiously awaited.[34]

When the President's address was postponed for two weeks, allegedly because of illness, the committee was exultant. Lindbergh termed the delay a "most unexpected and welcome development."[35] To Pinchot, the moratorium indicated that Roosevelt was "afraid to commit the great crime [instituting convoys or calling for war] against the country at the present moment."[36] *Uncensored* reported that public indifference or hostility to the speeches by cabinet officials had convinced the President that the country was not ready to support strong warlike measures. Noninterventionists, the publication maintained, had temporarily "checked the drift to war."[37]

The AFC confidence engendered by the postponement of Roosevelt's address was surpassed only by committee elation over the eventual presidential talk itself.[38] Finally delivered as a quiet "fireside chat" on May 27, Roosevelt's speech reasserted the doctrine of freedom of the seas, announced another expansion of neutrality patrols, but, with the exception of a proclamation of unlimited national emergency, took no concrete steps. The President bitterly attacked noninterventionists as a small group whose passion for peace had "shut their eyes to the ugly realities of international banditry and to the need to resist it at all costs." He also asserted that antiwar arguments were "echoes of the words that have poured out from the Axis bureaus of propaganda." The next day, in a press conference, he added flatly that he did not contemplate the use of convoys.[39] NYC-AFC leaders were sure that Roosevelt's pointed assaults on the committee, as well as his failure to call for convoys or war, indicated that the America First movement was having powerful effects. Pinchot termed the address a "timid, defeatist" one, and advised Lindbergh to speak out "calmly and objectively, as if the President were a silly, scared, and somewhat naughty boy. . . . It [Roosevelt's speech] shows a man in a desperate way, making a sorry sight of himself in public by giving way to fear, truculence, and the utterance of threats."[40] Flynn announced that the convoy issue had been resolved in a "dramatic and decisive . . . victory" for the noninterventionist cause.[41]

Following the President's talk, the NYC-AFC moved forward assuredly. A large anticonvoy rally, deemed by the committee to be a bellwether of Northeastern reaction to Roosevelt's address, was held by the Philadelphia AFC. Lindbergh, the featured orator, later summarized this meeting: "The country is not ready for war, and the people who are against it do not intend to be intimidated. Our meeting gave them a chance to express their attitude, and they took it."[42]

Flynn attacked the President's speech in a Memorial Day address to the national convention of the Keep America Out of War Congress. At this time he questioned White House reports that ninety percent of the mail regarding Roosevelt's talk was favorable. According to congressional insiders, Flynn claimed, the President was very disturbed and disappointed at the *lack* of public support reflected in his mail.[43] NYC-AFC efforts then concentrated on persuading the public that the declaration of unlimited national emergency did not in any way limit the constitutional guarantees of free speech and assembly. Committee leaders feared that administration spokesmen would attempt to make antiwar statements and actions appear unpatriotic in view of the declaration.[44] Flynn took pains to point out that the declaration granted the President additional superintending powers only in the fields of production, transportation, and the actions of aliens.[45] Pinchot maintained that the proclamation was "not important except as showing the President's inability to sell his war."[46]

In the weeks immediately following Roosevelt's speech, Flynn became convinced that the antiwar struggle was nearing a victorious end. There was "a general feeling," he maintained, that the President had "put the brakes on his surrender to the war party." Flynn claimed that persistent AFC publicity of America's lack of military preparedness had a sobering effect on many people: several senators known as staunch interventionists were "noticeably drawing back," he asserted, and a large segment of the public now favored a negotiated peace. "England needs to be saved from her friends," Flynn joked in defending a negotiated peace, and he was so sure that many citizens now agreed with him that he began to think seriously of a triumphant and imminent dissolution of the NYC-AFC.[47]

Unfortunately for Flynn and the NYC-AFC, their extreme optimism following their self-proclaimed victory in the convoy issue was not justified. Between April 1 and June 14, 1941, public support for convoys rose from forty-one to fifty-five percent.[48] By late May and early June, seventy-five percent of the American people felt that the effect on the future well-being of this country would be very serious if Germany and Italy won the war, and sixty-two percent felt that if the two fascist nations defeated England, they would start a war against the United States within ten years.[49] Sixty-two percent also opposed a negotiated peace, even if such a peace could be based on the unlikely terms of Britain retaining its empire and Germany keeping only the countries it had so far conquered.[50] Fifty-seven percent still felt sure England would win the war, and, perhaps most significant of all, eighty percent thought that even though the United States was not actually fighting, it was "so much involved that we are in it for all practical purposes."[51]

Aside from public opinion, an even more sinister tide of events was running against the noninterventionist cause: Roosevelt secretly instituted convoys by executive fiat. Under the guise of patrols, partial convoying was instituted as early as mid-April. Stimson has recalled that on April 10 he and the President opened an atlas and, "by drawing a line midway between the westernmost bulge of Africa and the easternmost bulge of Brazil, we [decided to] . . . patrol the high seas west of the median line. . . . The British [would then] . . . swing their convoys over . . . to the west of this line, so that they will be within our area. Then . . . we can follow the convoys and notify them of any German raiders or German submarines."[52] Complete transatlantic convoying by the United States Navy began in early July. At that time Knox announced that new orders to the navy went "further" than those in effect a few weeks previously, but he still did not disclose that formal convoying had begun.[53]

Along with its defeat in the convoy issue, the noninterventionist cause was struck with fresh losses in its fight to prevent further augmentations of aid to warring nations. In late June Roosevelt announced the extension of Lend-Lease aid to the Soviet Union, in response to Hitler's June 21 invasion of Russia.[54]

The invasion, a shock to most of the world, was a predictable move according to Flynn. He believed that Hitler had always wanted to expand eastward into the rich agricultural and oil fields of the Ukraine and Rumania. Flynn was convinced that the German dictator was not interested in conquering England or France because, with the exception of France's Alsace-Lorraine province, neither of these countries possessed sufficient natural resources. "That little island [England]," Flynn maintained, "cannot grow enough food for herself. If Hitler got England she would just be a big WPA [Works Progress Administration] project on his hands!" Nevertheless, the German dictator's original assaults to the east, specifically his seizure of Poland, provoked an unwanted intervention by England and France. In Flynn's view, these two countries attacked Hitler not out of altruism, but to prevent Germany from challenging their empires or their dominance of Europe. Russia and Germany, also acting out of self-interest, signed their Non-Aggression Pact of

89

August 1939 when England and France gave warning that they would not tolerate an invasion of Poland. Stalin entered the Russo-German agreement hoping to get the Allies to vanquish Hitler for him, and Hitler simply wanted to be able to choose his own time for fighting Stalin. Now that the Allies were nearly defeated, Flynn maintained, Hitler was again ready to pursue eastward expansion and "the real war [the Russian conflict]. Britain is a mere flea bite."[55]

Accepting Flynn's interpretation of the Russo-German war, NYC-AFC leaders saw "in the tangled course of events new reason for maintaining the fight to keep America out of war."[56] America Firsters believed that Hitler and Stalin should be left alone to fight each other to exhaustion. This course would give added safety to the United States: therefore, aid should not be extended to either side. Igor Sikorsky, helicopter inventor and NYC-AFC member from Bridgeport, Connecticut, declared that Germany would be so busy fighting Russia that it would not be able to attack the United States for at least a generation.[57]

In addition to their belief that the new war would deflect a possible attack from this country, NYC-AFC leaders opposed aiding Russia because they feared the spread of world communism. As Flynn graphically drew the issue: "If Germany wins, Russia will go Fascist. If Russia defeats Germany, Germany will go Communist. . . . The question now is, ARE WE GOING TO FIGHT TO MAKE THE WORLD SAFE FOR COMMUNISM?"[58] In his diary Flynn added that no matter which side triumphed in the conflict, "those peace aims we have heard about—freedoms, etc. . . . [can not] get a chance."[59] Sikorsky asserted that the Soviet Union would "use the results of any military success for the promotion and expansion of its own ideology."[60] Burton K. Wheeler maintained in later years that "evil as Nazi imperialism was, I suspected the Communist techniques would be even more dangerous and far-reaching."[61] Robert Stuart has said that both he and General Wood, throughout their tenure with the AFC, feared a long-range threat from Russia, and that in Wood's case, this fear was his primary motivation in working with the committee.[62] Lindbergh went so far as to say that he would rather see the United States allied with Germany, with all of its faults, than with the "cruelty, the Godlessness, and the barbarism" of Soviet Russia.[63]

Because of their belief that the Russo-German war made the interventionist position "more indefensible than ever," America Firsters

90

were horrified at Roosevelt's extension of Lend-Lease aid to the Soviet Union.[64] Herbert Hoover termed the aid "the gargantuan jest of all history," and Sikorsky labeled it "a betrayal of Christian idealism."[65] Pinchot raged that "the present intimacy between Roosevelt and Stalin is fairly disgusting!"[66] Flynn responded to the extension of aid with a hard-hitting series of newspaper advertisements that attacked the communistic way of life. In one such ad, captioned "No Red Allies for the United States," he hinted that Roosevelt might harbor the dual objectives of defeating Hitler and spreading communism.[67] In another, titled "Can the Reds Worship God?" Flynn attacked the President for having averred that Article 124 of the Russian Constitution gave guarantees to freedom of worship similar to those granted by the United States Constitution.[68] The NYC-AFC also helped to fund a poll by Brooklyn AFC chief William T. Leonard's Catholic Laymen's Committee for Peace. This poll revealed that ninety percent of the Catholic clergymen questioned opposed aid to Russia.[69]

Apparently the campaign against giving Lend-Lease aid to the Soviet Union had a noticeable effect on public opinion regarding that country. According to the Gallup polls immediately following Hitler's invasion of Russia, nearly seventy-five percent of the American people wanted to see the Communist state win the struggle against Germany. Only twenty-five percent agreed with the idea that because Hitler was engaged in Russia, it was now no longer as necessary for the United States to help Britain.[70] However, by late September, a Roper poll indicated that thirty-five percent of the American people felt that the Russian and German governments were equally bad, while an additional thirty-two percent found Russia to be only slightly better than Germany, and only eight percent rated Russia as far better.[71]

Before their view of Russia gained credence, however, noninterventionists experienced considerable uneasiness in early and mid-July. Other presidential actions, besides the extension of Lend-Lease aid to the Soviet Union, seemed to combine to make the period "a critical and somewhat discouraging time."[72] To NYC-AFC leaders, Roosevelt appeared to be announcing decisions casually and smugly, and pursuing his own timetable of war involvement. Earlier in the spring he had declared that the Red Sea was no longer a war zone, and thus made it possible for American ships loaded with war matériel for the British to enter the area. Flynn, at the time of this decision, termed the Red Sea region a "boiling cauldron of

91

war. . . . What in the name of God is the President trying to do?" Flynn raged. "Is he actually trying to create an incident?"[73] Then, on July 7, in a bold stroke that noninterventionists believed to be even more provocative, Roosevelt announced the American occupation of Iceland. Iceland was outside the Western Hemisphere, and on the day following the occupation the President declared in a sweeping statement that the United States would establish strategic outposts wherever they were deemed essential to the security of the hemisphere.[74]

The "Iceland coup," as it was termed by Connecticut Senator John Danaher, gave the AFC a great "sense of uneasiness."[75] Roosevelt was "submitting to the people as 'faits accomplis' one act after another," charged Danaher, and the senator believed that this constituted a grave danger to representative democracy.[76] Norman Thomas agreed. The Socialist leader charged that the President did or proposed things and then said to the people in effect that if they did not support him they were aiding Hitler. "That way lies ruin," warned Thomas, "not only in the sense of war but in the sense of any decent protection of democratic processes."[77]

Flynn was even more outspoken in his outrage at the occupation of Iceland than was Thomas. "This audacious act may well mean the beginning of the end of constitutional government in the United States," he fulminated. Roosevelt would not have acted so brashly had he not presupposed the "ignorance" of the American people and the shadowlike "servility" of the Congress![78] An equally aghast Lindbergh conferred with Flynn and declared the Icelandic move to be "the most serious step we have yet taken. It may mean war. . . . The President has very cleverly maneuvered us into a position where he can create incidents of war and then claim we have been attacked."[79] Pinchot, in an open letter, reviled Roosevelt as an outright dictator.[80]

The NYC-AFC's sense of despair and futility in the face of the President's "faits accomplis" was brief. The chapter soon threw itself into the fight over the Draft Extension bill of 1941, and noninterventionist spirits rose in the heat of the struggle. In August 1940 the first peacetime draft in United States history had been instituted. Flynn and Thomas, along with many other antiwar leaders, decried the law at that time. Consequently, they were wary when, eleven months later, army chief of staff General George C. Marshall formally recommended that Congress extend the selectees' term of service for an indefinite period and remove the restrictions against sending combat troops outside the Western Hemisphere.[81]

92

Marshall made his suggestions at the direction of Stimson, and a few days later, at the request of the War Department, three resolutions providing for consideration of Marshall's recommendations were introduced in the Senate. Within ten days congressional leaders advised Roosevelt that the restriction prohibiting American combat troops outside the Western Hemisphere (known as the no-AEF, or no-American Expeditionary Force, provision of the 1940 law) was impossible to dislodge in view of noninterventionist strength in Congress. A mid-July Gallup poll confirmed this judgment: only thirty-seven percent of the people favored removal of this restriction. This resolution was then withdrawn, and the two resolutions representing the extension of the terms of service eventually became the Draft Extension bill of 1941.[82]

The NYC-AFC led the noninterventionist fight against the bill, and the chapter viewed the contest as "the last and greatest phase of this historic [antiwar] struggle."[83] The America First national committee took no official position regarding the issue. General Wood believed that the public would perceive the draft-extension question as one of defense rather than of foreign policy, and he therefore decided that for the AFC to stand in direct opposition to the army chief of staff would cause the public to doubt committee patriotism. Consequently the national committee confined its role to advising America Firsters to fight the bill in a private capacity.[84] Flynn angrily dissented from this judgment. He berated Chicago headquarters by claiming that "this proposal for the extension of the draft has nothing to do with national defense. It is done for one purpose only —to whip up the tempo of the war hysteria. Certainly we here in New York are . . . protesting against this thing every inch of the way."[85] Norman Thomas agreed with Flynn: "The most logical explanation of the present demand [extension of the draft] is that it is a further step in the process by which an unwilling people are being put into total war."[86]

The NYC-AFC assault against the Draft Extension bill was begun by Gregory Mason, professor of journalism at New York University, chapter committee member, and leader of the Stamford-Greenwich-Norwalk (Connecticut) America First group. In testimony before the Senate Foreign Relations Committee, Mason emphasized that the British dominions of Northern Ireland and India had no draft laws whatever, and that South Africa, New Zealand, Australia, and Canada had conscription for home defense only. In Canada, he revealed, the term of service was only four months! Mason concluded that the real national emergency in the United States concerned not army size, but the "wide and growing resentment among our people over the proposal to ask them to do more than our British allies are doing in the British colonies and dominions."[87]

Flynn reiterated Mason's data in a radio speech, and labeled as a false smear tactic an administration assertion that the army would "melt away" if the Draft Extension bill were not passed. The draft operated on a rotating basis, Flynn maintained, and even if the bill were defeated, more men would be inducted into the army each month than would be processed out. He then charged that the bill should be viewed in light of a whole chain of "persistent and cunning efforts to get us into the European war."[88] To emphasize his viewpoint, Flynn devoted an entire issue of the *AFC Bulletin* to the draft-extension question. The headlines of this issue read: "War Bloc Pushes Draftee Bill to Drag U.S. Nearer Shooting."[89]

Noninterventionists were convinced that their efforts against the Draft Extension bill were effective enough to worry the President when events in the controversy took a surprising turn. Roosevelt sent a special message to Congress, urging that body to pass a declaration of unlimited national emergency to concur with the executive declaration of May 27. Had it passed, this course would have granted the President discretionary power to extend the draft, and it would have sidestepped specific congressional authorization for prolonging conscription.[90] Roosevelt claimed that the interests of saving time dictated this method, but NYC-AFC leaders were sure that the administration was becoming "desperate [and] . . . panicky over its inability to sway the American people from their opposition to war."[91] NYC-AFC executive committee member Adelaide Marquand asserted that she now believed "we are going to win out in spite of everybody in Washington," and Amos Pinchot maintained that he thought he saw "certain signs of returning [national] sanity."[92]

When Congress rejected the President's request for a declaration of unlimited national emergency and decided to vote on the specific Draft Extension bill itself, the tempo of the Great Debate reached a frenzied level. Gallup polls indicated a hopelessly divided public opinion on the conscription question, as fifty-one percent of the American people wanted the bill passed.[93] A Rooseveltian call for national unity provoked an angry outburst from Edward Reisner, professor of education at Columbia University and NYC-AFC chapter committee member. "The suggestion that the nation has made up its mind and that all opponents of our entering the war should shut up and get behind the President," Reisner charged in an address to a teachers' group, "is only a 'slick' and unscrupulous propaganda device. . . . It is simply an effort to weaken the opposition . . . with imputations of poor sportsmanship or even of disloyalty."[94] Harried proadministration members of Congress finally offered the concession of a time limitation of eighteen months of the extension of conscription. Hardcore interventionist Senator Claude Pepper of Florida, however, observed that a discussion of time limitations was "quibbling." The draftees would remain in service for at least five years, Pepper asserted, and possibly for ten years, or for a whole generation: "This contest shall not be over until Armageddon is fought!"[95]

The final vote on the Draft Extension bill was as dramatic as the debate. On August 12 an amended eighteen-month bill passed the House by only one vote. Five days earlier a similar measure had passed in the Senate by a comfortable margin. On the same day as the House vote, the Senate Appropriations Committee unanimously refused a presidential request for one billion dollars in additional defense funds. A nation at peace, the Senate committee maintained, had no need for such expenditures. Flynn was convinced that this refusal, the first such rejection for Roosevelt, coupled with the close House vote on the draft, was deeply shocking to the President. The events of August 12, the New York chapter chairman asserted gleefully, marked "the final turning of the tide against war." He added that any attempts by Roosevelt to take additional steps toward war would be summarily defeated.[96]

Amidst his general elation over the near victory in the conscription issue, Flynn was perhaps most pleased by what he saw as enormous NYC-AFC gains in the votes of Northeastern congressmen. Many Northeastern representatives, especially Democrats, he maintained, had switched from an interventionist position in the Lend-Lease vote to a noninterventionist stance in the Draft Extension vote.[97]

Apparently Flynn's statements regarding the NYC-AFC's effects on congressional votes were quite well justified. Of the 118 congressmen from the six New England states plus New York, New Jersey, and Pennsylvania, the total number of "yes" votes dropped from seventy-one for the Lend-Lease bill to forty-six for the Draft Extension bill. Of those votes that were changed from one bill to the next, thirty-one switched from "yes" to "no" or "no vote" (a shift to the noninterventionist cause), while six switched from "no" to "yes" or "no vote" (a shift away from the NYC-AFC position). Of the thirty-one changing in favor of the noninterventionist cause, twenty represented cities with strong NYC-AFC chapters and two more were congressmen-at-large from New York and Connecticut, two states strongly organized by the committee. Seventeen of those switching toward the America First position were Democrats, who had to defy strong administration pressure in order to vote against the Draft Extension bill.

The most notable Democratic shifts came in Brooklyn, Queens, and Manhattan, the areas of most intensive NYC-AFC activity. Fifteen of the eighteen representatives from these areas were Democrats: thirteen voted in favor of Lend-Lease while only seven voted for the Draft Extension bill.[98] Later in 1941 Flynn and Henry Christ, chairman of the Queens AFC, remarked that while they had begun the year with the support of only one of the Queens representatives, all three of the borough's other men backed the noninterventionist position by late autumn. At least two of the noninterventionist converts stated that they switched because of strong NYC-AFC influence.[99]

To consolidate and celebrate the gains in the draft issue, Flynn planned an NYC-AFC rally for late August. Shortly before the meeting, the Atlantic Charter agreement between President Roosevelt and English Prime Minister Churchill was announced. This agreement, conceived in a secret oceanic rendezvous between the two leaders, consisted of eight points designed to bring "freedom to mankind."[100] America Firsters objected to the document on the grounds that the President was formulating foreign policy covertly and singularly, and that the agreement's proposals were too vague. Flynn suspected that the agreement was a military alliance, and he demanded full disclosure. To some degree, however, committee leaders were exultant because they viewed the secrecy of the Atlantic Charter as further proof that Roosevelt was afraid to confront growing noninterventionist strength in Congress. New York chapter officers decided to make their upcoming rally a focal point of dissent against the document.[101]

The NYC-AFC meeting featured as speakers former Wisconsin Governor Philip La Follette, Vassar College president Dr. Henry Noble MacCracken, actress Michael Strange, and Flynn. MacCracken lashed out sternly against the Atlantic Charter's commitment to the "final destruction of Nazi tyranny." How could this goal be accomplished without the United States going to war, he asked.

How could the document's long-range pledges to uphold freedom for mankind be maintained without America becoming the "police force of the world? . . . The way to make peace," he concluded, "is to keep peace."[102] Chapter staff member Robert Bliss termed the rally an "outstanding success," and Flynn commented that the meeting, combined with the draft-extension vote, convinced him that the "war spirit" in the country was "breaking down."[103] Lindbergh claimed that he was "more than ever convinced that American citizens are opposed to intervention."[104]

The buoyant confidence of the NYC-AFC in late August was intensified when the President once more took time to attack the noninterventionist movement. Roosevelt termed the antiwar advocates "appeasers and compromisers," and charged that the course they recommended was "perilous to our national security."[105] As in the case of the President's late May barrage against their cause, America Firsters believed that Roosevelt would not have bothered to assault them if he did not perceive them to be a serious threat. Again, however, the committee's optimism was rather ill founded. The Gallup and Roper polls indicated that a growing number of Americans, seventy-two percent, felt that Hitler would not be satisfied until he tried to conquer the entire world. Seventy-one percent opposed a negotiated peace between England and Germany, and fifty-five percent felt that the President's foreign policies, including his summer measures, were "just about right."[106]

As the summer of 1941 waned, the NYC-AFC's most hopeful period was drawing to a close. The committee did not know this at the time, however. It had fought hard during the convoy debate, and emerged supremely confident that the noninterventionist position could prevail in American foreign policy. In reality, this optimism was quite naive in view of the attitudes expressed in the late-spring public opinion polls. Roosevelt's extension of Lend-Lease aid to the Soviet Union, following Hitler's June invasion of the country, combined with the American occupation of Iceland in early July, briefly disheartened and frightened the committee. However, a vigorous fight and near victory against the Draft Extension bill revived noninterventionist spirits. Public opinion polls again indicated a deepseated American determination that Hitler should not prevail, but the AFC failed to note this trend. Unforeseen national and international events would soon disabuse Flynn and the New York chapter of their optimism. By mid-September they would be seriously considering disbanding the committee.

6

A Time of Discouragement: New Decisions in the Autumn

The summer optimism of the America First movement was shattered suddenly in September 1941. A series of ship sinkings and other hostile naval encounters resulted in President Roosevelt's announcement of a "shoot-on-sight" order for the United States Navy against German vessels. This executive dictum was fully legitimized by the Congress nearly two months later in a decision to repeal the crucial portions of the Neutrality Act of 1939. Following the repeal, the America First Committee did not experience the profound gloom that plagued it after the passage of the Lend-Lease Act, but it did have a need for concrete new issues. New York chapter executive committee member Amos Pinchot warned in mid-November that "if our people . . . are not given a definite affirmative program . . . they will lose their enthusiasm and their confidence in America First. . . . We must get going or we'll be forgotten—and ought to be."[1] A plethora of new suggestions deluged the committee, and affirmative strategies were adopted in the areas of publicizing national economic problems, pursuing political involvement, and briefly highlighting the deepening conflict with Japan. The Pearl Harbor attack cut short all of these new endeavors, and posed another dilemma for the AFC. The committee's December 11 decision to disband entirely was the last in a series of complex autumn decisions.

The President's September 11 shoot-on-sight order came as a result of recent German attacks on American merchant ships and a destroyer. In late May the merchant ship *Robin Moor* had been sunk in the South Atlantic on its way to British bases in North Africa. Roosevelt termed the incident an act of "piracy," and declared that the United States would not yield to such tactics.[2] Two months later the *Sessa*, an American-owned merchant vessel under Panamanian registry was torpedoed near Iceland. One casualty was an American. Then in quick succession on September 4 and 5, the United States destroyer *Greer* was fired upon by a German submarine near Iceland and the merchant carrier *Steel Seafarer* was bombed in the Red Sea.[3]

The German naval assaults that prompted the President's hostile order had worried John Flynn and other noninterventionists for some months. Nothing would arouse popular war hysteria in this country so much, they believed, as the shedding of American blood at sea.[4] Although early-1941 public opinion polls tended to disprove this theory, later indices confirmed it. A February Gallup poll indicated that only twenty-seven percent of the people of this nation would be in favor of entering the war if American merchant ships with American crews were sunk carrying war goods to England. This figure was only twelve percent greater than the number of people favoring immediate war participation anyway.[5] However, a June poll found that sixty-five percent of the American people believed that full war participation could not be avoided if any part of this country's armed forces engaged in shooting incidents with those of Germany.[6]

America Firsters often accused Roosevelt of astutely fomenting shipping incidents in order to arouse war hysteria. The committee's worst fears in this vein seemed to be confirmed by one of Joseph Alsop and Robert Kintner's early-June columns. The two journalists, believed to have reliable sources inside the administration, avowed that Roosevelt was privately hoping for a shipping "incident" that could be used as an excuse to take the nation into war. The President, they said, was determined "to force the Germans to fire the first shot" and then to act as an outraged innocent.[7] Consequently the AFC was quick to respond to the sinking of the *Robin Moor* with a pamphlet charging that seventy percent of the ship's cargo was contraband! The committee based its claim on the World War I contraband classifications of the United States, England, and Germany, and on the World War II categories of the two latter countries. Forbidden industrial building materials, as well as actual armaments such as shotguns and cartridges, were included on the vessel's manifest. Had not America violated its own Neutrality Act and "invited attack?" the committee asked.[8]

America First denunciations of the shoot-on-sight order itself were even more vehement than those directed at the *Robin Moor* incident. Flynn, upon hearing of the President's September 11 order, termed Roosevelt "a deadly peril to the peace of this nation!"[9] When the next generation is told "this sorry war story," Flynn asserted, "no incident in it will assume a darker hue than this one—coldly calculated" to exacerbate armed conflict.[10] He and Pinchot decried the proclamation as an unconstitutional usurpation of power and a virtual declaration of war, and the NYC-AFC held a Constitution Day rally on September 17 to protest the order. This rally, a relatively small one, was held in Carnegie Hall and featured Senator Charles Tobey of New Hampshire as the main speaker.[11]

Soon after the angry vituperations at the shoot-on-sight order, a feeling of impotence and despair settled briefly over the America First movement. In the committee's view, Roosevelt seemed to be provoking war determinedly and brashly, in spite of popular noninterventionist gains. Ruth Sarles has said that America Firsters believed that their cause was being "dragged along with its heels dug in, stirring up dust but accomplishing little else." There was, Sarles records, no lessening of the opposition to involvement in war, but the American people seemed to be "succumbing to a sense of futility; they were beginning to feel that involvement was inevitable."[12]

Responding to the aura of noninterventionist gloom, AFC national chairman Robert E. Wood despairingly suggested disbanding the committee. However, Flynn, Charles Lindbergh, and national executive director Robert D. Stuart all counseled avidly against this course.[13] Flynn maintained that the shoot-on-sight order was "still not the speech the British want him [the President] to make . . . . He has agreed to put the American Navy more fully at their disposal but he has withheld the greater request [full intervention] . . . because he knows he cannot grant it."[14] Stuart and Lindbergh argued that dissolution would be interpreted by the administration as a sign of weakness, and would mean the abandonment of the millions of America First members across the country. Lindbergh summarized his objections to dissolution by advocating that the AFC "continue its activities until and unless Congress declares war, or unless it becomes obvious that we are no longer being effective—which is far from the case today. . . . I prefer to go down fighting for what we believe in, if we must go down at all."[15] Wood, moved by these arguments as well as by the urgency generated by new shipping incidents, rededicated himself and agreed to stay on as committee chairman.

The new shipping incidents, coupled with militant administration speeches in late September and October, increased the tempo of the Great Debate. In late September three more American-owned merchant ships flying Panamanian flags were torpedoed.[16] In an October 1 speech to the American Bar Association, Navy Secretary Frank Knox called bluntly for a more decisive and active United States naval role in helping to defeat Nazi Germany. He said that, as yet, America was contributing "only part of our share," but that he was confident that this nation would "proceed from one measure to another measure until we have taken adequate steps" to defeat Germany, Italy, and Japan. He added that after military victory was achieved, the United States and England should join hands for "at least one hundred years" to make certain that peace would be enforced.[17] Pinchot termed the Knox speech an "outrageous . . . performance. . . . The Administration no longer pretends to be for freedom of the seas, but for 'control of the seas.' "[18] The AFC Washington research bureau pointed out that British shipping losses during the third quarter of 1941 were well below those of the second quarter, and indignantly asked why England, with more merchant shipping capacity than the United States, could not transport more of its own supplies and save American ships from explosive incidents.[19]

During the final two weeks of October, dramatic developments brought the national debate over shipping incidents to a bitter and chilling peak. Noninterventionist David I. Walsh of Massachusetts, chairman of the Senate Naval Affairs Committee, forced from Admiral Stark, Chief of Naval Operations, the facts surrounding the early-September *Greer* episode. Stark revealed that the American destroyer, cruising near Iceland, had been informed by a British airplane that a German submarine was nearby. The *Greer* found the submarine, broadcast its exact location to the airplane, and then crowded it while the English craft dropped bombs on it. Only then did the submarine fire upon the *Greer*. When both of the German torpedoes missed, the *Greer* unsuccessfully attempted to destroy the craft. Stark admitted that the *Greer's* actions throughout the episode were "in accordance with existing orders" from Knox.[20]

Upon learning the truth of the *Greer* incident, a thoroughly alarmed and aghast Flynn decried the President's "deceit" in having made it "sound as if our ship was proceeding on a peaceful mission carrying mails and matériel to Iceland."[21] On the day of Flynn's statement, news arrived that another American destroyer, the *Kearny*, had just been torpedoed off Iceland with the loss of

102

eleven lives. Naturally, many America First releases denounced the *Kearny* incident as a "manufactured" crisis, "sure to be used . . . to increase the flame."[22] However, Amos Pinchot, in one of his open letters to Roosevelt, expressed the noninterventionist position most forcefully and eloquently. Referring back to the shoot-on-sight order, Pinchot declared: "Mr. President . . . you cannot cast yourself as a deadly, gun-toting aggressor and then rage to high heaven if you are last on the draw."[23]

Within the week the bitter sparring was repeated as Roosevelt termed Nazi submarine warfare an "attack on America," declared that he believed undeclared war was in progress, and pledged that the United States would "see it through" to the defeat of Hitlerism. "We Americans have cleared our decks and taken our battle stations," the President maintained in a Navy Day address.[24] Three days later reports were received of the torpedoing of the American destroyer *Reuben James*. One hundred fifteen lives were lost aboard the *Reuben James*, and Flynn rose to the height of his journalistic sarcasm. The administration, he said, was hoping for even more sinkings: "Oh, for a nice sinking or two or eight or nine. . . . Wouldn't that be jolly? Then Secretary Knox can grow apoplectic. The President can go on the radio and call on Americans to avenge the blood of their boys . . . while they [the administration] will be really very grateful and will call for an AEF."[25]

The grim dialogue over shipping incidents might have continued indefinitely, had it not been overshadowed in late October by the furious debate over repeal of the crucial portions of the Neutrality Act of 1939. The important sections of the law consisted of prohibitions against arming merchant ships, and against allowing American citizens or ships to enter combat zones. On September 21 Roosevelt called simply for repeal of the provision against arming merchant ships. He defended his request by claiming that it was a logical outgrowth of the sinkings, since implementation of his shoot-on-sight order meant violation of the existing law. He also termed repeal "a positive program for giving safety. . . . By the repeal . . . the United States will more likely remain at peace than if the law remains as it stands today."[26] A month later the Senate Foreign Relations Committee, under the control of proadministration Democrats, recommended repeal of the two important additional provisions of the statute.

America Firsters had been expecting formal proposals for repeal of the Neutrality Act for many months, and committee leaders saw this fight as their most important one thus far. As early as January interventionist spokesman Senator Alben Barkley of Kentucky had predicted that, in the interests of the Lend-Lease policy, revision or repeal of the neutrality statute would be necessary. In April Knox and Secretary of War Henry Stimson openly called for repeal.[27] When the actual debate on the issue began in October, Stuart established the tone for a climactic battle: "We have been saying 'this is the crisis' for many months," he confided to New York advertising executive Chester Bowles, "but. . . I'm convinced that within the next couple of weeks, we will face our most serious crisis thus far."[28] General Wood agreed. Passage of the repeal bill would mean that "we are virtually in the war." If the AFC could not impress this belief upon every member of Congress, the measure "probably" would pass.[29] Socialist leader Norman Thomas also saw the situation as explosive, and he declared gravely that he "never had less confidence in Roosevelt than now."[30]

To emphasize their belief that repeal of the neutrality law meant war, America First leaders considered a bold strategy. They discussed having noninterventionist Senator Burton K. Wheeler of Montana introduce to the repeal bill an amendment calling for a declaration of war! This move would graphically demonstrate to the public the committee position that repeal made war inevitable, Flynn explained as he urged Wood and Stuart to adopt the plan. An added advantage, Flynn maintained, would be that if the war declaration amendment failed in Congress, the President would be "obliged to respect that decision and take no further steps toward our involvement."[31] The AFC national committee adopted a modified version of Flynn's recommendation. Deciding that a call for a war declaration would "clear the way for a final fight," the noninterventionist governing body urged Roosevelt to submit such a proposal to Congress. Asking for a declaration of war, Wood asserted in an open letter to the President, was the only way to make the neutrality repeal contest an "honest debate."[32] Roosevelt chose to ignore Wood's letter.

Following the defeat of their bold plan, America Firsters adopted more conventional methods of fighting against repeal. Wood denounced the repeal bill as an "engraved drowning license to American seaman," and Flynn and several other committee leaders testified against it before the Senate Foreign Relations Committee.[33] In his testimony, Flynn termed the bill "part of a general pattern . . . the effect of which . . . is to create a state of war."[34] The NYC-AFC also held a huge no-repeal rally on October 30, at Madison Square

Garden. Nearly fifty thousand people made this the largest AFC rally ever held anywhere. Senators Wheeler, Gerald Nye of North Dakota, and D. Worth Clark of Idaho, as well as Lindbergh, Pinchot, Flynn, former ambassador John Cudahy, and the wife of Senator Bennett Clark of Missouri, all spoke. Lindbergh exulted afterward that "this was in many ways the most successful meeting we have yet held . . . . There is no better indication of how people feel about this war. . . . It seemed as though every man and woman in the crowd was behind us."[35] Flynn also termed the rally "a great success."[36]

In one important aspect, however, the NYC-AFC campaign against neutrality repeal was fundamentally different from its earlier battles against Lend-Lease, convoys, and the Draft Extension bill. Flynn made a very careful and exhaustive effort to identify undecided Northeastern congressmen and to exert selective pressure in their home districts. After an October lobbying trip to Washington, he arranged for almost daily reports on the words and actions of those who were wavering. Shortly before the mid-November House vote, he sent barnstorming America First orators into the home districts of the undecideds and solicited the aid of prominent local noninterventionists to press their congressmen to vote no. For example, on November 4 he telegraphed several Binghamton, New York, leaders: "Congressman Edwin Hall getting equal mail for and against Neutrality Repeal. Undecided on vote. Urge special effort to promote telegrams asking him vote no."[37]

Flynn's increasing politicization of the neutrality repeal fight was matched by an equally close monitoring of the public opinion polls. Gallup polls taken between April and early November 1941 indicated a rise from thirty to sixty-one percent in the number of Americans favoring repeal.[38] Even an AFC poll taken in late October showed fifty-two percent in favor of repeal.[39] After viewing these results, Flynn privately cautioned Wood that "there is a chance of our winning despite the rosy claims of the opposition. But I think we must admit it is only a chance."[40] Norman Thomas, also viewing the autumn polls, grew even more pessimistic than Flynn. Thomas pointed to a late-October Gallup reading that saw Roosevelt placed first on a list of those agitating for war, and third on a list of those agitating for peace. Terming these poll results "characteristic of the muddled public," Thomas gloomily concluded: "We are definitely losing ground simply because people have . . . a sense of fatalism and confusion."[41]

Despite the lack of confidence regarding the outcome of the neu-

105

trality repeal vote, Flynn was convinced that even defeat on this issue should not mean the end of the AFC. He asserted that "if we quit on the thin assumption that repeal [means] . . . war . . . this would be a tragedy of the first order. . . . Whatever the consequences . . . we must stand fast . . . and let the war-mongers, if they dare, say that it [repeal] equals war."[42] This determination was soon tested, as neutrality repeal passed the Senate by a vote of 50–37 on November 7, and passed the House by 212–194 nearly a week later. Flynn's fighting spirit prevailed, however, and he comforted the distraught General Wood by maintaining that "we are acutely conscious of our own troubles. We probably overlook the difficulties of our opponents. . . . There is much we can do and plenty to hope for."[43] Publicly, Flynn issued the strong and optimistic proclamation that the NYC-AFC had "just begun its fight against war. . . . We represent the conscience and common sense of America, and we are going confidently forward to win."[44]

Flynn based his postrepeal assurance on several factors concerning the House vote. He consistently labeled the vote "a staggerer for the President," or "a startling setback for the war-makers."[45] The closeness of the total vote itself encouraged Flynn: a change of only ten votes out of over four hundred would have meant victory for the noninterventionists. Second, in the thirty-four states north of the Mason-Dixon line, in which states over fifty percent of the population lived, the vote ratio was nine to five against repeal. Thirdly, twenty-eight Democrats who had consistently voted with the administration in the past turned against it in the repeal vote. Among the most surprising and gratifying converts to the noninterventionists was Democratic House Judiciary Committee Chairman Hatton Sumner of Texas. Third, many of the administration's old supporters who voted for repeal, alleged Flynn, "did so with misgivings and plain indication that they will not hold out further . . . if the President attempts to embark upon more provocative war steps." Fourth, Flynn was convinced by several leading congressional noninterventionists that "unprecedented" pressure and even outright bribery had been exerted by the administration to change last-minute votes to favor repeal. Perhaps most important of all to Flynn was the fact that "even the most rabid interventionists" asserted during the debate that repeal would not lead to war. "They knew their overwhelming defeat would be certain," he claimed, "if the issue were presented on a 'war or peace' basis."[46]

Flynn's determined confidence regarding the neutrality repeal vote was shared by many other leading noninterventionists. Burton K. Wheeler counseled that "the important thing is that we got as far as we did. If anyone had said to me, at the outset, that we could have come as close as we did, I would not have believed it."[47] Marie Hennessey, official in the NYC-AFC branch on Manhattan's Second Avenue, credited the committee with securing the votes of at least a score of downstate Democrats.[48] Ruth Sarles even went so far as to say that "barring an accident—the accident that actually occurred [the Pearl Harbor attack]—the anti-war group was in a stronger position on November 15, 1941, than it had occupied for some months."[49]

In reality, the NYC-AFC optimism regarding the voting record on neutrality repeal in the Northeast was not as well justified as it had been regarding the draft-extension vote. A consideration of the total vote of the 118 congressmen from the six New England states, New York, New Jersey, and Pennsylvania reveals that a majority of sixty-four voted against repeal, fifty-one voted for repeal, and three did not vote. Although the number voting against repeal was larger than the number who voted against the Lend-Lease bill, it was smaller than the number who voted against the Draft Extension legislation. While seven of the nine congressmen who changed their votes from yes on draft extension to no on neutrality repeal came from districts with strong AFC chapters, so also did twelve of the seventeen who changed their votes in the opposite direction. Nine of the seventeen representatives who changed their votes away from the noninterventionist position were Democrats, but so were four of the nine who changed toward that position. Therefore, Flynn's contention that undue administration pressure changed many votes is confirmed somewhat, but not to an overwhelming degree, in the Northeast. Finally, in relative terms overall, New York City and Long Island, the most heavily organized NYC-AFC area, lost two votes on the neutrality repeal issue as compared to the draft-extension vote.[50]

Following the defeat of the noninterventionist forces in the neutrality repeal battle, the general NYC-AFC membership experienced a wave of despair. Resignations, many of them from long-time members, increased sharply. A resigning New York City man explained on the day of the repeal: "In view of present developments . . . it is my personal opinion that we now must have a united stand behind the Administration in order to face the problems that are ahead."[51] Eastern regional field representative Joseph Boldt urged Flynn to make a radio speech reaffirming the NYC-AFC viability. "Northeastern chapters," Boldt claimed, "are yelling for something that will show the AFC is still aggressive and which will serve as a morale booster."[52] A national committee memorandum two weeks later confirmed the fact that, nationwide, "comparative inactivity is chafing at the members."[53]

Plagued with the dissatisfaction and despair of the membership, New York America First leaders in late November abandoned their buoyantly optimistic postrepeal statements and set to work proposing new, affirmative actions to inspire their followers and caution the administration. Norman Thomas feared that some of the more irresponsible elements among the NYC-AFC membership might attempt "some foolish . . . 'direct action' . . . which could damage the cause" if aggressive new proposals were not forthcoming from the legitimate leadership. He suggested that the committee renew the drive for a national advisory referendum on the question of war versus peace, push for a formal congressional resolution opposing an AEF, and critically publicize Roosevelt's newest appropriations request and "the dangerous Japanese situation."[54] The NYC-AFC executive committee, following a recommendation from treasurer H. Dudley Swim, voted to link together the names of Hitler, Stalin, Mussolini, and Roosevelt in future publicity and advertisements.[55]

Amos Pinchot also posed several suggestions for America First actions in late November. Fearful that the administration planned to avoid the "old-fashioned" method of calling for a formal war declaration and to proceed immediately with unabashed warfare, Pinchot counseled that the AFC hire full-time, paid congressional lobbyists. He also advised a vigorous new series of speaking tours, scored the administration for "provoking a war with Japan," and recommended that the committee emphasize the fact that neutrality repeal gave the President the right, but not the duty, to send American ships into war zones. If Roosevelt sent ships to their doom, Pinchot asserted, the responsibility for loss of lives would rest "squarely on his shoulders, a responsibility he should not be permitted to shift." Although Pinchot believed that the noninterventionist cause still might prevail if the public could be persuaded to direct its anger over ship sinkings at the President, he was not highly optimistic. "The President is sitting on so many kegs of dynamite," he admitted to several friends, "that I should think, on the law of averages, one might blow up in the near future."[56]

Many America First supporters, including Thomas, Pinchot, and New York executive secretary Edwin Webster, also favored the crea-

108

tion of an auxiliary committee of educators and ministers to call for a negotiated peace. The AFC national committee was proceeding with plans for such a surrogate when it was dissuaded by Lindbergh. The American people had been led to hold an unrealistically optimistic view of England's military position, the aviator counseled. Consequently, the only type of peace settlement that the people would accept "could not possibly last."[57]

John Flynn, reviewing all of the suggestions for new America First activities in late November, found them inadequate. The committee must take fundamental new directions, he asserted. Instead of hammering at symptoms and specifics of the intervention problem, the AFC must work on establishing an overall public conception of the hardships, realities, and disadvantages of war. One way to engender this public awareness, he maintained, was for the America First movement to become temporarily silent and circumspect. "Murmurs, even loud wailings" of discontent against Roosevelt and war, he stated, were "coming from many quarters wholly unconnected with us." He asserted that peace threatened "to bob up in London at any moment," and he proposed that the explosive domestic and foreign situations be "allowed to boil up without any open and direct heat from us."[58]

Another technique that Flynn suggested for achieving an increased public realization of the hardships of war was the creation of a professional publicity agency. This bureau, he recommended, could be funded by the AFC but remain publicly independent of committee ties. He would head the department, and would do "a propaganda job, or what might be called an educational job" on long-range issues connected with war and the economy. The regular America First publicity channels would continue to handle committee responses to daily events. After hearing of Flynn's new publicity idea, the AFC national committee decided to implement it, and General Wood personally pledged three thousand dollars for the fledgling agency's first month of operation.[59]

Flynn immediately began his new bureau's work by planning a series of articles and advertisements designed to demonstrate that despite the economic boom experienced by defense industries, war and war preparations were "not all skittles and beer." He directed his appeals specifically at small businessmen, investors worried about inflation, and conservative, tax-conscious groups. He pointed to gasless Sundays and evenings, rising prices, tax increases, shortages of priority items in some areas, and the looming specters of wage controls and possible national bankruptcy. "It is difficult to escape the feeling that it is possible for a nation to go mad," he admonished in one article. "The United States, which two years ago was fearful that a continuance of a WPA for America would sooner or later bankrupt us is now setting the stage to establish a WPA for the whole world."[60] In an advertisement entitled "The Handwriting on the Wall," Flynn depicted a small business establishment bearing a "Going Out of Business" sign.[61] Recalling the slogan that "the customer is always right," he also predicted a loss of freedom in the United States if the federal government became the chief consumer in a wartime economy.[62]

Flynn's economic offensive was apparently unnecessary, however, as prominent polls indicated that by late November 1941 a clear majority of the American people were already aware that war would bring severe hardships. Looking ahead to postwar conditions, Roper polls showed that sixty-nine percent believed that people would have to work harder, sixty percent thought that people would be paid less and that there would be "lots" of unemployment, and forty-three percent felt that prices would rise. Fifty-two percent of the American people were convinced that the postwar economic system would include governmental takeover of many formerly private services, but would still leave some room for private enterprise. An additional thirty-six percent believed that postwar America would see a semisocialized society that left very little room for the profit system. At the same time, Gallup and Roper polls indicated that an overwhelming majority of Americans were determined that Hitler should not prevail.[63]

While Flynn pursued his special propaganda job following repeal of the Neutrality Act in November 1941, the AFC national committee formulated plans for another new activity. The America First leadership decided to engage the committee on a nonpartisan basis in the congressional elections of 1942.[64] While the AFC had previously attempted to influence the votes of existing members of Congress, it had never entered the election process itself. In fact, the committee scrupulously strove to avoid political involvement, reasoning that it might appear to be an anti-Roosevelt interest group and might thereby divide its heterogeneous membership.[65] On many specific occasions, the strictly nonpolitical nature of America First was emphasized in both the national and the New York offices.[66]

Disagreement with directives to keep committee work faithfully apolitical was voiced by many NYC-AFC leaders in the late summer and autumn of 1941. Brooklyn chairman William T. Leonard proposed at a national meeting in July that America First work to defeat any prowar member of Congress "because he is an interventionist, not because of his party."[67] A few weeks later, General Wood contacted Webster, asking him to explore the possibility of getting Democratic candidate William O'Dwyer to turn the upcoming New York mayoralty race into a noninterventionist-interventionist fight with incumbent Fiorello La Guardia.[68] Webster, along with Chester Bowles, favored the more radical step of transforming the AFC into a third political party. Webster envisioned the committee as the last bastion standing for free enterprise and strict constitutionalism against the "ravages" of the New Deal.[69] Bowles, more centrist than Webster, predicted that, whether or not America entered the war, a vast disillusionment would sweep this country within a few years. The "honeymoon days of 1941," he was convinced, would reap a bitter harvest among idle workers or returning soldiers and sailors. Therefore, he believed, the AFC should ready itself to assume a strong, steady, and healing position between the divided major parties.[70]

Perhaps more than any other New York leader, John Flynn favored nonpartisan political involvement by the America First movement. He reasoned that the "unscrupulous" Roosevelt was manufacturing and exploiting war hysteria in order to continue his "gigantic spending spree." Heavy spending kept the administration in power, Flynn postulated, and in straightforward political debates the American people should be informed of how they were being manipulated.[71] By mid-September Flynn was formulating plans for a surrogate NYC-AFC women's committee "as a device for the representatives of anti-war groups to function in a political way."[72] The neutrality repeal battle, however, truly fueled his enthusiasm for political involvement. At the end of the fight, he wrote a personal note of thanks to each Northeastern member of Congress who voted with the noninterventionist position. Incensed at what he believed had been undue presidential pressure on congressmen, he then made an extensive analysis of those who voted with the administration. After deducing a list of "wobbly" congressmen, he journeyed to Washington to study and lobby with each of these. He also directed a new NYC-AFC organization drive for each congressional district where the representative voted for repeal.[73]

While alleged Rooseveltian pressure on members of Congress in

111

the neutrality repeal contest angered Flynn and inspired him to sharpen his political focus, so also did it prompt the long-discussed AFC national committee decision regarding political involvement. Stuart explained that the new position was necessary, because "fascism results when the legislative branch of government surrenders to one man its power to make decisions for the people."[74] The America First action, he believed, would "serve as a warning to those who have slavishly supported the administration's war policy against the will of their constituents."[75] When national committee lawyer Clay Judson warned that AFC political involvement was illegal under the Federal Corrupt Practices Act, Stuart and Wood were undismayed. They began work on a technical reorganization of the committee that would have sidestepped the law, and invited Raymond Richmond, administrator of former President Herbert Hoover's National Committee on Food for the Small Democracies, to come to Chicago and direct the new political program.[76]

Northeastern America Firsters reacted overwhelmingly in favor of the committee's political plans.[77] A few, however, were skeptical or hostile. Norman Thomas resignedly termed the move "logical—almost inevitable under the circumstances—but [it] will require considerable watching."[78] Amos Pinchot was disappointed, feeling that the course was not one "that will inspire anybody. . . . It isn't enough."[79] One national committee member from the Northeast, Mrs. Ellen French Vanderbilt FitzSimons of Rhode Island, resigned over the nonpartisan political decision because she was also a Republican national committeewoman.[80]

Flynn, "greatly pleased" by the new program, was convinced that it would "steam up our whole organization."[81] He plunged immediately to work, having each New York City block catalogued and organized in the manner of the old Tammany machine.[82] He also examined the circumstances surrounding two upcoming congressional by-elections in Massachusetts and Connecticut, and he wrote General Wood of definite plans to involve the NYC-AFC in the latter race.[83] He was determined, however, to oversee the political program carefully and personally. The new activity might attract "a considerable number of the hair-brained fringe [as well as] . . . even more dangerous recruits—gentlemen who are by no means hair-brained and know precisely what they want and who are professional."[84]

The NYC-AFC's political involvement was cut short, only a few days after Flynn officially began it, not by pernicious schemers but by the Japanese attack upon Pearl Harbor. The raid, later denounced by many America Firsters as part of a presidential plot, was a complete shock at the time it occurred. In general, throughout 1941 the committee did not concern itself except to a minimum degree with Japan. A national speakers' bureau manual advised AFC orators to emphasize the belief that "nations act in general in their own best interests. . . . [Japan] is not going to pull Germany's chestnuts from the fire. . . . Obviously Japan . . . is not overly anxious to fight us." The manual added, almost as an aside, that America would be at fault if war came with Japan.[85] Flynn and Burton Wheeler both believed that Japan, even if it captured the Dutch East Indies and Southeast Asia, would not likely attack the United States or withhold the valuable tin and rubber of the new territories. Economic suicide for Japan and its dependents would result from either of these courses, they maintained.[86]

An intensification of America First interest in Japan had occurred in July, as Japanese forces occupied Indochina. Two years before, the President had placed a "moral embargo" on the export of munitions to Japan. This move was followed in 1940 by a formal prohibition of the sale of scrap iron and steel to the Pacific island country, and in 1941 by the freezing of all Japanese assets in the United States. The July 1941 occupation of Indochina was met with a formal protest by the Roosevelt Administration, and the AFC grew concerned over the possibility of imminent war. The America First Committee passed a resolution opposing American armed conflict in the Pacific on the ground that war there would make adequate defense in the Atlantic more difficult.[87] The New York executive committee denounced the "dangerous . . . monstrous" proposition that America should "spill a drop of blood" to protect an area as "remote" as Indochina. Flynn declared further that France, England, and the United States, in professing an altruistic concern that Southeast Asia not be colonized by Japan, were simply looking for an opportunity to exploit the region themselves.[88] Norman Thomas concurred in Flynn's beliefs, and added: "If we go to war over empire in southeastern Asia, neither our descendants nor history will forgive us."[89]

The flurry of interest in the Japanese situation waned by late August, however, and it did not reappear until late November. Flynn reported in his diary on August 30 that he was convinced that an arrangement between the United States and Japan was approaching. The two nations had been "brought . . . to their senses," he asserted, by the realization that "neither party can afford a war there [the Pacific], least of all us."[90] The fall from power of moderate Japanese Premier Konoye in mid-October elicited from Flynn only the brief comment that the "situation in Asia [is] deteriorating swiftly. . . . Talk of war in Orient (about what no one knows)."[91] Until the exhausting battle over repeal of the Neutrality Act was finished, America Firsters said no more about Japan. News of the termination of diplomatic negotiations between Secretary of State Cordell Hull and the Japanese in late November occasioned a spate of worried telegrams to chapter offices.[92] Thomas and Pinchot expressed concern, and Flynn headlined the December 6 issue of the *AFC Bulletin* with the words: "Blame for Rift with Japan Rests on Administration." Roosevelt's and the State Department's "inability or unwillingness" to adjust the Japanese question peacefully, Flynn accused, was producing an explosive situation.[93]

The AFC's failure to perceive the severity of the impending crisis with Japan was quite similar to the lack of awareness of a majority of the American people. While some people did see a confrontation developing throughout 1941, a great number had no interest and no opinion concerning the Far Eastern situation. February Gallup polls revealed that sixty percent of the American people believed that this nation would be threatened if Japan seized Singapore and the Dutch East Indies, but only fifty-six percent thought the United States should take steps to prevent these actions and only thirty-nine percent felt that America should be willing to go to war over the issue. In the case of all questions involving Japan at this time, nearly twenty-five percent of the people had no opinion at all.[94] By early December sixty-nine percent believed that Japan should be stopped, even at the risk of war, but only fifty-two percent thought that war actually would result. Still, twenty percent held no opinions on the subject. Even two weeks after the Pearl Harbor attack, only fifteen percent of the American people saw Japan as a greater threat to this country's future. Sixty-four percent believed that Germany posed a worse danger, and another fifteen percent perceived the threats as being equally bad.[95]

The December 7 Pearl Harbor attack was immediately preceded by the appearance of a government report as bewildering as the attack, at that time, was surprising. Four days before the raid a copy of a secret government document labeled "Victory Program" was given to Senator Wheeler by a noninterventionist army officer. The report was a huge prospectus containing estimates of the manpower

114

and production requirements needed for the United States to defeat Germany and Italy in a global war. It recommended a total American armed force of over ten million men. Wheeler was appalled. "The document," he later confessed, "undercut the repeated statements of Roosevelt and his followers that repeal of the Neutrality Act, Lend-Lease, the Destroyer Deal, and similar measures would keep us out of the European conflict."[96] Wheeler contacted a trusted noninterventionist newspaper correspondent, Chesly Manly, and the two men released excerpts from the report to the *Washington Times-Herald.*

When the newspaper account of the "Victory Program" reached the public on the morning of December 5, the nation's capital was "stunned." Work in government offices came to a virtual halt, as people sat reading the story. The officer responsible for writing the army portion of the report, Albert C. Wedemeyer, later admitted that he was frankly amazed to see his work published, and he termed the leak "political dynamite." Secretary Stimson condemned those responsible for the report's publication as being guilty of a lack of "loyalty and patriotism," and the Federal Bureau of Investigation began a search for the source of the revelations. The investigation bore no fruit, however, and Wheeler kept his secret for twenty-one years.[97]

Two days after the publication of this startling government document, the Japanese attacked Pearl Harbor. America Firsters, along with other citizens, were stunned and confused. The national uncertainty was exemplified by Lindbergh, who listed in his diary several unanswered questions as to the circumstances and severity of the raid and then confessed that he found it "impossible to keep my mind off the war or to concentrate." He added that although he felt the United States had invited attack, there was "nothing to do under these circumstances but to fight." Wood was equally determined to retaliate against the Japanese, but he cynically maintained that Roosevelt had gotten this country into the war "through the back door."[98] An even more skeptical Senator Gerald Nye of North Dakota was addressing an America First rally when news of the raid arrived. "It's just what the British planned for us," he quipped bitterly.[99] Wheeler put aside sarcasm and asserted simply: "Let's lick hell out of them [the Japanese]."[100]

The initial cynicism of some America First leaders regarding the Pearl Harbor attack was magnified in later years. Lindbergh, touring military installations in the Pacific during the war, spoke to some of those present at the raid and gained the impression that the United States had been provoking war by dropping depth charges on Japanese submarines for several days before the attack.[101] Wheeler has stated that America might have avoided war "if the President had required Hull to negotiate seriously and realistically with the Japanese."[102] Ruth Sarles, focusing on the administration's November 26 note demanding that Japan cease its conquests in China and elsewhere, has said that this note "could have been dispatched only with the full realization that . . . war was the only answer."[103]

The most censorious attitude struck in later years toward the Pearl Harbor attack, however, came from John Flynn. He provoked considerable controversy in the United States during 1944–45 with two scathing pamphlets. In these booklets Flynn argued that Roosevelt knew beforehand of the raid and deliberately allowed it to occur in order to galvanize popular sentiment for war. Flynn claimed credit for precipitating a second congressional investigation of the attack in late 1945 and early 1946. When the second probe again found the President blameless, a bitter Flynn maintained that "Pearl Harbor, which began as a military scandal . . . now comes to an end, as is befitting, as a legislative scandal."[104] At least one other America First leader, former national organization director Page Hufty, has said that he finds Flynn's Pearl Harbor thesis "completely accurate." Hufty adds that he has had independent confirmation of Roosevelt's culpability from a friend close to the former President.[105]

Flynn was much less trenchant regarding the Pearl Harbor attack at the time that it actually occurred, however.[106] He immediately announced his agreement with an AFC national committee statement calling for a declaration of war. He also directed all NYC-AFC activities to cease forthwith, decreed that chapter offices remain open only to transact business relating to liquidation, and returned all contributions received after December 7.[107] He reaffirmed his belief in the noninterventionist cause, saying that history would vindicate the America First movement and that he did "not regret one hour, one minute of the fight we made." Nevertheless, he now thought that the time for debate had passed, and that it was "the duty of every citizen to stand behind the government to the uttermost" in the prosecution of the war. In a radio speech entitled "Unity In Wartime," Flynn asked only that the war be conducted "in the interest of American aims and ideals." He wanted no secret treaties "committing America to imperialistic aims or vast burdens in other parts of the world," no profiteering or suspension of civil

116

liberties, no extensive borrowing against the future, and a positive role for Congress in determining the nation's long-range goals and policies. "We cannot for one moment lose sight of the fact that the war means for every one of us a period of sacrifice. This is not the time . . . to be thinking about getting better prices . . . wages . . . profits . . . to be grumbling over taxes or weeping over defeats."[108]

Flynn's opinion that the America First movement should disband immediately and support the war effort sprang from several sources. The committee had been founded as a "temporary emergency organization, not interested in [becoming a] permanent anti-war organizational entity."[109] When Flynn agreed to join the group in August 1940, Wood promised him that it would dissolve totally and immediately once its specific purpose of keeping the United States out of the European war was fulfilled or rendered impossible.[110] In the light of Pearl Harbor, Flynn was more than ever convinced that this policy was wise. The AFC's membership was too diverse, he asserted, to agree upon any principles regarding the war effort or peace aims. Furthermore, he contended, continuation of the committee in any form would provide its enemies with an easy excuse to question its patriotism. "No matter what we would do or say, our motives would be misunderstood," explained a Northeastern chapter chairman in agreement with Flynn.[111] Most important, however, Flynn feared that subversive, profascist elements in and around the NYC-AFC would attempt to "grab this movement, at least its machinery, when its war job is done." Throughout 1941 Flynn lived "in continual fear of the rise of some kind of fascist movement in America," and he did not want a fumbling and divided wartime or postwar America First movement to be infiltrated and used as a fascist front group.[112]

Flynn's opinion that the America First movement should disband was by no means shared by all committee leaders, however. The congressional declaration of war voted at Roosevelt's request on December 8 applied only to Japan. Germany and Italy did not invoke the Tripartite Pact and join Japan in its struggle until three days later. During these three days the AFC underwent a deep internal struggle to determine its future course. The committee debate centered around four options posed by Stuart: complete termination of the group, continued opposition to the war in Europe, transformation of America First into a civil defense service organization such as the Red Cross, or a brief adjournment with the intent to reactivate the committee as a political lobby. According to the last possibility, the AFC might serve as a sentinel to assure civil liberties and the two-party system during wartime, to defeat Union Now (a New York movement advocating political and military union between the United States and England), and to "express principles relative to the conduct of the war and the peace terms."[113]

The last option, the adjournment and reactivation idea, was overwhelmingly the most popular choice among Northeastern America Firsters. Pinchot, Webster, and Swim enthusiastically supported the concept, believing that anti-New Deal principles would be espoused by the new AFC. Edith Newby, chairman of the Bergen County, New Jersey, chapter, spoke for many lesser committee members when she asked, "Why not a platform of national reforms? Why lose a great nucleus we have been building toward better constitutional government?"[114] In Chicago, General Wood had changed his mind and now believed that "our going into the war . . . should not mean the end of the committee, though our energies may have to be diverted into other channels." Early on the morning of December 11 he drafted a proposal recommending the adjournment alternative.[115] A few Northeastern committee leaders urged that America First treat the Japanese attack as a mere "incident," and remain "steadfast against war," but these activitsts were rare exceptions.[116] A somewhat larger minority agreed with Flynn's position.

The national committee debate over the AFC's future course, scheduled for the afternoon of December 11, took a surprising turn. The German and Italian declarations of war on the United States were received only moments before the meeting, and the committee's governing body was so shocked that it hurriedly voted for complete dissolution.[117] Many leaders issued final statements proclaiming their conviction that history would vindicate the America First cause. If the administration had followed the committee's principles, maintained Wood, "war could have been avoided, and America and the world would have benefitted. . . . Our principles were right . . . and are right today. . . . We firmly believe that history will prove that we were right."[118] Chester Bowles asserted that the President had led the country into "an unrealistic policy" that could have but one result. "In the future," he argued, "the exact point at which the explosion took place will not seem important. . . . I am as confident as I have ever been in my life that the future will prove the rightness of the policies" of the AFC.[119] Norman Thomas was so convinced of the veracity of the noninterventionist position that in early 1942 he helped to found the Provisional Committee Toward a

118

Democratic Peace. This group, a technical reformation of the Keep America Out of War Congress, strove to protect civil liberties during wartime, assure an equal distribution of the economic burdens of war, and arrange an early negotiated peace between the Allied and Axis powers.[120]

Following the decision to disband completely, the AFC remained in existence only for the few months that it needed to liquidate. Chapter records were called in to Chicago headquarters for safekeeping, and recalcitrant local organizations were reminded that "if . . . part of our files are missing or are inaccessible, they [present and future investigators] can always say, 'We couldn't tell that you weren't subversive, etc.' "[121] Where chapters were laggard in dissolving, field representatives were advised to contact Flynn for "plenty of arguments in case you do not already have enough of your own."[122] In the end, all save a few local organizations cooperated.[123] Flynn shipped eleven cases of NYC-AFC records to Chicago, but, still fearful of subversive interest in the committee, stipulated that no one be allowed to inspect them.[124] General Wood first secretly stored all America First records in a Sears, Roebuck and Company warehouse, but in mid-1942 donated them to the Hoover Library at Stanford University in California. This institution was chosen because Stanford's president, Ray Lyman Wilbur, had been a strong committee supporter and former President Hoover was the university's board chairman. In the interests of national unity, Wood directed that the AFC papers be closed to research for the duration of the war.[125]

During the last four months of 1941, John Flynn had played a crucial role in America First affairs. The period was a stormy and confusing one, and many new decisions faced the committee. A spate of explosive shipping incidents, Roosevelt's shoot-on-sight order, and the repeal of the crucial portions of the Neutrality Act of 1939 combined to shake AFC confidence deeply. Leaders realized that the committee must engage in affirmative new programs or forfeit its role as chief spokesman of the noninterventionist cause. Decisions were made to pursue nonpartisan political involvement and to have Flynn operate a special publicity bureau, but these new initiatives were cut short by the Japanese attack on Pearl Harbor. The raid, a shock to most America Firsters, provoked a sharp debate over the future of the committee. In the end, startling international developments and not Flynn's fears of subversive infiltration prompted the AFC decision to disband. When Flynn sent the sealed

119

New York chapter records to Chicago and terminated his full-time work in the committee's Manhattan headquarters in late December 1941, he was convinced that any "hair-brained" attempts to continue and subvert a wartime America First movement had "died aborning."[126] Though he never admitted it publicly, Flynn had been plagued since the birth of the NYC-AFC by worries over chapter infiltration by profascist and anti-Semitic elements.

7

Anti-Semitism and Profascism in the NYC-AFC: Fact and Fiction

The New York chapter of the America First Committee encountered the most severe and persistent attempts at infiltration by anti-Semitic and profascist elements of any chapter in the entire America First movement. Although some permeation by undesirables did occur, these groups never gained a significant or controlling influence in any portion of the chapter. Far more pressure on the NYC-AFC and its ability to function as a viable agent of the noninterventionist cause was exerted by the accusations of anti-Semitism and profascism that were directed against the committee. As assistant national organization director Harry Schnibbe has said, the New York chapter became a nationwide "target for abuse. . . . It was smeared . . . imputed . . . [and] accused of every imaginable 'ism.' "[1] Slurs against the NYC-AFC's tolerance and patriotism emboldened the area's actual "hate groups" to seek an active role in chapter affairs.[2] A more serious consequence of the charges, however, was their effect upon John Flynn. "No one will [ever] know," he lamented in June 1941, "what . . . odium has been heaped upon honorable men and women because they dared to lift their voices for peace and for our country."[3] While the AFC national committee often refused to dignify the assaults made against it with replies, Flynn waged an exhaustive personal crusade to defend the America First reputation. As 1941 progressed, he found himself spending more time refuting recriminations than creatively espousing the noninterventionist cause.[4]

Flynn's policy throughout his tenure as NYC-AFC chairman was stricter than that of the national committee in regard to screening the membership for undesirable elements. The chronically understaffed Chicago headquarters required only that each prospective member sign a pledge promising that he or she was not affiliated with any pro-Nazi or Communist groups.[5] Furthermore, all donations of one hundred dollars or more were investigated before they were accepted. Harried national chairman Robert E. Wood believed that the committee's best protection against subversive infiltration was a reliable, intelligent, and experienced chapter leader.[6] Flynn, taking his mandate from Wood very seriously, maintained tight personal control over the NYC-AFC. He attempted to preserve the chapter's integrity by dominating the selection of branch chairmen and then holding these lieutenants personally responsible for the probity of their respective memberships. Many persons who did apply for local memberships or who sent contributions were spurned on the grounds of affiliation with undesirable groups.[7]

Flynn was most particularly on guard against a small number of militantly anti-Semitic groups. Drawing their membership from the lowest economic classes, these organizations also espoused a confused version of "egalitarian" fascism. They saw potential advantage to themselves in any new order. Chief among these groups was the German-American Bund, founded by Fritz Kuhn and now led from its New York headquarters by G. Wilhelm Kunze. Another noteworthy hate group, headed by Edward James Smythe, was an Eastern affiliate of Detroit radio priest Charles Coughlin's Christian Front. Joseph McWilliams' American Destiny Party in New York also claimed a Coughlin tie. In addition to these organizations, William Dudley Pelley's Silver Shirts, the Ku Klux Klan, and a surfeit of smaller groups plagued the NYC-AFC. Flynn publicly maintained that these societies and their leaders were "literally nobodies—people without following who command no support. . . . We would have been mad to have either sought or accepted the support of such groups."[8] He also labeled all suggestions that America First in New York was seriously affected by these organizations "an outrageous falsehood."[9] Nevertheless, these groups did have some following, although the extent of it is not easily judged, and Flynn did worry privately about their infiltration into his chapter.[10]

Other AFC leaders were, in later years, more candid in admitting that some degree of subversive penetration of Northeastern America First units did occur. However, they asserted, the extent of the infiltration was not serious. Senator Burton K. Wheeler acknowledged

122

that "the haters were as hard as maggots to shake off," and Ruth Sarles agreed that some anti-Semites and profascists managed to "wriggle like termites" into the NYC-AFC.[11] New York chapter staff members Robert Bliss and Edward Atwell, as well as Eastern regional field representative Joseph Boldt and Boston AFC co-chairman Paul Killiam, all granted that undesirable infiltration did take place. They cited rapid committee growth, inexperienced personnel, and tough persistence by the subversives as the major contributing factors.[12] Socialist leader Norman Thomas also conceded that unsavory elements tried repeatedly to join the NYC-AFC, but he maintained that the chapter did "a great job of keeping its hands clean."[13] NYC-AFC executive secretary Edwin Webster remained as steadfast as Flynn in denying any permeation.[14]

Objective evidence of subversive infiltration into America First in New York is available, but a thorough examination of the facts reveals that such penetration was extremely slight. The most notorious case was that of Laura Ingalls, famous in 1935 as the first woman to pilot a nonstop transcontinental airplane flight. Ingalls became a frequent orator for the NYC-AFC, and although Flynn barred her as a speaker in the fall of 1941 because of her "foolish and irresponsible remarks," she continued as a member until dissolution. In February 1942 Flynn was shocked and dismayed to learn of her conviction for having failed to register as a paid agent of the German government. At her trial Ingalls aggravated her damage to the AFC reputation by revealing that her superior in the German embassy in Washington, Baron von Gienanth, had told her that "the best thing you can do for our cause is to continue to promote America First." A leading American news magazine commented that it was "impossible to avoid the conclusion that the [Ingalls] trial was a severe indictment of the America First Committee."[15] In another sensational 1942 trial an aide to Hamilton Fish, the NYC-AFC's greatest champion in the House of Representatives, was convicted of helping a paid German agent in New York to distribute pro-Nazi propaganda. The aide, George Hill, had conducted his illicit activities without the knowledge of Fish or Flynn, but still the America First name was further damaged.[16]

On an unknown number of occasions concentrated subversive infiltration into various parts of the NYC-AFC on the grassroots level was temporarily successful. In one such case, Flynn revoked the charter of the Forest Hills–Kew Gardens unit of the Queens AFC because several locally prominent Christian Fronters had gained control.[17] In other cases, Joseph Boldt simply reorganized some of the local units in Connecticut and elsewhere in order to shake out Christian Front lieutenants.[18] In the early, formative stage of the Philadelphia AFC, Flynn intervened through national headquarters to cancel a rally at which Edward James Smythe was scheduled to speak.[19] At a later time, Flynn and national executive director Robert D. Stuart took strong action to prevent two local Coughlinites from speaking at a Brooklyn AFC rally.[20]

Despite the fact that actual subversive permeation of the NYC-AFC was minimal, the committee was beset by a cannonade of accusations of anti-Semitism and profascism. Many noninterventionists, although they expressed "amazement" at the time the assaults began, later came to believe that such attacks were "inevitable." Speaking of the committee's early reputation, University of Chicago vice president and leading AFC spokesman William Benton has maintained: "It never occurred to any of us that we had any taint on us."[21] Ruth Sarles found the barrage of accusations predictable "because it was to Germany's advantage for the United States to stay out of war." In addition to this factor, New York's reputation as the "melting-pot city" gave powerful impetus to rumors that the NYC-AFC was a collection of hyphenated Americans who did not have the best interests of their new land at heart.[22] Flynn explained the slurs against his chapter by asserting simply that they were "too good a weapon, however disreputable a one, for them [the interventionists] to overlook."[23]

The presence of a massive number of accusations of profascism and anti-Semitism soon affected America First decisions and actions. In December 1940, for fear of aggravating Jewish groups already suspicious of the movement, the AFC asked Henry Ford to withdraw as one of the original national committee members. Ford was well known for the anti-Semitic views expressed in his publication, the *Dearborn Independent.* Six months after requesting his resignation, the AFC also rejected a gift of two hundred and fifty thousand dollars from Ford.[24] By late 1941 America Firsters, especially those in New York, were "everywhere on the defensive, explaining that they were not Nazis." As historian Geoffrey Smith has pointed out, the verbal assaults and "the very existence of an extremist fringe [Bundists, Christian Fronters, etc.] . . . and the latter's support" thrust an extra obligation on the America First movement. Constant criticism and the need to respond to it and defend the committee's integrity overwhelmed AFC leaders and achieved its aim of hampering the organization.[25]

124

To John Flynn, the plethora of accusations against America First and the committee's inability to respond adequately to all of them were tragic. The attacks were made, he charged, "primarily to rouse the Jewish population in New York . . . against our committee. . . . There is not the slightest doubt that they succeeded." Unfortunately, he believed, Jewish people and other minority groups that shunned the noninterventionist movement because of the slurs of intolerance against the AFC and other antiwar groups would be the ones to suffer most if war came. War would bring such hardships and disillusionment to the United States that a wave of conservatism and scapegoating, similar to the Red Scare and the resurgence of the Ku Klux Klan immediately following World War I, would sweep the nation. Jewish people especially, he maintained in 1941, had already begun to suffer the effects of intolerance by becoming the "football" of both sides of the Great Debate in their accusations against each other. Flynn was joined in this analysis by Norman Thomas who asserted that war would "unleash the dreadful forces of bigotry" in America.[26] Consequently, when the three top Jewish members of the NYC-AFC staff resigned in early 1941 because of a charge that Flynn was "determined to work with everybody," presumably including Nazis and Communists, in the antiwar struggle, the chapter chairman was sad, angry, and filled with foreboding.[27]

At the same time that Flynn was experiencing the first wave of Jewish resignations and criticism, the NYC-AFC was under attack on at least two other grounds. The first charge concerned catering inflammatory rallies to hatemongering audiences, and the other accusation stated that the committee was accepting Nazi money. Immediately following the NYC-AFC's first large rally, held in February 1941 to protest the Lend-Lease bill, prominent local interventionists and prowar committees launched pointed assaults based on the nature of the rally crowd. Leaders of New York's "hate groups" had been present, the interventionists contended, and the audience booed the names of Roosevelt and Churchill. "The so-called patriots who spoke at tonight's [NYC-AFC] meeting . . . proved beyond a doubt . . . that intentionally or not . . . the America First Committee [spokesmen are] . . . making their appeal to the Nazis, Fascists, Communists, and their fellow-travelers in this city," charged Frank Kingdon and Herbert Bayard Swope, leaders of the New York Committee to Defend America by Aiding the Allies (CDAAA).[28] Norman Thomas, a featured speaker at the rally, defended the crowd as being "mixed and representative . . . genuinely American . . . whether Mr. Joe McWilliams [of the profascist American Destiny Party] was there or not."[29] Flynn and Webster, under questioning from Stuart, readily admitted that some "unsavory characters" were present at the rally. The two NYC-AFC leaders could no more control the attendance of undesirables, they maintained, than prevent prowar advocates from picketing the chapter's large public meetings. "This is simply the type of thing we have to face here in New York," Webster concluded philosophically.[30]

As the year progressed NYC-AFC rallies were continually criticized because locally prominent subversives often attended.[31] Charles Lindbergh, a frequent America First speaker in New York, often took it upon himself to defend the meeting crowds. The people were "an unusually good cross section . . . far above the average of New York," he stated. The opposition press, he asserted, deliberately "picks out and emphasizes the radical and fanatical types who attend."[32] Shortly before the May anticonvoy rally, Wood instructed Flynn to make a public repudiation of Nazi, Communist, Bundist, and other undesirable support for the AFC. The New York chairman arrived at the meeting to find Joseph McWilliams seated in a front row and surrounded by photographers. "I don't know whose stooge he is," thundered Flynn from the platform, "but newspapermen can always find him where they want him." A long and impassioned denunciation of subversive America First supporters followed, and even vitriolic NYC-AFC critic and author John Roy Carlson (Avedis Derounian) later admitted that Flynn's sincerity was "unmistakable."[33]

In addition to imputations against its rally crowds, however, the New York chapter and the entire America First movement was plagued in early 1941 by allegations that it accepted Nazi money. On New Year's Day, the *New York Herald-Tribune* challenged both the CDAAA and the AFC to publish a complete list of their donors of one hundred dollars or more. The CDAAA agreed almost immediately, but the America First national executive committee decided that "since in some communities the issue of 'war or peace' has become so surcharged with emotion," it would be unfair to release contributors' names without first seeking individual permission.[34] Requests for individual authorization, unfortunately, were denied in nearly one-third of the cases. Those donors who refused, many from the "interventionist capital" of New York, explained that "intolerable business and social pressure would . . . result" from disclosure.[35] Flynn, convinced that the interventionist *New York Herald-Tribune* had issued the challenge simply to "intimidate po-

126

tential contributors," refused to reveal any of the NYC-AFC's large donors except to authorized government bodies.[36]

Prowar leaders responded to the AFC refusal of complete cooperation with vehement charges that the committee was hiding embarrassing foreign contributions. CDAAA national chairman Ernest Gibson announced that "pro-Nazi organizations are out soliciting support for the America First Committee. . . . If the supporters [of the AFC] . . . are so pure and holy, why are they afraid?"[37] Presidential aide Robert Sherwood, the CDAAA's largest donor, charged that "as long as any contributors to the America First Committee are ruled by this fear of exposure, the committee itself will remain under suspicion of enjoying the support of those who believe, not in putting America first, but in making America next."[38]

NYC-AFC supporters defended the committee with stinging offensives, but their efforts did little to clear the air of charges. New York executive committee member Amos Pinchot asked how Sherwood could accuse another group of secrecy and deception when he was part of an administration and a committee that were attempting to "sneak" this nation into war.[39] A Jewish NYC-AFC supporter, Sidney Hertzberg, also lashed out against the interventionists: "I have seen," Hertzberg maintained, "the way pressure is put upon members of this committee and upon persons who sympathize with its point of view but are afraid to say so publicly, particularly Jews. I therefore think that General Wood's insistence that contributors first be asked was reasonable and justifiable, although I knew from the beginning that the committee's enemies would make hay."[40] However, as late as October Interior Secretary Harold Ickes was still asserting that the America First movement was financed, at least partially, by Nazi money.[41]

Not long after the worst of the donors' controversy quieted in mid-March 1941, the accusation was made that Flynn termed "the most shocking . . . of all the outrageous smears" against the AFC. The new charges appeared in the pamphlet "America First: The Nazi Transmission Belt," published by a New York interventionist group called Friends of Democracy. Aside from several allegations of overt collaboration between the AFC and various Nazi officials and pro-fascist groups, the tract suggested that the committee might be an unwitting tool of nazism. "Thus, it [the AFC] is more effective than any Nazi agent or organization for it does not bear the stigma of an alien loyalty," the pamphlet argued.[42] To many moderate Americans unwilling to believe that reputable people such as Flynn and Wood

127

were fascist converts, this last imputation of unintentional duping and Nazi collusion was the most plausible one advanced thus far against America First.

The question of a response to this difficult charge produced a split in AFC ranks. The leader of Friends of Democracy, Leo Birkhead, was "a very disreputable character," the America First national executive committee stated. "It would just play into his hands to dignify such a communication [the pamphlet] with a reply, because all that he wants is publicity."[43] Flynn disagreed. Several respected national personalities, including the eminent philosopher John Dewey, were members of Friends of Democracy's board of directors, and Flynn feared that the presence of these names would lend credibility to Birkhead's accusations. The New York chairman moved quickly to secure telegrams repudiating the tract from several of the interventionist board members. One such telegram that greatly pleased Flynn was from writer Will Durant: "The notion that every opponent of America's entry into the war is a Nazi agent is a disgrace to the American reputation of fair play."[44]

The response that hurt and embittered Flynn more than any other came from John Dewey. "The actual text [of the pamphlet] say[s] America First Committee is *used* as [a] 'Nazi Transmission Belt,' which cannot be denied," the philosopher maintained in response to Flynn's original query. The New York chairman read Dewey's communication with "amazement." He wrote the philosopher a long letter explaining his belief that American participation in the war would "crush and crack up and enervate our own social structure so that the next chapter here will be fascism." He asked Dewey to consider the AFC's concern for the preservation of civil liberties in this country, and warned him that if war came, "every [liberal] principle that you . . . have fought for all your life . . . will go into the scrap-heap." He pleaded with the philosopher not to join the "witch-hunt on Americans who are struggling to keep this country out of war," and to "accord to men like me . . . the intellectual integrity and moral fibre not to be used as a transmission belt by . . . anybody." Flynn summarized his growing sorrow and disgust at the acerbity of the charges against America First by asserting that he would preserve Dewey's letter "as one of my melancholy souvenirs of this wretched era."[45] Dewey responded that he did not like the "catchword 'America First.' It's too much like the nationalism that is a great cause of the war." He maintained that he had not meant to imply to Flynn that the AFC was deliberately collaborating with

128

Nazis, but held firmly to his original contention that "others were *using* it in that way."[46]

Following the "Nazi Transmission Belt" episode and partially as a result of it, the New York America First Committee began to have added difficulties with eager subversives. Hearing their names mentioned in connection with the committee emboldened undesirables to establish firm connections. In late April the official newspaper of the German-American Bund, the *Free American and Deutscher Weckruf und Beobachter,* openly urged its readers to join the NYC-AFC. Flynn responded with an emphatic letter to Bund president G. Wilhelm Kunze, affirming that America First did not want "men who support the philosophy of Hitler's government, because we do not believe them to be good Americans."[47] Shortly thereafter Flanders Hall Publishing Company, a firm registered with the State Department as a German-supported propaganda organization, published a book bearing the large cover imprint: "A Flanders Hall–America First Book." Company president S. H. Hauck wrote Flynn, asking him to assist in distribution of the book. The AFC had no knowledge of, or connection with, this or any other project of the company, and both Flynn and Wood wrote to Hauck demanding that this false impression be corrected.[48]

Father Coughlin's organization also increased its attempts to infiltrate America First in the summer of 1941, and an incident having disastrous consequences to the committee's reputation occurred. General Wood ordered out of a Chicago AFC rally some men trying to sell Coughlin's magazine, *Social Justice.* "We don't want you in America First," Wood angrily explained to the men. Shortly afterward *Social Justice* featured an article treating Wood's rejection as an example of religious discrimination. The AFC national chairman became fearful of alienating either Roman Catholics as a whole or those among Coughlin's supporters who were naive, unprejudiced, and attracted simply to the radio priest's economic appeals. As a result, he sent an ambiguous letter to *Social Justice* stating that he "welcomed" the support of Coughlin followers "in our common objective—preventing the country from getting into war." When *Social Justice* triumphantly printed this letter in late July, along with similar correspondence from Lulu Wheeler, wife of Senator Burton K. Wheeler and an official of the Washington AFC, Flynn was aghast.[49] He was sure that the "ill-advised" letters would be construed as an open invitation to pernicious Coughlinites in the East who already had given him considerable trouble.

The *Social Justice* letters invited not only increased attempts at infiltration but massive criticism of the AFC. Norman Thomas joined the official Socialist Party condemnation of the communications, terming them "indefensible, even if they were made to answer a charge of religious discrimination. Father Coughlin and *Social Justice* do not speak for a religious movement."[50] Thomas further demanded a private meeting with Wood and Stuart, and warned them that in the Northeast there was "pretty strong unfavorable reaction to America First" because of the two letters. "I do think we have to lean over backward not to aggravate . . . this anti-Semitic issue," he cautioned the two Chicago leaders.[51] Liberal journalist Dorothy Dunbar Bromley resigned her position on the NYC-AFC sponsoring committee as a result of the *Social Justice* letters. "I could not keep my self-respect and be associated with any antiwar group that embraces totalitarian-inspired elements. . . . You, for the sake of rolling up a mass membership . . . invite either openly . . . or indirectly . . . the support of anti-Semites who have only cheers for Hitler," she reproached Flynn. The New York chapter chairman, dismissing Bromley's charges as "wholly inadequate," maintained that she was allowing an isolated incident to "obscure the main objective" of keeping out of war.[52]

As pressure from subversive elements increased in the spring and summer of 1941, accusations against the AFC from all sectors of the Great Debate mounted sharply. Criticisms from liberal noninterventionists such as Bromley and Thomas were drowned out by more vicious denunciations from American Communists after Hitler's June 21 invasion of the Soviet Union. In a large rally in New York's Madison Square Garden in July the American Communist Party called for the defeat of Hitler's "friends in the United States, the Lindberghs, Hoovers, Wheelers, Norman Thomases, and all other appeasing Munich-men." In August William Z. Foster, party chairman, vilified the AFC as "traitorous." America Firsters, glad to be rid of their Communist "supporters," now parried interventionist charges that profascists attended AFC rallies by citing instances of Communist attendance at prowar meetings. "Those who have been crying that the AFC has been giving comfort to Hitler, may now very justly be accused of giving comfort to Stalin if they continue to urge us into war," gloated NYC-AFC staff member Richards Emerson.[53]

The most damaging attacks against America First in the spring and summer of 1941, however, came from "respectable" and well-known interventionists. In April Secretary Ickes charged that the AFC was composed of "anti-democrats, appeasers, labor baiters, and anti-Semites."[54] In August James Sheldon, official of the New York prowar Fight for Freedom committee, asserted that "America First is only a thinly disguised front for Adolf Hitler. . . . America First should be destroyed along with Hitler." Frank Kingdon, New York CDAAA leader, argued that leading AFC spokesmen "should be muzzled," and former city magistrate Joseph Goldstein contended that the antiwar committee was "merely a cloak for Nazi propaganda." He demanded Flynn's removal from the New York City Board of Higher Education because of his connection with America First.[55] Unpleasant incidents also increased around the Northeast, as Carnegie Institute of Technology in Pittsburgh, Ohio University, and Ebbets Field in Brooklyn all denied the AFC permission to hire space for speakers. In the Ebbets Field case, Brooklyn Dodgers' president Larry MacPhail declared that he had "no use for . . . Colonel Lindbergh, Senators Wheeler and Nye, the German-American Bund, the Christian Front . . . or Adolf Hitler. I believe the propaganda which these groups and individuals are sponsoring is extremely dangerous in this emergency."[56]

The reactions of New York America First leaders to the unpleasant accusations and incidents throughout the spring and summer were varied but generally subdued. William T. Leonard, Brooklyn AFC chairman, responded to the Ebbets Field episode by scoring it as "a sample of the intolerance which has led to the whole campaign of smearing those Americans who want to save America from a foreign war . . . a totalitarian idea."[57] Flynn had come to believe that the incessant obloquies against the committee were merely "red herrings" designed to shift attention away from the force of the AFC's arguments. He answered the wave of verbal abuse in August with a calm statement: "Once and for all let it be said that the charge that the AFC is anti-Semitic is a shameful calumny and is made merely to injure the committee."[58] He confided ironically in his diary that it looked as if "the warmakers have been caught in the fires of their own hysteria . . . declaring that . . . [America First] should be muzzled. . . . Pretty exhibition. I wonder what process they would use—the concentration camp? How does this differ from Hitler?"[59]

Despite their rather restrained rhetoric, Flynn and others were chafing bitterly at the flood of accusations. The New York chairman received "a flock" of anonymous, denunciatory letters every day, and he admitted that "gibes and hostile criticism" were his daily diet. There was "scarcely anybody . . . actively connected" with the NYC-AFC "about whom I have not heard the most outrageous stories," he revealed sourly.[60] In addition to disparagement from the outside, Flynn earned almost constant censure from America First members who wanted a more vigorous response to the attacks. One Queens member warned that "the tolerant attitude" assumed by Wood, Flynn, and Webster "in failing to demand retraction of these statements has been the cause of wide discussion of members of AFC."[61] During the summer of 1941, Flynn consequently began to amass evidence in a thorough study of the sources of interventionist charges against America First.[62] Before his investigation could bear fruit, however, he saw the public initiative in answering criticisms seized dramatically away from him by Charles Lindbergh.

Lindbergh's personal views and some of his actions had made his noninterventionist beliefs controversial even before he became associated with the AFC. He voted for Herbert Hoover in 1932 because he feared that the New Deal would be socialistic and he did not "trust" Roosevelt. The President was "unstable," Lindbergh was convinced, and possessed the dangerous "ability to persuade himself that whatever he wants himself is also to the best interests of the country." The aviator was sure that Roosevelt "would, consciously or unconsciously, like to take the center of the world stage away from Hitler."[63] On a complimentary tour of the German Luftwaffe in the late 1930s Lindbergh gained "disturbing insight into the magnitude of Hitler's intentions." Like Flynn, the aviator believed that Hitler wanted to expand eastward into the Soviet Union. Lindbergh warned the countries of western Europe to rearm defensively as a preventive measure, but he urged them not to intervene in Germany's offensive against Stalin.[64] He viewed the French and British intervention against Hitler in 1939 as "one more of those age-old struggles . . . a war of politics and possession."[65]

Lindbergh's methods of emphasis and expression caused him to be labeled a racist and a defeatist by many persons. He spoke often of the glories of "Western civilization," and he advocated that Americans not "dissipate our strength, or help Europe dissipate hers [in war]. . . . It is only by [peaceful] cooperation that we can maintain the supremacy of Western civilization."[66] War would bring "race riots, revolution, destruction . . . to our race, or culture, or whatever you want to call it."[67] It was foolish, he maintained, for "Western nations," including the United States, England, and Germany, "to

132

carry on a prostrating war among themselves." Such a course would make them too weak "to resist" Russia and the other nations of "the East."[68] Lindbergh also openly predicted a British defeat throughout 1941. American interventionists, he contended, failed to recognize the extent of the "decadence in England or the virility in Germany."[69] He militantly attacked prowar advocates, charging that they gave "comfort to the enemy . . . for their policy has led to the defeat of every country that followed their advice since this war began."[70]

As a blunt speaker Lindbergh aggravated many people inside and outside the America First movement. He readily admitted that he did not intend to have his thoughts or expressions "held back by the question of influencing the mass of people." Furthermore he thoroughly distrusted the press, and believed that it would distort his statements to the point of being inflammatory no matter how tactful he might try to be.[71] Consequently, he refused to heed repeated requests from Norman Thomas to modify and clarify his racial and religious views. The distraught Thomas, under heavy criticism from Socialists and liberals for appearing with Lindbergh on America First speaking platforms, ruefully complained to General Wood that it was "an enormous pity that . . . [Lindbergh] will not take the advice on public relations which he would expect an amateur in aviation to take from an expert."[72]

Lindbergh's most controversial step before joining the AFC was the acceptance of an honorary medal from German Field Marshal Hermann Goering in 1938. The decoration was presented without warning at a dinner in the American embassy in Berlin shortly after the Munich Pact. He accepted the medal, Lindbergh later recalled, because at the time "there was a decided effort to improve the relationships between European countries in the hope of avoiding war." When the decoration became the grounds for many accusations of German sympathy during 1941, the aviator refused to return it. It had been given "in times of peace and as a gesture of friendship," he maintained, and returning it could have "no constructive effect."[73]

The very act of Lindbergh's joining the AFC national committee in April 1941, over the objections of some of America First's Jewish advisers, increased the controversy surrounding him.[74] The aviator's partisans rejoiced: Ruth Sarles stated that "the anti-war forces now had a popular hero, and the AFC was incalculably strengthened." William Benton was convinced that "Lindbergh in a certain sense

133

gave it a character, a uniqueness. He brought something extra
. . . and gave a kind of lift to the group." Wood was so happy about
the aviator's connection with America First that he repeatedly urged
him to become national chairman.[75] However, Lindbergh's addition
caused many problems for the NYC-AFC's reputation for anti-Semitism and profascism, even though the flier never officially joined the
chapter. He was associated with the NYC-AFC in the public eye
because he lived on Long Island at the time and he delivered three
of his twelve major America First addresses before the committee's
New York rallies. Flynn's Manhattan headquarters also handled
Lindbergh's nonpersonal correspondence for much of the year.[76]

The principal early damage done by Lindbergh to the NYC-AFC's
reputation for being anti-Semitic and profascist came because of his
previous connection with a disreputable noninterventionist group
called the No Foreign Wars Committee (NFWC). The NFWC existed briefly for the five months following November 1940, and it was
directed from its New York headquarters by Verne Marshall, editor
of the *Cedar Rapids* (Iowa) *Gazette*. Marshall, who frequently made
anti-Semitic statements, has been called by one America Firster "the
eccentric problem child of nonintervention." Stuart described the
editor as "a wild man . . . who certainly helped to discredit us in the
eyes of the public."[77] William R. Castle, an AFC national committee
member familiar with Marshall for many years, warned General
Wood very early that Marshall was "an unreliable egoist . . . [who] is
inclined to run over the mark. . . . [He] confuses issues badly . . .
[and] his ideas are often violent. . . . Marshall believes anything that
is told to him which reflects on the Jews or the New Deal. Heaven
knows that his auspices are thoroughly bad."[78]

The America First Committee decided early to have nothing to do
with the NFWC.[79] The NYC-AFC and the NFWC competed for a
time in late 1940 for leadership of the noninterventionist cause in
New York, but the America First movement was able to seize the top
position when Flynn convinced Charles Payson and Jeremiah Milbank, two conservative multimillionaries close to the NFWC, to
switch their support to the AFC. Flynn gained the allegiance of the
two men, who reportedly had promised to spend one million dollars
to keep America out of war, by pledging that America First would
distribute part of its money to various other antiwar groups in the
Northeast.[80] The AFC subsequently redeemed its promise by giving
at least five thousand dollars to several groups within the Keep
America Out of War Congress during early 1941. There is no evi-

134

dence, however, that America First ever gave money to the NFWC.[81]

Lindbergh, who was in close contact with the NFWC during its formative period, broke with the group in January 1941. Although Lindbergh was never officially a member, Marshall boldly and continually asserted in meetings with the press that the aviator would "do anything this committee wants [him] . . . to do."[82] Lindbergh eventually repudiated Marshall because of the editor's "erratic . . . disturbing . . . violent . . . [and] nervous behavior," and because the NFWC had accepted contributions from, and aligned itself with, some definitely anti-Semitic and profascist backers.[83] Nevertheless, the aviator's name was ineradicably linked with Marshall and the NFWC in the public mind, and Lindbergh's later connection with the America First movement effectively formed a strong and damaging nexus between the AFC itself and its public reputation for anti-Semitism and profascism.[84]

Lindbergh's next major blow to America First prestige, after establishing a public tie with the NFWC, came in a speech delivered at an AFC rally in Des Moines, Iowa, in September 1941. The famous Des Moines speech had severe repercussions for the committee nationwide, but nowhere was the injury so harsh as in New York. The address resulted partially from Lindbergh's desire to quell the urging of his friends that he enter politics and lead a new conservative, isolationist coalition against Roosevelt. Lindbergh firmly maintained that he "wasn't suited to, or trained for" a life in politics, and he insisted that he had "no intention" of being pushed into it. He confided mordantly in his diary: "I *can* avoid it [politics] . . . by making one address [that would] . . . discuss truthfully and openly the fundamental issues which face this country today. One need only . . . speak what he actually believes, and in these times he need have little fear of being pushed into politics—even by his friends."[85] Actually, Lindbergh's fears of unwanted political success may have been chimerical. A May Gallup poll indicated that only sixty percent of the American people were familiar with his views on foreign policy, and of this number only twenty-four percent agreed with them.[86]

A desire to avoid political involvement was only one of Lindbergh's primary reasons for delivering the Des Moines speech, however. He was also convinced that an incisive counterblast would give pause to the interventionists that were smearing America First with charges of anti-Semitism and profascism. Consequently, without consulting any other AFC leaders, he delivered the notorious

135

Iowa address entitled "Who Are the War Agitators?" "The three most important groups who have been pressing this country toward war," he charged, "are the British, the Jewish and the Roosevelt Administration. . . . If any one of these groups . . . stops agitating for war, I believe there will be little danger of our involvement. . . . If it were not for this [agitation] . . . I believe England would have negotiated a peace in Europe many months ago, and be better off for doing so."[87]

Although Lindbergh qualified his remarks in Des Moines by stating that he could understand and sympathize with Jewish hatred of Hitler, the Iowa speech brought a storm of controversy and criticism upon the entire America First movement. "Tolerance," the aviator asserted at Des Moines, "is a virtue that depends upon peace and strength. History shows that it cannot survive war and devastation." Thus he expressed his agreement with Flynn's and Thomas' view that Jewish people in the United States would be the first to suffer if war came.[88] Nevertheless, in a world familiar with Hitler's specious explanations of all of Germany's problems as being caused by Jewish manipulators, it was easy for critics to infer that Lindbergh might be fomenting the claim that America's entry into war, should it come, was "caused" by Jewish propagandists. Dorothy Dunbar Bromley, recently resigned from the NYC-AFC, expressed these fears most succinctly when she charged that the aviator "must have known it [the speech] would incite race hatred and lay the groundwork for charges that this is a Jew's war."[89]

The storm of abuse against the America First movement as a result of the Des Moines speech came from leading interventionists and noninterventionists alike. Former Republican presidential candidate Wendell Willkie termed the address "the most un-American talk made in my time by any person of national reputation," and Roosevelt's press secretary, Stephen Early, found a "striking similarity" between Lindbergh's speech and "the outpourings of Berlin."[90] NYC-AFC sponsoring committee members Philip Liebman, Ernest Wheeler, and Charles Fleischer resigned because of the address, and New Jersey utilities magnate Thomas McCarter and others also left the America First national committee.[91] Norman Thomas joined the Socialist Party's official condemnation of the talk, and temporarily refused to appear on any AFC speaking platforms. He was convinced that Lindbergh was not personally anti-Semitic, but he believed that the aviator had been "a great idiot" to make the speech. "Not all Jews are for war," Thomas contended,

136

"and Jews have a right to agitate for war if we have a right to agitate against it. The point is . . . a great many besides Jews have been at fault."[92] Even Burton K. Wheeler took pains to point out that he was not actually a member of the AFC. Because his wife was an officer of the Washington, D.C., chapter and his son John was chairman of the Los Angeles chapter, however, Wheeler's disclaimer was not widely acknowledged.[93]

No other noninterventionist in the Northeast or elsewhere was more adamant in condemning the Des Moines speech than John Flynn. Flynn agreed with Lindbergh that Jewish leaders were prominent in the interventionist movement, but the New York chairman did not "want to see this fine movement [America First] degenerate into intolerance."[94] He was "greatly irritated . . . by the virulence with which some of their leaders [Jewish Americans] have attempted to brand everyone opposed to war as anti-Semitic and pro-Nazi. It has seemed to me that their responsibility for this should be brought home to them. But this is a far different matter from going out upon the public platform and denouncing 'the Jews as the warmakers.' "[95] Flynn viewed the address as an "incredible . . . open attack upon the Jews," and he believed that "it might be almost fatal" to the AFC. He was sure that real undesirables would regard the speech as an "open invitation" to join the committee, and he clearly perceived the "added ammunition" that interventionists would gain against America First. "Here in the East," he ruefully chided Stuart, "we are right on the firing line. . . . You have no idea how much concern there is here about this whole thing." Flynn also threatened to resign from the AFC if Lindbergh were allowed to continue "playing a lone hand."[96]

The problems the Des Moines speech caused for the New York chapter and the rest of the America First movement were compounded by the fact that a large portion of the committee's membership was happy about the address. Tired of the AFC's chronically defensive posture, many members were attracted by Lindbergh's bold, aggressive talk. Stuart reported that in the week following the speech, ninety percent of the messages delivered to Chicago headquarters from America First members revealed approbation.[97] NYC-AFC official Marie Hennessey declared that the chapter's street speakers met their most favorable crowd responses of the year just after the Des Moines address. "At the mention of Lindbergh's name," Hennessey claimed, "there was loud applause. Everywhere people voice respect for his courage and straightforward honesty."[98] Amos Pinchot spoke for many moderate America Firsters when he defended Lindbergh's speech by maintaining that there was "something wrong" in America when the "deeds, words, or attitudes . . . [of] any group (in this case the Jewish people) . . . should be unmentionable. . . . And there's something wrong about the idea that the person who does mention them, fairly and objectively, should be accused of trying to incite prejudice."[99] Lindbergh himself, surprised at the controversy caused by his speech, believed that he had phrased his comments at Des Moines "carefully and moderately. It seems that . . . today in America . . . the very mention of the word 'Jew' is cause for a storm." The aviator offered to issue a statement affirming that he had spoken only for himself in Iowa, but he refused to retract any of the speech.[100]

In order to resolve the split in America First ranks caused by the Des Moines address, the national committee held a special meeting on September 18. Flynn confided to a friend shortly before the meeting that "our problem . . . [is] one of clearing the AFC of this taint without at the same time breaking it up or weakening its influence."[101] As it happened, the parley resolved nothing, and Flynn came away confirmed in his impression that Lindbergh was "a man who cannot work with others." The national committee issued a statement that, in the words of Chicago member Janet Fairbank, "really took no stand at all."[102]

The aftermath of the ambiguous national committee declaration was perhaps more damaging to America First's reputation for anti-Semitism and profascism than the Des Moines speech itself. Certainly liberals such as advertising executive Chester Bowles and Norman Thomas became increasingly alarmed over the AFC's degenerating prestige. "It would almost have been better to make no statement at all," Thomas reproached General Wood. "The repudiation of anti-Semitism in it was perfunctory."[103] Immediately following the national committee parley the highly interventionist New York tabloid *PM* carried the headline: "America First Splits: OK's Lindbergh's Attack on Jews."[104] As Flynn had predicted, New York's real subversives increased their efforts to burrow into the NYC-AFC. "I have had to step into [Manhattan] HQ to spend all my time there to straighten out kinks," he recorded in mid-October.[105] Joseph Boldt disclosed at the same time that "Coughlinites, Christian Fronters, etc., have regarded this [episode] as a come-ahead to them."[106]

The most serious, lasting effect of Lindbergh's speech was the deep rift that it exposed between Flynn and his lieutenants, Webster

138

and NYC-AFC treasurer H. Dudley Swim. The root problem among the three men had existed since early 1941, when Webster urged that the fledgling chapter cooperate with any other willing noninterventionists, regardless of their other beliefs or allegiances.[107] From that point forward Flynn was convinced that Webster and his close companion Swim were encouraging anti-Semitic and profascist persons and groups to enter the NYC-AFC. Flynn also suspected that the two men were personally anti-Semitic. At least one high-ranking NYC-AFC staffer, Robert Bliss, agreed with the chapter chairman's views of Webster and Swim. Everyone in the NYC-AFC offices seemed to love Flynn, Bliss has reported, while Webster sought friends, novelty, and adventure through extravagant parties and the courting of notorious undesirables. For their part, Swim and Webster resented Flynn's belief that only he was competent to steer the chapter through the "idological reefs and shoals" of New York. They established friendships with Pinchot and Lindbergh, and continually fought Flynn on large and small matters affecting the NYC-AFC.[108]

The intrachapter feud had been smoothed over at least superficially by late summer, but the Des Moines speech fired the tensions anew. In August Flynn reported that "headquarters . . . [is] in pretty good shape so that I bother very little with administrative detail."[109] However, Webster, Swim, and Pinchot took positions on Lindbergh's address that were exactly opposite to that of Flynn. The chapter chairman later recalled arriving at Manhattan headquarters on the morning following the speech to find the three men "delighted at what Lindbergh had said and . . . all for backing him up . . . . They were busy whipping them [the office staff] into a demand for the support of Lindbergh and into a state of fury against me because I refused to do this."[110]

A blatant NYC-AFC power struggle ensued.[111] Swim, Webster, and Pinchot introduced at a chapter executive committee meeting a resolution providing that the executive secretary be given complete control over the hiring and firing of personnel. Such an arrangement would emasculate Flynn and leave him as essentially "a glorified publicity man." Although the three friends controlled a majority of the executive committee votes, Flynn faced them down by threatening to quit and split the NYC-AFC irrevocably if they limited his authority.[112] Flynn then unburdened himself to Wood. Early in the year, the New York chairman claimed, he had discovered Webster to be "quite incompetent . . . running the office with disorganization, confusion, and lack of proper accounting of funds." Webster's behavior was annoying, he contended, but presented no serious troubles until the Des Moines speech escalated the NYC-AFC's problems with "undesirables. . . . The difficulty of keeping them in their place calls for the understanding of such things and for some strength of character. . . . This enormous organization we have here is filled with danger." Webster, Flynn insisted, was completely unable to guard against subversives. "The man," Flynn concluded, "is hopelessly and tragically incompetent . . . futile, feeble, confused, without strength of character, without understanding."[113]

The Flynn-Webster dispute was never resolved. It persisted even after the dissolution of the NYC-AFC and it continued to have serious consequences concerning America First's reputation for being anti-Semitic and profascist. In late November 1941 Stuart informed Wood that "all reports indicate that John Flynn and Ed Webster are continuing to clash bitterly."[114] Shortly after the Pearl Harbor attack and the AFC's decision to disband, Webster held a dinner at his home in honor of his fiancée Jean Bennett, an NYC-AFC volunteer street speaker. Flynn did not attend, but some of the America Firsters present vehemently expressed their disagreement with the national committee's decision to terminate. However, Lindbergh, the featured speaker at the gathering, counseled them that "no matter what we did or advocated . . . we would have been viciously and bitterly attacked if we . . . continued our activities after the start of war."[115]

Webster's dinner soon began to haunt and damage the defunct NYC-AFC. In January 1942 press reports appeared, stating that the executive secretary and the chapter's most radical elements had held a formal, secret meeting to arrange for an underground continuation of the America First movement. Lindbergh vehemently denied these charges, terming Webster's dinner "a sort of last get-together and farewell party. . . . The dinner was in no sense an America First organization meeting." Nevertheless, Flynn's irritation at Webster increased, both because of the damage the press rumors did to the AFC's reputation and because the chairman feared that the gossip might be true.[116]

Flynn's last clash with Webster and Swim was a protracted struggle over the financial liquidation of the NYC-AFC. Again, the chapter's prestige in the face of accusations of anti-Semitism and profascism was at stake. After December 1941 Swim retained care of the NYC-AFC account books, and he delayed payment of the group's final debts for several months.[117]

In May 1942, after continually pressing the treasurer to make a final settlement, Flynn confided to Wood his deep and recurring worry that Swim and Webster were planning to reactivate a secret and subversive version of the chapter. "My own belief," Flynn maintained, "is that Swim and Webster have been purposely delaying this [final dissolution] in the hope of making some use of it."[118] One month later, using the threat of a court suit, Flynn and Wood persuaded the two executives to clear all NYC-AFC accounts and dissolve the chapter as a corporation. This late action, however, made the NYC-AFC the last America First organization in the nation to disband, and rumors accusing the chapter of continued covert profascist activities were already rampant.[119]

The NYC-AFC was infiltrated to a limited extent by anti-Semitic and profascist individuals and groups. However, Flynn maintained a tight personal guard over the chapter and prevented the permeation by undesirables from becoming dominant in any area of committee affairs. A storm of accusations of harboring subversives directed at the NYC-AFC by various interventionist organizations presented a far more serious problem to the chapter than did the actual infiltration. First of all, the charges emboldened real anti-Semites and profascists to attempt to enter the NYC-AFC. Second, the imputations were so persistent and severe that an inordinate amount of John Flynn's time and energy was spent in combating them. Finally, Charles Lindbergh, in his famous Des Moines speech, aggressively and tactlessly reacted to the many recriminations. His address brought massive additional criticism and problems to the entire America First movement. In New York, the most serious consequence of the Des Moines talk was a worsening of the relations between Flynn on the one hand, and Webster, Swim, and Pinchot on the other.

In late 1941 and early 1942, Flynn became increasingly suspicious that Webster and Swim were plotting a secret, subversive continuation of some elements of the NYC-AFC. These fears were shared by some of the press, and America First's reputation for being anti-Semitic and profascistic became even worse after the nation went to war. Flynn, in seeking to defend the committee's good name both during and after 1941, became convinced that the AFC was a victim of a well-organized conspiracy aimed at discrediting it and involving the United States in war. These new beliefs changed his entire outlook on life in America, and he devoted nearly the rest of his life to proving the existence and the insidiousness of this conspiracy.[120]

8

Relations with the Media and the Interventionist Committees: A Conspiracy Theory

"The plain and terrifying fact is that this great and peaceful nation is in the grip of one of the most subtle and successful conspiracies . . . to embroil us in a foreign war."[1] John Flynn uttered this charge at a Chicago rally in December 1940, in his first important speaking role for the America First Committee. The interventionist *Chicago Daily News* commented sarcastically that for forty years Flynn had thrived on unearthing intrigues. Since the death of muckraker Lincoln Steffens, the newspaper stated, Flynn had become "the authentic dean of the conspiracy and demonology school of journalism."[2]

It is true that a conspiracy theory of war involvement was prominent in the thinking of many AFC leaders, but Flynn extended this thesis to much deeper levels. Most noninterventionists blamed the Roosevelt Administration and British agents, at least to a limited extent, for fomenting prowar propaganda. Flynn, acutely aware of the barrage of assaults against America First's reputation throughout 1941, became convinced that a concerted effort to vilify and discredit noninterventionists was being made by the same sources he believed were responsible for interventionist propaganda. The "propaganda offensive against our peace and security," he asserted, "has been directed by some central intelligence. . . . Future students of propaganda will study this drive as a model just as military strategists study the battles of Napoleon and Lee."[3]

To prove his conspiracy hypothesis, Flynn undertook investigations of the public media and the interventionist committees within the United States. He concluded that the motion-picture industry, the major radio networks, most of the press, and the prowar associations were dominated by Roosevelt and British Prime Minister Winston Churchill. Official English sources supplied interventionist propaganda, according to Flynn, and a tightly knit cabal within the American media and prowar committees distributed it in response to threats and coercion from the White House. War came before the New York chapter chairman was able to amass convincing proof of all of his suspicions, and he dropped his queries in favor of national unity.

Flynn's background rendered him especially prone to a conspiracy theory of war involvement. Shortly after World War I he was profoundly impressed by two books: *Now It Can Be Told,* by Philip Hamilton Gibbs, and *The Genesis of the World War,* by Harry Elmer Barnes. Gibbs, a British knight, served as a war correspondent with the French and Belgian armies in 1914 and with the British forces from 1915 to 1918. Barnes was a young New York history and sociology professor. Both of these books maintained that a negotiated peace could have been concluded in Europe in 1916 or 1917, had not English hopes of total victory been kept alive by the belief that the United States could be persuaded to enter the war. In order to assure American involvement, Britain saturated the United States with fabricated atrocity stories regarding the "terrible Huns." American intervention, according to this theory, prolonged the war by nearly two years and readied the German people for Adolf Hitler by deepening their scars of total defeat and resentment.[4]

Flynn's conspiratorial view of war involvement deepened as a result of his tenure as economic adviser to the 1934 Senate investigation of the World War I munitions industry. After probing the so-called merchants of death, North Dakota Senator Gerald Nye's Committee on Banking and Finance concluded that American industrialists inordinately pressured the Wilson Administration and propagandized for war. The munitions makers wanted war, according to the Nye report, in order to salvage their profits in defense contracts and in loans to belligerents.[5]

In 1938 Flynn became suspicious that England was planning another public relations blitz designed to involve the United States in the imminent European war. His fears were aroused by a book entitled *Propaganda in the Next War,* by commercial British propagandist Sidney Rogerson and English military authority Liddell Hart. The book asserted that only fright could convince the disillusioned, isolationist American people to enter the upcoming conflict. "To persuade her [the United States] to take our part . . . will need a definite threat to America . . . which will have to be brought home by propaganda to every citizen," the two Britons boldly contended. After reading this volume, Flynn harbored only disdain for the interventionist argument that "this is our war, that we are next on Hitler's list . . . that England is fighting our war."[6]

Flynn's series of caustic, journalistic attacks on war profiteers during 1940 epitomized his conspiratorial view of war involvement. He coupled suggestions that Roosevelt and the financiers of Wall Street were using war as a "boondoggle" to escape from the economic malaise of the Great Depression with strong assaults on the British.[7] In an article titled "The Multi-Million Dollar British War Propaganda Budget," Flynn accused the English of spreading misinformation and German atrocity stories in order to goad the United States into war. He also reacted angrily against the "appeasement label" already being flung at noninterventionists. "There are Americans here," he fulminated, "real Americans who are thinking about America, her interests . . . her democracy, her recovery, all of which would probably be destroyed by entering this war. Apparently it is quite proper for English propagandists to work here to get us into a war. But an American who wants to keep us out is a 'fifth columnist.' "[8]

By early 1941 Flynn was castigating the Roosevelt Administration, England, and the interventionist Committee to Defend America by Aiding the Allies (the CDAAA) on a regular basis from AFC speaking platforms. The three were acting together "in a conspiracy to terrify the American people," he asserted to a Massachusetts rally audience in April.[9] The Lend-Lease Act, the convoy proposals, and other measures were merely ploys to increase the American stake in a British victory by inflaming American passions when goods, ships, and men were lost. "How can any sane man doubt" collusion? Flynn asked, pointing to a letter written by Churchill during World War I to a friend in the United States. "Nothing will bring the Americans in on our side quicker than a little American blood spilled," the British leader had maintained.[10] To Flynn, the letter symbolized a calculating and selfish English plot to involve the United States in war.

Several Northeastern AFC leaders agreed with Flynn's analysis of Churchill's letter and with other alleged indications of a prowar conspiracy. New York advertising executive Chester Bowles decried

145

the "vicious methods . . . used by the interventionists . . . in their efforts to trick us into this war in Europe."[11] NYC-AFC executive committee member Amos Pinchot contended that the situation in 1941 was "really . . . an existing conspiracy—to put this country, unprovoked, unprepared and unwilling into war."[12] Socialist Party chairman Norman Thomas charged that for various selfish reasons a "curious association" of persons and groups wanted America to be drawn into the war, and aviator Charles Lindbergh and New Hampshire Senator Charles Tobey voiced similar accusations at NYC-AFC rallies.[13]

This "anti-English line," however, met with strong disapproval from the America First national committee, and in the late spring the ruling group asked Flynn to "drop it."[14] Executive director Robert D. Stuart and others feared that derogatory comments made about Britain would alienate potential AFC supporters, especially in the Northeast where sympathy for the besieged country was most intense.[15] National chairman Robert E. Wood believed that a full America First endorsement of Flynn's conspiracy theory would give the committee a reputation for being "an anti–New Deal or hate-Roosevelt campaign."[16] Furthermore, Stuart was convinced that any intrigue theory represented an oversimplification of social forces. "Things just don't work out that way," he insisted to Lindbergh. Many "very sincere persons," the young director maintained, favored intervention "not because of a great conspiracy . . . but because they honestly believe that it[intervention] is the best way to preserve the American Republic."[17]

Flynn resented being asked to discontinue his direct attacks against alleged presidential and English propagandists, and he determined to try a new approach to exposing the conspiracy he was sure existed. "This committee [America First] made an initial blunder when it began pulling its punches about Britain," he contended angrily in July.[18] Nevertheless, he secured Wood's permission to undertake an independent investigation of interventionist leaders and sponsors, and by midsummer Flynn and a small private staff were thoroughly immersed in this task. The probers raised their own funds from special donations, and interested noninterventionist Senators Wheeler and Nye, and others in pursuing the findings in congressional hearings. Flynn termed the investigation "critical and much the most important thing we have to do." He asserted gleefully that the facts uncovered would produce "some real trouble" for "our dear President. . . . May his woes increase."[19]

Flynn hoped that his probe could salvage the rapidly deteriorating credibility and reputation of America First by exposing the committee's persistent accusers. Throughout the investigation he focused on: "Who are the culprits [attackers of the AFC]? Who are these people who are furnishing the money, etc.? Who, Who, Who?" He concentrated on the CDAAA and other prowar committees, the motion-picture industry, and interventionist press and radio commentators, because these groups and individuals were the most vocal AFC critics. He was convinced that among these hostile forces he would discover an interlocking core of donors, sponsors, and leaders. Foreign and Jewish names would predominate, Flynn believed, because people in these categories had overwhelming personal reasons for wanting Hitler defeated. The New York chairman insisted that he did not intend a racial vendetta; he simply wanted to reveal the "biased" sources of what he perceived to be specious, emotional, interventionist propaganda. The prowar cabal, he contended, acted as a "gestapo to supply commentators and others with the calumnies [sic] they have been using" against America First. By divulging the sources of the "red-herring" character smears against AFC spokesmen, Flynn asserted, he could undercut the effectiveness of interventionist charges and propaganda, and provide renewed "enthusiasm [for] all the people who are with us and are tired of being pushed around."[20]

Flynn was most concerned with the motion-picture industry. Many prominent movie stars such as Melvyn Douglas, Errol Flynn, and others made frequent broadcasts favoring intervention, and their support seemed to give the prowar cause a glamorous appeal.[21] Moreover, the NYC-AFC chairman was positive that the Roosevelt Administration had a subterranean arrangement with the film industry to promote subtle, emotional, interventionist propaganda. A "seemingly purely legal antitrust attack on the movies . . . wound up by their going under unofficial but complete government domination," insisted Flynn and David Munro, a fellow editorial sponsor of the antiwar weekly publication *Uncensored*. The two men were referring to the November 1940 antitrust complaint filed by Attorney General Robert Jackson against eight major film companies. The suit was never tried, but was terminated in what John Flynn termed a "meaningless" consent decree. Flynn was sure that the suit was dropped in exchange for favors the movie-producing cartel agreed to extend to Roosevelt.[22] "There is plenty of evidence of collaboration between the film magnates and the government to whip up [war] hysteria," the chapter chairman confided to Wood.[23]

Flynn began the film industry exposé in early August by writing a

147

scathing speech that Nye delivered before a St. Louis AFC rally. In the talk Nye charged that "the movies have ceased to be instruments of entertainment. They have become the most gigantic engines of propaganda in existence to rouse the war fever in America." Naming several motion pictures that he believed to be flagrantly prowar, Nye emphasized *That Hamilton Woman* and *The Great Dictator*. The former movie portrayed a love affair between Lady Hamilton and the historic British Admiral Nelson. In the latter film English actor Charlie Chaplin rendered a comedic, lampooning version of Hitler, and then startled audiences at the conclusion by delivering a serious, impassioned speech against fascism. These and other motion pictures, Nye insisted, delivered insidious, emotional appeals glorifying British warfare and manhood, and ridiculing Germans. Whether or not these portrayals were accurate, he maintained, they were dangerous and unfair, given the current world situation. They were "designed to drug the reason of American audiences," and to engender in this country an interventionist spirit impossible to dislodge by rational debate. Nye added later that even more direct prowar appeals might soon be made through American films. A script under consideration in Hollywood, he alleged, depicted a German battleship sinking an unarmed English vessel carrying only children and pregnant women. The story, he cried angrily, showed "Nazis gleefully wringing their hands and glorying in the opportunity" of destroying two generations of Britons at once.[24]

The most sensitive portion of Nye's speech came when he discussed the ethnic backgrounds of Hollywood's top operatives. Among the seventeen owners and highest executives of the ten major movie-producing companies were twelve Jews. These magnates, Nye declared, used the facade of the industry's own obscenity policing agency, the Hays Production Code Administration, to veto all noninterventionist films. An unusually large proportion of Hollywood's directors, Nye asserted, were Russian or Balkan, and many actors were British. The antiwar senator insisted that he meant to imply nothing derogatory against these religious and national groups, but he maintained that the public should be aware that "at this highly emotional time in history, this mighty engine of propaganda is in the hands of men who . . . are peculiarly susceptible to these emotions." Nye concluded by citing a December 1940 study undertaken by a Wall Street firm, which indicated that because of direct English investments and the profits gained by showing American motion pictures in British theaters, seven of the eight major

United States film companies would go bankrupt if England lost to Hitler. "Are you ready to send your boys to bleed and die in Europe," he fulminated, "to make the world safe for [movie executives] Barney Balaban and Adolph Zukor and Joseph Schenk?"[25]

Within a few days of Nye's address Flynn orchestrated a similar, though less thorough, denunciation of Hollywood by Wheeler on the Senate floor. The NYC-AFC chairman also prepared a resolution calling for a Senate investigation of war propaganda in motion pictures. Nye and noninterventionist Bennett Champ Clark of Missouri introduced this resolution into Congress. Flynn and the antiwar congressional bloc were determined to act in a concerted manner, since three previous 1941 Senate resolutions demanding examination of propaganda and defense contracts had been smothered by powerful interventionists in key committees. Now the noninterventionists planned carefully to refer the Nye-Clark resolution to the Interstate Commerce Committee, chaired by Wheeler. Wheeler then appointed a subcommittee composed of strong, senior antiwar advocates and only one freshman prowar spokesman. Funds for a preliminary investigation were procured from the Interstate Commerce Committee, and hearings were scheduled to open on September 9.[26]

Preparations for the hearings were hectic on both sides. The movie industry retained 1940 Republican presidential candidate Wendell Willkie as its counsel, and demanded that some of the films in question be shown at the hearings. Flynn, busy preparing lists of questions for the subcommittee members, as well as writing the testimony of principal witnesses such as Nye and Clark, advised the senators to accede to Willkie's demand. He also suggested that earlier, antiwar motion pictures such as *Peace on Earth* and *J'Accuse* be shown. Both of these movies, Flynn contended, contained "terrific scenes . . . illustrating the frightful waste and cruelties of war. . . . The question can then be raised as to what would have been the effect on the public if massive numbers of these types of films had been shown during the last year."[27] America First aided Flynn to the extent that it urged chapters across the nation to boycott and campaign against war films at local theaters. However, Wood always carefully maintained that in directing the probe Flynn "acted as an individual and was in no way sponsored by the AFC."[28]

The hearings opened on a combative note, as Willkie condemned the proceedings as "a barefaced attempt at censorship and racial persecution." Subcommittee chairman D. Worth Clark of Idaho dismissed Willkie's charge as "drivel" and Nye declared that he refused to allow the anti-Semitism accusation "to cover the tracks of those who have been pushing our country . . . to war with their propaganda. . . . I detest . . . race prejudice . . . and I shall be found in the very front lines of those who give battle to" it.[29] Flynn, in his testimony, accused Willkie of confusing the issues by implying that all of those against fighting Hitler automatically supported the dictator. Hitler was "merely an excrescence" hated by all decent men, Flynn maintained. However, the NYC-AFC chairman warned, film propagandists capitalizing on the emotions of the masses to arouse fear, hatred, and war hysteria in America were imitating Hitler's methods. The moviemakers themselves, he insisted, were the true pioneers of fascism in this nation.[30]

Following Flynn's testimony, Lindbergh's Des Moines speech intervened and caused a delay in the hearings. Flynn admitted that the Iowa address had given the hearings "a terrible kick in the pants," and he feared that Lindbergh's remarks would strengthen Willkie's contention that the noninterventionists were conducting a racial vendetta. He termed the Des Moines talk "all the more tragic in view of the immense patience and industry we have been going through to bring this issue to light in an entirely different way. . . . Just as that is blossoming into almost undreamed of success Lindbergh had to blab the issue out and hang it on America First."[31]

In spite of Flynn's worries, the public seemed to take very little notice of the hearings. Roosevelt, in a press conference, simply denied bringing any pressure to bear on Hollywood to produce interventionist propaganda. He then ridiculed the hearings by pointing out that the Bible was written by mostly "foreign-born and Jewish people," and he displayed a cartoon of Charlie Chaplin lampooning the investigation. The caricature portrayed Chaplin studying his Senate subpoena and asking: "Now what could I possibly tell those past masters about comedy?"[32]

The hearings resumed on September 23, with Willkie presenting the movie industry's defense. One after another, film magnates such as Harry M. Warner, president of Warner Brothers, and Darryl F. Zanuck, head of Twentieth Century-Fox, testified. All of the executives confessed to very strong personal feelings against Hitler, and admitted that they would support the President in a war against Germany. However, they emphatically denied using their positions to promote interventionist propaganda. Zanuck, recalling that he had pioneered gangster films when the public was interested in the underworld, maintained that now his company was "simply keeping abreast of the times" by catering to public curiosity about the European war.[33]

At the end of the film makers' testimony the hearings terminated inconclusively, but the antiwar forces proclaimed victory. The preliminary budget from Wheeler's Interstate Commerce Committee was exhausted, and Scott Lucas, interventionist chairman of the Senate Audit and Control Committee, refused to grant funds for a full investigation. Nevertheless, Nye asserted that the initial probe "very clearly revealed the existence of propaganda in the motion-picture industry." Soon afterward, Wheeler triumphantly declared to a Los Angeles AFC rally that "the modern Benedict Arnold is the silver screen."[34]

Certainly Nye's and Wheeler's sweeping charges of prowar collusion between the movie industry and the government were unwarranted, at least in light of the evidence amassed at the time, but the noninterventionists did produce a strong circumstantial case. For example, they cited a September 1941 magazine article written by Lowell Mellett, head of the Office of Government Reports. Mellett, a strong prowar advocate, had been nicknamed by *Time* magazine "the George Creel of WWII . . . Roosevelt's Censor-in-Chief." In his autumn article Mellett maintained that the government would not itself engage in interventionist propaganda since the movie and radio industries already were doing such a fine dissemination job. Motion-picture "owners, producers, directors, actors, writers, distributors, exhibitors, all have been putting their hearts into it. . . . And so with the radio. . . . What would or could the government do better?"[35]

Noninterventionists also obtained evidence of attempts to promote the prowar cause from within the film industry itself. In one case Flynn uncovered a 1940 interview in which Charlie Chaplin spoke of his role in *The Great Dictator*. When asked why he abandoned his traditional comedic pose at the end of the movie to deliver his call-to-arms against fascism, Chaplin admitted: "I had to do it . . . . There was no other way I could adequately express how strongly I felt. . . . I wanted to make them [members of the audience] stop being so damned contented. This isn't just another war. Fascism means the end of our world."[36] Flynn also obtained a 1941 letter written to theater owners from Louis de Rochemont, foreign-born producer of the newsreel series "March of Time." The letter, concerning a newsreel entitled *Peace—By Adolf Hitler,* asserted: "The Hitler peace offensive is on, and lots of good, well-meaning people will be taken in by it. We at the 'March of Time' are not. . . . I have had our staff put the whole thing down in film. . . . This film is . . . vital and brutal."[37] The de Rochemont letter was shown to Flynn by the owner of a small chain of local theaters. The owner complained that he was "powerless to reject" such motion pictures "because . . . it is not one company that is putting out such propaganda films but all of them, because the same interests control all producing companies."[38]

Perhaps the most compelling evidence of Hollywood complicity in the interventionist cause came to Flynn from the AFC. In late summer 1941 Lillian Gish, America First national committee member and actress who gained fame in the antiblack movie *Birth of a Nation,* confided to Wood that she had to make an agonizing decision. Since becoming active in the AFC, she revealed, she had been "blacklisted" by motion-picture studios throughout Hollywood. She was unemployed for several weeks, but then obtained a lucrative contract with the understanding that she resign from America First, refrain from publicly stating her reason for this action, and cease all activities in behalf of the noninterventionist cause. Gish accepted the contract, and Wood announced her resignation in early October.[39]

Flynn was concerned and upset over the Gish resignation and the collapse of the film hearings, but there is evidence that from the beginning he overestimated the power of motion-picture propaganda on public opinion. A majority of the papers presented at the Conference on Communication Agencies at the University of Chicago in August 1941 indicated that "the most evident single effect of mass communications is the reinforcement of existing predispositions. People select what they want to hear and listen only to what they agree with." The Chicago conference did report agreement with Flynn's theses that the movie industry was controlled by a tight production cabal and that indirect emotional appeals in films affected audiences on a subtle, irrational level. Nevertheless, the papers concluded, the need for support by advertising and audience patronage caused American mass communication media, in general, to follow rather than lead public opinion.[40]

Following the motion-picture investigation, Flynn turned his attention to the radio industry. He had been wary of interventionist radio propaganda since the formation of the NYC-AFC. In January 1941 he visited the National Broadcasting Company studio to arrange air time for the chapter. Frank Mason, his NBC contact, appeared reluctant to talk to him in his office and asked him to wait and go home with him. Once at home Mason explained to Flynn that he could not speak freely at the radio offices because there were "spies, FBI agents, and company pressures all over the building." The mere fact that the vocally antiwar Flynn came to confer with him, Mason alleged, "would be reported." The intrigue at NBC existed, Mason stated, because network president Niles Trammell was a militant prowar advocate and "this percolates all through the company. . . . Also, broadcasting companies are scared stiff of the government." Mason asserted that a similar situation prevailed in the Columbia Broadcasting System and in other radio companies, and he advised Flynn that, regardless of promises of equal time, "the only way the anti-interventionists can get time on the air is to watch the programs closely and every time the other side has time, to demand . . . time for their own side."[41]

After Mason's warning Flynn intermittently monitored the various radio stations in New York, and much of what he heard disturbed him. For one thing, he found several radio dramas that he said carried subtle and emotional interventionist appeals similar to the alleged appeals in movies.[42] Second, he believed that radio debate forums were often distorted by biased, prowar interlocutors. "The chairman," he explained, "does the dirty work . . . on these shows. What looks like a two-man discussion turns out to be a two-to-one-man discussion."[43] Third, Flynn was convinced that English shortwave broadcasts to the United States were spewing direct and flagrant interventionist propaganda. In one shortwave broadcast British Broadcasting Company commentator Leslie Howard declared to his American audience: "We have arrived at the stage at which we must tell each other openly what is in our hearts and minds. . . . I say to hell with whether what I say sounds like propaganda or not. . . . I don't think it matters any more." At least one *Public Opinion Quarterly* article agreed with Flynn, citing a great upsurge in English shortwave propaganda after December 1940. The militantly interventionist 1941 broadcasts, the article asserted, were as different from the former British broadcasting equilibrium "as acquaintance is from marriage."[44]

The most important radio problem for the noninterventionist forces, Flynn believed, was regular, American announcers and commentators "who pepper their talks with . . . a fairly incessant plugging for the Administration's war policies." The NYC-AFC chairman explained to David Sarnoff, prowar president of the Radio

153

Corporation of America, that "these little plugs aren't fair." Antiwar advocates could demand equal time to structured interventionist programs, but it was difficult and time consuming to respond to one-line sneers and asides.[45] Two commentators, Walter Winchell of NBC, and Burnett Hershey of WMCA, proved to be Flynn's continual sparring partners. Winchell, in reporting the NYC-AFC's activities, consistently referred to the group as "the Hitler First—America Last—Committee." Hershey's "violently interventionist pronouncements" were finally acknowledged by WMCA, and station managers promised to "quell" him.[46]

Many other Northeastern AFC spokesmen agreed with Flynn's analysis of radio's tie to the prowar cause. Committee historian Ruth Sarles has claimed bitterly that "from the day it was born America First had to scratch and claw at the networks, to cajole and humor, to plead and threaten, in order that it might present a small percentage of the aggregate propaganda of its opponents."[47] Norman Thomas became incensed at the radio industry in 1941 after he worked hard to raise funds and obtain a contract to present a series of antiwar lectures over the air. At the last minute the National Association of Broadcasters invoked against him the radio code governing public issue broadcasts, and canceled his series. A deeply angry Thomas complained to Flynn that "we are dealing with a situation on the radio in which practically all commentators are on one side, in which people who talk on public affairs or sponsored programs are almost always, without exception, interventionists. Then . . . the Code is suddenly enforced against me. . . . If that isn't discrimination, what is, and the issue is certainly more than personal."[48]

As 1941 progressed, Flynn tried different approaches to exposing what he believed was radio's prowar bias. In a speech before the Keep America Out of War Congress in February he denounced the interventionist commentaries.[49] In April he published an article entitled "Radio, Intervention's Trump." In this piece he maintained that he had no quarrel with "frank and labeled" prowar broadcasts, but he charged that "the war hysteria in America has been worked up by those innumerable five and ten and fifteen minute sustaining programs . . . news-croonings, and commentators that flood the mind of the listener all day." He hinted darkly that perhaps there was "some central intelligence . . . conspiring . . . thus to monopolize the time of the broadcasting stations on the side of the war propaganda." Flynn admitted that he was not currently prepared to prove the existence of such a conspiracy: proof, he asserted, could not be

154

established until "the whole war episode is over and the gentlemen who are responsible begin to boast of their achievements."[50]

Flynn took more concrete steps against the allegedly unfair radio policies as war drew closer. In May he sought to coordinate all America First radio relations work from New York by persuading the AFC national committee to hire a radio liaison officer to work out of Flynn's office. With the major radio company headquarters close to the NYC-AFC Manhattan lodgings, Flynn believed that the young coordinator, Benson Inge, could demand immediate and personal accountability from the network chiefs. However, Inge's position was eliminated after only one month when Robert Stuart decided that radio liaison work should be done from America First's national publicity bureau in Chicago.[51] During the summer probe of the motion-picture industry Flynn assigned a small portion of his staff to investigate prowar collusion within the radio empire. The researchers' most appalling discovery, in Flynn's view, was that in an August broadcast Archibald MacLeish, interventionist Librarian of Congress, had impersonated the voices of subjugated people in Europe calling on the United States for help.[52]

After the MacLeish revelation Flynn became grim and determined to move forcefully against the radio networks. For three days in early October he had four New York stations carefully monitored from early morning until midnight. Counting sponsored and unsponsored commentaries, he found 127 interventionist and six noninterventionist broadcasts. Then, shortly before the October 30 antineutrality repeal rally, Flynn publicly charged an overt radio conspiracy. "There wasn't one fifteen-minute period for three days," he contended, "when some[one] . . . wasn't whooping it up for intervention. . . . In good time I will prove . . . [that] if and when this country is plunged into war, the heaviest and darkest stain of guilt will rest on the hands of the radio companies, whose chiefs are interventionists and who have gone all-out on the air to entangle this country in Europe's war."[53] Flynn and the NYC-AFC executive committee also wired the Federal Communications Commission to protest the behavior of the networks as "an outrageous proceeding in a democracy."[54]

By provoking a public confrontation right before the October rally Flynn hoped to prompt New York radio stations to broadcast the rally live. Nevertheless, the networks refused. NBC president Niles Trammell termed Flynn's charges an "unfair, unreasonable, and unjustifiable attack on the radio industry." Trammell added that it did not "seem fair" for America First "to assume a martyrdom which the facts do not justify."[55] At the rally itself Flynn and the other speakers severely denounced the radio empire: "For every hour we have had on the air, the other side has had twenty," Flynn fulminated to the crowd.[56]

After his failure to coerce the radio industry into greater cooperation with the AFC, Flynn turned his attention to a probe of the interventionist press. Several aspects of press coverage of the war versus peace issue, as well as the reporting of America First actions and statements, disturbed Flynn. For one thing, he believed that subtle and emotional periodical fiction with a prowar bias similiar to that of many movies and radio dramas was systemically being printed. At least one authority agreed with Flynn. In a May 1941 survey for *Public Opinion Quarterly*, Vernon McKenzie, director of the School of Journalism at the University of Washington, found that a large majority of stories about war recently published in American popular magazines "could be expected to influence the reader in favor of the British."[57]

Another primary Flynn concern regarding the press was the overwhelming percentages of major newspapers and periodicals that took flat editorial positions for war during 1941. An August *Public Opinion Quarterly* survey indicated that sixty-seven percent of the prominent newspapers in the nation supported an interventionist position.[58] In New York, only the *New York Daily News* and the William Randolph Hearst chain's *New York Journal-American* were strongly noninterventionist. The *New York World-Telegram*, a Scripps-Howard paper, adopted a middle position and advocated strictly limited aid to England. All other major newspapers in the city were completely prowar.[59] Among the principal magazines, only the *Saturday Evening Post* was antiwar for part of 1941. Editor Wesley Winant Stout confided to Lindbergh in December 1940 that the *Post* intended to continue its noninterventionist stand but that it looked "like a losing fight." Five months later the journal dramatically shifted to support of Roosevelt's foreign policy.[60]

Although overt editorial stands in favor of war bothered Flynn, he was perhaps most disturbed by what he believed were journalistic distortions of news stories. Newspapers and magazines, he was convinced, inflated Allied military triumphs to boost circulation and to persuade the public that victory could be easily achieved if America entered the war. Lindbergh, notorious for his distrust of the press, shared Flynn's convictions. Accounts of the war were "so prejudiced and confused that it is almost impossible to obtain an accurate picture," the aviator contended. "The result is that the impression given by our newspapers is far more favorable to the British cause than is warranted by the facts . . . .[The American people] have no accurate source of information to which to turn."[61]

From late June onward Flynn and Lindbergh despaired of reading any truthful war reports in major United States newspapers. Concerning Hitler's invasion of the Soviet Union, Flynn insisted in his diary: "Russia is withdrawing at many points before Germans, but as usual the papers announce that Russia, after administering heavy defeats to Germans, withdraws to other positions."[62] Lindbergh concurrently maintained that "results of R.A.F. raids over the Continent are exaggerated, while results of German raids over England are minimized."[63] At the time of the Pearl Harbor attack Lindbergh was so skeptical of press reports that he wondered if the assault were not "just a hit-and-run raid by a few planes, exaggerated by. . . commentators into a major attack."[64]

Lindbergh, Flynn, and other America First leaders were also wary of what they believed were press distortions of committee actions and statements. "What you say is invariably twisted," Lindbergh complained. "They [reporters] make you seem like a different person than you are or want to be."[65] General Wood warned Flynn to "lean over backwards" in New York to keep the AFC "clean, so that the unfriendly press cannot make capital of any missteps on our part. . . . So many editors and columnists throughout the country look to the New York papers for hot news."[66] Yet it was the unsuspecting national chairman himself that fell into a clever reporter's trap. In an interview with the interventionist New York tabloid *PM*, Wood was asked to what point in Latin America he would permit a Hitler conquest to penetrate before he would favor armed United States intervention. A military tactician by training, Wood answered, "To the bulge of Brazil." *PM's* next headline cried: "General Wood Willing to Give Hitler Lower Half of South America!" The shocked AFC chairman protested that "under no circumstances could the interview have justified such a conclusion," and the committee "closed the door" to *PM* on future interviews with America First officials.[67]

AFC concern over press distortion of committee activities reached its zenith immediately following Lindbergh's Des Moines speech. "I can think of nothing to do but avoid the newspapers," Flynn complained desperately on the morning after the address. "I am at my wit's end what to say" to them.[68] The America First national committee requested that "due to very unfair treatment and inaccurate reporting in the past" the New York chapter grant no immediate interviews concerning the speech.[69] When New Jersey utilities magnate Thomas McCarter renounced the AFC because of Lindbergh's address, Stuart urged him not to publicize his resignation "as it would be eagerly seized upon by a hostile press."[70] A month after the speech Flynn was still decrying "all the misrepresentations to which I and many of my colleagues have been subjected."[71]

As 1941 progressed alleged press distortions and smears against America First turned to actual accusations. In June the *New Republic* labeled the AFC "the most powerful single potential Fascist group in this country today—the group that is polarizing every Fascist force among us."[72] Shortly afterward *Life* magazine charged that "despite the lofty rhetoric of its hired orators, America First en masse . . . [is] emphatically anti-British, furtively anti-Semitic, and possibly pro-Nazi."[73] Chester Bowles deplored the "verbal stink bombs which have been tossed in our general direction by *Life*, *PM*, etc.," and New York antiwar minister and KAOWC leader John Haynes Holmes mourned the "low degraded state . . . [to which] liberal journalism in this country has fallen."[74]

As the Great Debate became more acrimonious several journalistic outlets flatly closed their doors to Flynn and other noninterventionist writers. In June 1940 prominent antiwar spokesman and "dean of American liberals" Oswald Garrison Villard resigned the post he had held over forty-six years as editor of the *Nation*. Villard blamed "differences of opinion" over the European war for his unhappy departure. "I regret all the more," he explained bitterly, "that my retirement has been precipitated at this time by the [other] editors' abandonment of the *Nation*'s steadfast opposition to all preparations for war, to universal military service, to a great navy, and to *all* war, for this in my judgment has been the chief glory of its great and honorable past."[75] Five months later Flynn was dropped by the *New Republic*, after spending seven years as an economic and financial commentator. The *New Republic* editors explained that Flynn apparently "lacked sufficient material" to write on the subject of business, and that he had "ranged far afield and has frequently collided head on with the views of the editors."[76]

Flynn, rancorous over his dismissal, had been expecting it for a long time. For many months the *New Republic* had published editorials or appended notes to Flynn's column, "Other People's

158

Money," disclaiming personal agreement with, or responsibility for, his views. By October 1940 these disclaimers were personal and insulting. One note charged that the "Other People's Money" of that week was "an amazing instance of the blindness to which prejudice may lead." Another maintained that if Flynn "wants to imply that the reason President Roosevelt began to arouse the people about the international danger was merely that the domestic program was going badly, his opinion is nonsense."[77] When dismissal came Flynn was convinced that the threat of war was already limiting basic civil liberties such as freedom of the press in the United States. Although he could not yet prove that the Roosevelt Administration had pressured the *New Republic* into discharging him, Flynn mockingly asserted to editor Bruce Bliven that the journal "at least now is in a position to quiet [Interior Secretary] Mr. Ickes with the assurance that it has cleaned house and [been] restored . . .to freedom."[78]

After remaining publicly silent about his dismissal for three months, Flynn decided to air his views regarding the incident in an effort to link it to an overall White House attempt at journalistic suppression. On the basis of their old friendship, Flynn persuaded Bliven to print a long communication outlining the NYC-AFC chairman's beliefs. "I was liquidated," he charge balefully, "and I think it of the utmost importance that the foremost liberal weekly journal . . . in this country, which has for years thundered against . . . the war-makers and militarists, should almost overnight . . . plunge headlong into the forefront of the war party, [and] suppress a columnist who remained at least one voice for its old opinions."[79] Later in 1941 Flynn's view that a conspiracy was operating to silence him was strengthened when he was dropped as an associate editor of *Collier's* magazine. The Scripps-Howard newspaper chain also canceled his "Plain Economics" column, and *Harper's* magazine stopped accepting his freelance articles after 1942.[80]

The closing of these journalistic avenues limited Flynn and other antiwar writers to AFC publications and to *Scribner's Commentator*. The latter was a small monthly magazine owned by the wealthy and extremely conservative NYC-AFC donor Charles Payson and his young associate Douglas Stewart. It was reputed to have strong ties with the profascist German-American Bund, although it is doubtful that the magazine received money from the inept and financially struggling Bund.[81] *Scribner's Commentator* was permeated by a tacit anti-Semitism, however, and Norman Thomas termed it "a dubious magazine. . . . I would not care to have an article in it." Flynn and Lindbergh did use the periodical to publish several antiwar articles during 1941, and thereby received substantial criticism from those convinced of America First's profascist and anti-Semitic reputation.[82]

Flynn's loss of access to prestigious magazines brought a severe loss of income as a journalist. In late 1941 he confided to Wood that the result of his connection with the NYC-AFC "has been that I have sacrificed all of my own personal income and even the connections out of which I made that income." Until the 1949 publication of his popular book *The Road Ahead,* Flynn never again achieved an annual income that exceeded the twenty-six thousand dollars he made in 1940.[83] Finally in 1950, evidence emerged that seemed to Flynn to prove indubitably that his career had been wrecked on purpose, when a private 1939 letter from Roosevelt to *Yale Review* editor Wilbur Cross was published. "John Flynn . . . should be barred hereafter from the columns of any presentable daily paper, monthly magazine, or national quarterly," the President had insisted.[84] However, the embittered NYC-AFC chairman was never able to establish conclusively that Roosevelt took active steps to enforce his wishes.

Long before learning of the President's letter, however, Flynn amassed enough evidence of a pervasive prowar conspiracy to sour his belief in American liberties. As he pursued his 1941 investigations of the motion-picture industry, the radio networks, and the interventionist press, Flynn noticed "a kind of coherence and unity in the character of the smear attacks on our committee [the AFC]." The assaults, he concluded, "were not sporadic or casual, but . . . they originated in some central or unified group."[85] Yet his probes of the media did not lead him to the cabal that he was positive was supplying the various commentators and filmmakers with the venomous charges. The elusive clique, he decided in late 1941, must lie within the interventionist committees themselves.

The prowar forces, like the antiwar, consisted of a myriad of provisional committees.[86] The total membership figures for the two sides were approximately equal. A November Gallup poll indicated that truly committed interventionists and noninterventionists each composed about twenty-five percent of the American people. The remaining fifty percent was undecided.[87] However, the prowar community commanded far more financial resources and prestigious names than did its opposition, and there were many more small,

160

splinter interventionist groups.[88] The prowar phalanx was led by the CDAAA (also known as the White, or Aid-Allies, committee), founded by William Allen White and Clark Eichelberger. White was the venerable old editor of the *Emporia* (Kansas) *Gazette*, and Eichelberger was director of the League of Nations Association and the Union for Concerted Peace Efforts.[89]

For approximately six months after its formation in May 1940, the CDAAA advocated a simple aid short-of-war policy, but then it became decidedly more militant. In November 1940 it issued a policy statement demanding "repeal or modification of restrictive statutes which hamper this nation in its freedom of action when it would cooperate" more fully with Britain. The statement also asserted that "no one can guarantee that the United States can avoid active military involvement."[90] White, in an effort to soften the warlike tone of the Aid-Allies declaration, published a letter in which he contended that "the only reason in God's world I am in this organization is to keep this country out of war. . . . If I were making a motto it would be 'The Yanks Are Not Coming.' "[91]

White's remarks produced a split in Aid-Allies ranks that eventually pushed the committee farther toward outright advocacy of war. Flynn maintained that White's "colleagues leaped upon him with fury . . . and drove him by force from the committee which bore his name."[92] Actually, many interventionist leaders, especially in New York, did accuse White of "appeasement," and the old editor was stripped of his power as chairman. He remained as honorary chairman, while former Vermont Senator Ernest Gibson assumed the actual CDAAA leadership.[93] An extremely bellicose wing of the committee broke away and formed the Fight for Freedom committee (FFF) in New York. The FFF commenced operations in April 1941 by affirming flatly that "we are at war. . . . We must do whatever is necessary to insure a Hitler defeat." America First asserted that FFF was designed to appeal to "those who are for bloodcoated, instead of sugarcoated, phrases. . . . [It is] a tailormade-for-war group with a holier-than-thou title."[94]

Flynn was initially wary of the Aid-Allies committee and the FFF because of their close ties to the Roosevelt Administration and to the British embassy. Leaders of both interventionist groups held frequent conferences with the President, cabinet officials and aides, and English ambassadors Lord Lothian and then Lord Halifax. White described the relationship of the CDAAA and Roosevelt as "morganatic. . . . I knew I had his private support. . . . I never did

161

anything the President didn't ask for, and I always conferred with him on our program."[95] Mark Lincoln Chadwin, historian of the FFF, attested to an "extensive relationship [between the White House and the FFF] . . . beneath the level of public awareness." Roosevelt and his aides, Chadwin confirmed, "treated the FFF as an unofficial propaganda instrument for the administration."[96]

As close collaborators with the President, FFF and the Aid-Allies committee often launched "trial balloons" to prepare public sentiment for various interventionist policy steps. For example, the CDAAA called for United States naval convoys as early as March 18, a full month before cabinet officials spoke out on this subject.[97] In early May FFF and Aid-Allies spokesmen urged a declaration of unlimited national emergency, and Roosevelt "complied" in his May 27 address.[98] Both of the power groups also publicly recommended complete and specific repeal of the crucial portions of the 1939 Neutrality Act several weeks before the President broached the subject to Congress.[99] Finally the CDAAA cooperated with several interventionist journalists and motion-picture producers when it helped to promote a film series featuring discussions among prominent prowar journalists such as Dorothy Thompson, Linton Wells, and William Shirer. Aid-Allies headquarters asserted that the movie series "follows closely the policy of this Committee on the question of aid to Britain."[100]

The close ties between the leading interventionist committees on the one hand, and the Roosevelt Administration, the English, and some of the prowar sectors of the media on the other, gave powerful impetus to Flynn's conspiracy theory when he observed "the great sums of money . . . being spent on [interventionist] literature and advertisements, frequently by persons or organizations which could hardly be supposed to have such funds at their disposal."[101] Senator Wheeler concurred. "In the last war," Wheeler charged, "the British boasted of the fact that they spent . . . more than one hundred million dollars to carry on propaganda in this country. That they are spending more than that amount . . . through these committees [CDAAA, FFF, and others] . . . at this time cannot be doubted by anyone."[102]

Flynn's intrigue theory was also intensified as he watched hostile pickets and spies disrupting NYC-AFC rallies and other activities. One such spy, working in Flynn's Manhattan headquarters, became converted to the noninterventionist cause and went to the chapter chairman and confessed his true identity.[103] On several occasions Flynn appealed directly to prowar leaders to refrain from sending pickets to his New York rallies. The potential for violence and injury by "a few irresponsible people" was too great, the NYC-AFC chairman protested to Leo Birkhead, chief of the interventionist Friends of Democracy. "Can Americans not discuss great differences of opinion on national policy peacefully and rationally?"[104] When pickets continued to arrive, and fistfights and adverse publicity resulted, Flynn became convinced that the rally disruption was a deliberate machination to allow the prowar press to report that America First meetings were violent.[105] Lindbergh agreed. When a man shouted "Hang Roosevelt" at the NYC-AFC October meeting in Madison Square Garden, the aviator ruefully maintained: "The . . . shouter . . . was almost certainly an opposition 'plant.' They will now say there were demands to hang Roosevelt at our meeting."[106]

Flynn's suspicions regarding interventionist plants at his 1941 rallies and within the NYC-AFC organization were well founded. William Stephenson, head of the British security services in the United States, recruited agents of the FFF, Friends of Democracy, and other prowar groups to disrupt America First in New York. Stephenson was positive that the AFC was "a fifth column—a channel for enemy propaganda." He dispatched spies and hecklers throughout Flynn's organization and procured a "mass of information about its propaganda themes, its financing and its backers." Stephenson's co-worker H. Montgomery Hyde has argued that while the English-interventionist campaign against America First "did not cause its disintegration, it did considerably reduce its usefulness . . . and [pave] the way . . . for the great disrepute into which it shortly fell."[107]

On only one occasion, Hyde has boasted, "did a plan for harassing America First miscarry." The occasion was the large October rally, and Stephenson had printed and distributed to members of various pro-British groups scores of duplicate tickets to the rally's reserved-seat sections. He planned to have the spurious ticketholders arrive at the meeting early. When the genuine audience members appeared, they would, Stephenson hoped, "start trouble by demanding the accommodations to which their tickets ostensibly entitled them. Thus it seemed there was a good chance of disrupting the whole proceedings." According to Hyde, however, such a small audience attended the rally that there were enough seats for all who came. As a result, "Lindbergh addressed a considerably larger audience than he would have . . . without Stephenson's benevolent assistance."[108] Actually, unbeknown to the interventionists, Flynn anticipated their tactics and had a special printer's code inscribed on the genuine rally tickets. The unauthorized tickets were recognized by NYC-AFC ushers, and the prowar advocates were quietly shown to seats in the unreserved sections of Madison Square Garden. The meeting drew nearly fifty thousand people, but it is unknown how many of these were interventionist would-be disrupters.[109]

Toward the very end of 1941 Flynn's conspiracy hypothesis of war involvement began to coalesce around a nucleus of leaders and backers of various New York prowar organizations. However, war came before he was able to identify and attack the core group conclusively and forcefully. "While it would perhaps not be fair to say that all of the groups which functioned to attack the America First movement were brought into existence and directed by [this] one central body," the NYC-AFC chairman contended privately, "I found an organization whose name was never mentioned but which, I satisfied myself, sat more or less at the center of this web of propaganda, intrigue and calumniation." When the United States plunged into the war he dropped his investigations in favor of national unity. He warned, however, that after the war it would become "the duty" of the American people "to inquire into . . . that [pivotal] organization and its connections . . . with the United States government [and] . . . with other governments that were interested in involving us in war."[110]

Flynn had begun his involvement with the AFC with the general tendency to believe that Roosevelt and British propagandists were deliberately conspiring to bring America into war. Many antiwar advocates shared this view, although not as deeply as Flynn. The plethora of interventionist motion pictures, radio broadcasts, press articles and editorials, and committees, coupled with a growing stream of verbal abuse against noninterventionists, caused Flynn to look even more closely at the possibility of an organized prowar intrigue. His 1941 investigations led him to believe that the White House was collaborating with others to perpetrate a terrible injustice against free and fair debate. Government threats and coercion were perverting the media into tools of the state, he believed, and interventionist leaders were supplying vicious invective against dissenters. When war came Flynn expected his former opponents in the Great Debate to cease their activities. However, when attacks against America First continued for years after the committee dissolved, Flynn became angry and renewed his investigations. His discoveries were to shock him deeply and to have a seminal effect on his later view of life in the United States.[111]

9

Aftermath: Two Turning Points

Soon after America's entry into World War II, John Flynn returned to his office to begin reorganizing his "own very much disordered personal affiars." Although he was sometimes given to very sarcastic private comments regarding the United States' lack of military preparedness and President Roosevelt's "grandiose schemes to organize and save the entire world," Flynn supported the war effort completely.[1] He discontinued all of his investigations of the interventionist movement, and turned his attention to what he believed was constructive criticism of both America's mushrooming federal debt and this nation's early attempts to forge postwar global commitments. A large debt, he was convinced, would strangle small investment and lead to a corporative and eventually fascist economy in this country. Roosevelt's efforts in the area of postwar global commitments, Flynn asserted, were cynical, ill-conceived, and sure to pave the way for future wars. As Flynn tried to leave behind the rancor of the Great Debate of 1941, however, he found that he had recurring problems in finding publishing outlets and that attacks against the defunct America First Committee continued. Finally in late 1943 a shattering assault on the AFC was published in the book *UnderCover*.[2] Flynn, Senators Burton K. Wheeler of Montana and Gerald Nye of North Dakota, Socialist leader Norman Thomas, and other former noninterventionists joined forces to investigate *UnderCover*'s author and backers. Their probe revived and extended Flynn's 1941 conspiracy theory.

Throughout the rest of his life Flynn believed that his noninterventionist position in 1941 had been correct. The essentially undemocratic tactics that he thought the interventionists employed, as well as the overall global results of World War II, assured him that the interests of the United States and the world would have been better served had the massive conflict not been fought. Thirty years later many other America First leaders, together with some historians, agreed with Flynn's view of the AFC and the war.

Immediately following the Japanese attack on Pearl Harbor, Flynn rallied the New York chapter of the America First Committee to the war effort, and he eschewed all activities that might impair national unity. Throughout 1941 he had consistently maintained that he would "advocate a declaration of war, and a war to the utmost," if Germany or any other country "attempted to invade or attack the United States, Canada, Mexico, or any part of the South American continent."[3] In mid-December he publicly urged all NYC-AFC members to work to win the war "not as partisans of the furious debate which preceded the [conflict] . . . not grudgingly, not angrily . . . but as Americans to whom the safety and honor of their country is precious beyond all else."[4] He rested over the holiday season, and in early 1942 resolved that he would become connected with no more mass movements.[5] When some of his former associates from the AFC and the Keep America Out of War Congress formed a "Peace Now" organization to work for an early negotiated peace, he refused to become involved. Although he personally supported a negotiated peace, Flynn believed that such a movement was improper during wartime.[6]

Even though Flynn refused to do anything that might disrupt the American war effort, he did believe he should speak out against that "particularly poisonous system of politics and government known as the New Deal, which I believe is a prelude to fascism."[7] During 1942 he exercised this right by collaborating with Texas Senator Thomas Connolly on an article arguing against the possible wartime suspension of congressional elections. "We [Americans] will reject all canons of rule by a single mind and a single hand," Flynn declared. To his chagrin, the article was never published.[8] Nevertheless, he did manage to print an article decrying the "dangerous and destructive," spiraling federal debt imposed by the war. If Americans were sincerely committed to fighting fascism, he was convinced, they would have to sacrifice and pay for military expenses through greatly increased taxes. Financing the war by building up a huge debt could only lead to profiteering and to inflation. Inflation in turn would scare small investors out of the market, deliver the nation to the control of giant money cartels, and eventually result in fascism.[9] Flynn retained his interest in the debt problem, and generated several more articles on this topic over the next three years. Most of the works were never published, but one did find an outlet under the byline of fiscally conservative Maine Senator Ralph Owen Brewster.[10]

Flynn's deep concern with what he believed was the inevitability of a fascistic United States if the federal debt were not curbed led him in 1943 to seek new outlets for his views. He undertook an overall study of the problem of fascism, and in August he finished his most concise and important book on the subject, *As We Go Marching*.[11] He was also hired by *Reader's Digest* as a "roving editor" to write occasional pieces, but was disappointed to find that editor-in-chief DeWitt Wallace refused all but parabolic human-interest stories from him.[12] Flynn then retained Clark Getts, operator of a New York speakers' agency, to arrange a lecture tour for the winter of 1943–44. Flynn planned to focus his lectures on his salient concerns: war financing, the postwar economic outlook, what he perceived as the dangerous fascist trends in America, and his distress over Roosevelt's early approach to forging a postwar world organization.[13]

"Globaloney" was the label Flynn affixed to the President's overtures to England and the Soviet Union concerning postwar world commitments. The March 1943 Ball Resolution and the Moscow Pact seven months later raised the New York journalist's suspicions. Both documents proclaimed a general, preliminary intention to establish an international organization somewhat similar to the League of Nations.[14] Flynn feared that Britain, Russia, the United States, and possibly China were actually contemplating a "power alliance . . . for imperial aggrandizement but not for peace." England and the Soviet Union would use the moral authority of the organization to expand their empires, America would go along as the "idealistic sucker," and China might be included for "window dressing." In any case, Flynn was sure the league would be a cynical military alliance among the big powers: a modern triple or quadruple alliance.[15]

Throughout 1944 and 1945 Flynn retained and intensified his objections to Roosevelt's version of a postwar global organization. He denounced in turn the Bretton Woods Conference of July 1944, the Dumbarton Oaks Conference two months later, the Yalta Summit Conference of February 1945, and the San Francisco Charter drafted two months afterward. The United Nations concept endorsed by these meetings, Flynn contended, would "create and recognize and enforce spheres of influence and 'special arrangements between dominant powers'. . . . [It] can hardly be described as according sovereign equality to all peoples . . . and will include the subjugation of many. . . . *That is not cooperation for peace and justice. It is cooperation for peace and imperialism.*"[16] In July 1945 Flynn testified before the Senate Foreign Relations Committee in opposition to the United Nations charter. He asserted that the plan was being foisted upon the American people by organized propaganda, and he scored the charter as a calculated and deceptive scheme "not to protect the rights of little nations but to preserve the privileges and ambitions of a few . . . to perpetuate those very forces . . . which are the causes of all wars . . . [and] to deny human rights to hundreds of millions of people."[17]

Long before the United Nations charter was finally formulated, however, a seminal event occurred in Flynn's life. In the autumn of 1943 Armenian immigrant Avedis Derounian, using the alias John Roy Carlson, published a devastating attack on America First in a book entitled *UnderCover.* This book was promoted as an authentic directory of subversive, profascist groups and individuals in the United States. The AFC was denounced by Carlson as "America's Doom Squad . . . a spearhead aimed at the heart of democracy," and the Armenian author charged that the committee's goal had been fascist domination of the nation. Almost every America First leader was personally attacked in the volume, and only Flynn was portrayed as anything other than a confirmed fascist. The former NYC-AFC chairman was termed an appalling dupe, and his Northeastern chapter was described as the most flagrantly and notoriously profascist of all.[18]

UnderCover was not the first wartime assault on America First, but it disturbed Flynn far more than previous accusations. In January 1942 Carlson had denounced the AFC in a journal article, and later in the year Albert Kahn and Michael Sayers, employees of the interventionist committee Friends of Democracy, published a condemnation of America First in a book entitled *Sabotage! The Secret War Against America.*[19] Neither of these efforts attracted much public notice and Flynn did not bother to respond to them. He contended that there was no "need in America for this kind of thing now."[20] However, *UnderCover* seemed to be popular and credible. It sold nearly one million copies within six months of its publication, and

168

the distributors stated that they had extensive additional demand that could not be satisfied because of the wartime paper shortage.[21] Flynn spoke to several people, many of whom were "earnest opponents of everything that Roosevelt stands for, including . . . the war," who believed the charges leveled in *UnderCover*.[22] In addition to these factors, the book distressed Flynn because of its pointed attack on the AFC's New York chapter and because nearly two full years of war had not produced more national unity.

The most important reason for Flynn's intense anger over the Carlson book, however, concerned the America Firster's conspiracy theory. Many of the same persons that had been staunch noninterventionists in 1941 were currently criticizing both Roosevelt's financing and conduct of the war, and his initial steps toward postwar global commitments. Flynn asserted in early 1944 that Roosevelt and foreign agents, working through Carlson and others, had now resumed their orchestration of old smears in order to discredit and intimidate critics of the President's current policies. *UnderCover*, Flynn was convinced, was only part of a larger conspiracy "to frighten legitimate American patriotism underground." All persons mentioned in an uncomplimentary manner in the book, he maintained, had "only one thing in common—they opposed the efforts of others to plunge this country into war before there was justification."[23]

Flynn, Burton Wheeler, Gerald Nye, Norman Thomas, and some other former noninterventionists met together over the holiday season of 1943 and decided to launch a congressional investigation of Carlson and the book's backers. "These fellows [Roosevelt's agents] are now about to get busy with their smear tactics in a very industrious way," Flynn explained as he began amassing data for the probe. "There is simply nothing [that] can be done in opposition to this except to expose them. . . . Attack must be met with attack, vigorous and relentless."[24] He raised some preliminary funds by private solicitation and hired a researcher, Ike McAnally, to help with the investigative work.[25] For the first three months of 1944 the two men labored to establish the presence of a "conspiracy which has put not only this book but others out for a very definite purpose."[26]

The facts that Flynn and McAnally discovered convinced them that such collusion did exist. Carlson, they found, had done his "undercover" detective work concerning profascist groups and individuals under the auspices of three old interventionist, anti-Nazi

169

organizations: Friends of Democracy, the Anti-Defamation League, and the Non-Sectarian Anti-Nazi League to Champion Human Rights. Flynn traced alleged ties between several of the leaders of these heavily Jewish groups and the American Communist Party, and concluded that the three organizations were "acrawl with fellow-travelers."[27] He also discovered that Carlson himself had published several articles in Communist journals, and he adjudged the Armenian to be "an instrument in their hands."[28] Flynn then decided that the Communist Party was directing an organized "effort to create disunity among Americans." Realizing that economic and social disarray would provide the most fertile ground for promoting their revolutionary philosophy in this nation, he argued that the Communists were directing smears against respectable American groups and individuals. The confusion and internal strife generated by these accusations, Flynn maintained, were part of a deliberate and dangerous plot to ready the United States for Communist domination.[29] Furthermore, Flynn contended, Roosevelt knew of, and countenanced, Communist-led attacks against his political critics. The President was not a Communist himself, but he allowed the enemies of 1940–41 intervention policies and his wartime spending programs to be assaulted for the benefit of political expediency.[30]

Flynn encountered considerable trouble in publishing his ideas about a Roosevelt-Communist smear conspiracy. In late March 1944 the Senate refused to grant funds to underwrite an extended Flynn-Wheeler investigation, and in order to galvanize public support Flynn published a portion of his initial findings in an article titled "Uncovering *UnderCover*: The Real Facts About the Smear Book's Odd Author."[31] Martin Dies, conservative chairman of the House Committee on Un-American Activities, was attracted by Flynn's piece, and agreed to publish the full exposé under his own name. Flynn then hurriedly completed a small book entitled *Wake Up, America!* but two months later Dies, under intense pressure from the Rooseveltian Democratic Party, abruptly announced that he would not stand for reelection in the fall of 1944. When Flynn could not locate a publisher for the book, Dies lost interest and left a very chagrined Flynn with an unmarketable manuscript.[32]

Flynn's disappointment at not finding an outlet for his views led him to the nadir of pessimism and despair in the autumn of 1944. He was convinced that he was being deliberately silenced in favor of supporters of the President. In his resentment against Roosevelt he worked for the 1944 Republican presidential candidate, Thomas

170

E. Dewey. Although he had no real enthusiasm for Dewey and believed that the nominee did not possess the "sacred fire" of political charisma, Flynn was determined to see Roosevelt defeated.[33] The President's loss, he predicted, would end the demand for war hero stories and initiate "the 'Now-It-Can-Be-Told' type of story. . . . I have not the slightest doubt that there are phases [exposés of the war] which . . . are crying aloud to be printed." The journalist indicated a delighted readiness to "investigate" Roosevelt, "our planetary Santa Claus."[34]

Roosevelt's election victory came as yet another blow to the disillusioned Flynn. He was positive that the President should have been voted out in overwhelming disgrace because of the fourth-term issue, the huge federal debt, and the brutality of the war. Flynn concluded that the stress of war, as well as a deliberate, persistent propaganda effort had corrupted the American mind. The national consciousness "has been invaded and occupied by alien ideas," he fulminated. "Old, Constitutional principles" had been replaced by "blind Collectivism." He asserted that only a "sustained . . . campaign to recondition the minds of the people . . . to make them again hospitable to . . . American ideas of government and business" could save the nation.[35]

In order to mount the propaganda offensive needed to alter the "dangerous" new trends in American thinking, Flynn joined forces with several anti-Roosevelt writers and economists to form the Foundation for Foreign Affairs. Felix Morley, Merwin K. Hart, and former Indiana congressman and AFC national committee member Samuel Pettingill were prominent among the members. This amorphous group first met in December 1944, and formulated plans for a propaganda agency to "re-educate the American mind away from collectivism and toward Constitutional government."[36] The foundation, they anticipated, would select a "definite group of principles to which the loyal American employer and . . . worker and farmer can agree," and then saturate the nation's consciousness with these beliefs. "An effort on an ambitious scale to check the whole movement of the present program of Planned Capitalism must be made," Flynn contended.[37] The foundation proved to be an abortive endeavor, however, primarily because its original conception was too ambitious for its small funds and following. Its failure left Flynn even more embittered, and intensified his growing tendency to view American society in a "we versus they" manner. "Roosevelt's . . . New Order," he maintained shortly after the organization folded,

171

"is in no sense the result or mere chance or drift. . . . [It is] the result of deliberate and highly intelligent plans made and carried out by men who understand well what they are doing."[38]

Following the demise of the Foundation for Foreign Affairs, Flynn dedicated the remaining years of his life to exposing the various aspects of what he believed was a pervasive Rooseveltian-Communist conspiracy in the United States. The media were some of his chronic targets because he was positive that the President was orchestrating an extensive campaign to silence critics.[39] Let any writer attempt to reveal Roosevelt's collusion with Communists, Flynn asserted in 1945, "and see how far he will get in finding the printed page, the radio or any other medium of communication at his disposal. The extent of intimidation is beyond belief."[40] Two years later he again contended that the smearing and silencing of critics "must be ended. Is America to be governed by boycotters and smearers? Are public questions to be discussed in terms of libel and slander?"[41]

In an effort to secure an outlet for his views in 1947 and 1948, Flynn wrote a comprehensive study of the President entitled *The Roosevelt Myth*.[42] This book distilled Flynn's earlier analysis of Roosevelt as a man fundamentally without convictions or philosophy save that of political expediency. The President's one consistent theme, according to Flynn, was the power of his office and its increase: "The Presidency became in his hands an instrument of appalling consequences."[43] Roosevelt's two greatest crimes against the United States, Flynn was convinced, were his delivery of the nation to the poisonous sustenance of militarism and debt, and his collusion with communism. The former misdeed, Flynn charged, was committed because the President was unable to produce "any recovery whatever" from the Great Depression during the first eight years of his leadership.[44] Communist penetration of the New Deal took place "not because he [Roosevelt] was interested in revolution but because he was interested in votes." The President, Flynn again insisted, had "not . . . a grain of conviction on the side of the Communist philosophy," but collaborated with the party for political expediency.[45]

As Flynn described the course of events in *The Roosevelt Myth,* World War II increased Communist permeation of the Roosevelt Administration. Flynn termed the war a "bureaucrat's paradise" in this country, and maintained that the potpourri of wartime agencies was assembled so hurriedly as to make it impossible to check adequately the backgrounds of those hired. Many Communists "wriggled in" and worked in the midst of the confusion to break down the American economy. "In the financing and supervision of the war effort from Washington," Flynn contended, "practically every fiscal crime was committed. . . . The blindness of the White House opened the way for the Red conspirators into almost every important function of political, economic and educational life."[46]

At the time Flynn was working on *The Roosevelt Myth* he was writing a controversial article also accusing Roosevelt of Communist collusion, but he encountered difficulty in publishing either piece. His article, "Why the Americans Did Not Take Berlin," charged that at the Yalta Summit Conference in 1945 the President had secretly agreed to hold back the Allied armies and allow Russian dictator Stalin to capture the German city. Roosevelt's decision in this case, Flynn asserted, was "one of the most fateful mistakes" of the war because it gave the Soviet Union a vastly improved bargaining position for retaining control of large portions of Central and Eastern Europe.[47] Although Flynn swore that the facts in his article were "completely beyond dispute," the piece was never published.[48] He also spent several months during 1948 despairing of finding a publisher for *The Roosevelt Myth.* "For the first time in my life," he angrily wrote in May, "I am peddling a book around like a fresh unknown. . . . I am at my wits' end. . . . I have no means of . . . expressing publicly the facts which I think I am in possession of."[49] Later in the year, however, Flynn met Devin Garrity, anti-Roosevelt owner of the Devin-Adair Publishing Company, and this firm disseminated *The Roosevelt Myth.*

Flynn continued to speak and write publicly for twelve more years but was compelled to find more and more conservative backers to sponsor his works. America's Future, Inc., a militantly anti-Communist educational group, underwrote for several years during the 1950s a weekly Flynn radio broadcast, "Behind the Headlines."[50] Devin-Adair circulated his next, and last, four books. Written between 1949 and 1955, these volumes attacked President Harry Truman's continuation of Roosevelt's high government spending, taxation, and internationalism, warned of "creeping socialism" in the United States, contended that Communists in the federal government had obstructed American efforts to aid Chiang Kai-shek and led to Mao Tse-tung's victory in China, and warned of other alleged Communist penetration of the American government and economy.[51] Flynn's last books also recommended a virtually com-

173

plete repudiation of the substantive decisions of Roosevelt's presidency. He counseled invalidation of all Supreme Court decisions since 1937, dissolution of the United Nations, legislation prohibiting deficit spending, termination of all federal powers not specifically and literally granted in the Constitution, and passage of the Bricker Amendment negating international executive agreements not approved by Congress. Flynn also prescribed repeal of the graduated income tax embodied in the Sixteenth Amendment.[52] During 1956 he revised *The Roosevelt Myth* to make it even more strongly opposed to Roosevelt. Two years later his health began to fail. Flynn reluctantly retired in 1960, in his seventy-ninth year. He died in 1964.[53]

John Flynn never regretted the ideological positions that he took during his lifetime. He remained proud of his association with the America First Committee, and he continued to blame Roosevelt for this nation's war involvement. In 1956 he went so far as to charge that the dead President decided to enter the European war as early as October 1940. From this initial date forward, Flynn asserted, Roosevelt's "public avowals were the precise opposite of his secret intentions. He did not tell the truth to the American people from the beginning to the end."[54] Flynn also persisted in his belief that the financial burdens of total war between 1941 and 1945, and the subsequent deficit/defense spending cycle, would result in the collapse of the English and American economies and bring fascism to both of these countries.[55] His long years of watching President Roosevelt expand the powers of the executive branch taught Flynn to fear big government more than he had feared the power of big business in the prewar period.

Many other NYC-AFC leaders followed a pattern similar to that of Flynn during the years after 1941; they supported the war effort itself but sustained the conviction that World War II was unnecessary, futile, and deplorable. However, most America Firsters did not embrace Flynn's extreme anti-Communism. In May 1941 William T. Leonard, chairman of the Brooklyn AFC, expressed the prevailing sentiment of most committee members toward an actual national emergency. "If the American people go to war," Leonard promised, "the America First Committee will give its utmost efforts and will support and back the President in a war against the Axis."[56] Shortly after the Pearl Harbor attack many AFC leaders and members in New York and elsewhere redeemed Leonard's pledge. Eastern regional field representative Joseph Boldt and ranking NYC-

AFC staff member Robert Bliss, both became lieutenant commanders in the navy, and national director Robert D. Stuart served as an army artillery major in Europe. New York America First sponsoring committee member Archibald Roosevelt, a lieutenant colonel, became a battalion commander in New Guinea and was severely wounded by shrapnel at Biak. Colonel Theodore Roosevelt, Jr., another NYC-AFC sponsor, died of heart attack at Omaha Beach.[57]

Despite the admirable service records of some America Firsters, others, according to national chairman Robert E. Wood, were "debarred from any really important post in the war effort."[58] The most prominent AFC leader prevented from playing the role that he sought in the nation's war mobilization was Charles Lindbergh. Within three days after the Pearl Harbor raid Lindbergh volunteered his services to the U.S. Army Air Corps, but his offer was met with official silence. "Definite limits exist to the Administration's desire for 'unity,' " he ruefully complained to Wood. "Those limits do not extend very far into the group of people who have disagreed with the policies of the President."[59] In January 1942 the aviator attempted to penetrate the governmental rebuff by speaking to Secretary of War Henry L. Stimson and to General Henry H. ("Hap") Arnold, chief of the U.S. Army Air Forces. Both officials informed Lindbergh that in order to be allowed to serve he would have to issue a statement retracting or greatly modifying his 1939–1941 noninterventionist views. Arnold later admitted that these orders to Lindbergh came directly from Roosevelt, and that the famous flier's America First involvement "had alienated him permanently from [the] President's . . . good will." Deeply shocked and offended, Lindbergh refused to recant his earlier antiwar views, and ceased trying to regain his air corps commission. "After all," he declared, "we're supposed to be fighting for democracy and one's right to express his own political views, aren't we?"[60]

After his offer to enter active military service was refused, Lindbergh endeavored to aid the war effort from inside the aviation industry. However, he again found governmental pressure directed against him. He was first encouraged and then rejected by Pan American Airlines, Curtiss-Wright Aircraft Company, and others. In all cases company officials maintained that they wanted to welcome him but that the White House had informed them that the President would be "very angry" if Lindbergh were hired.[61] In early March the famous aviator, heartened by Roosevelt's press secretary, Stephen Early, almost accepted a post with United Aircraft Company.

175

He then learned that the firm was being investigated by the Senate for selling equipment to Germany and Japan in the immediate prewar years. Positive that the President was encouraging the connection with United in order to embarrass him, Lindbergh backed away from the offer.[62] "I am beginning to wonder whether I will be blocked in every attempt I make to take part in this war," he cried desperately in the late winter of 1942. He had always believed, he asserted, that every American citizen possessed "the right and duty to state his opinion in peace and to fight for his country in war. But the Roosevelt Administration seems to think otherwise."[63] Finally, in April, he joined Detroit auto manufacturer Henry Ford as supervisor of Ford's bomber plant at Willow Run, Michigan. Two years later Lindbergh became a civilian pilot trainer in the Pacific and shot down at least two Japanese Zeros.[64]

Despite his support of the war effort itself, Lindbergh continued to hold his noninterventionist beliefs for the rest of his life. In mid-1944 he encountered Archibald Roosevelt in the Pacific and they talked of "the now obvious hypocrisy of the prewar [interventionist] idealists."[65] A quarter of a century later he contended that "it is alarmingly possible that . . . in a broader sense . . . we lost it [World War II], for our Western civilization is less respected and secure than it was before." He pointed to what he perceived as the menacing threats of the Soviet Union and the People's Republic of China, the reduction of England to a "secondary power," the "mild dictatorship" of France, and the dissatisfaction and unrest within the United States. "Most of the challenges . . . that tower before us with unprecedented magnitude in almost every field of modern life . . . were, at least, intensified through the waging of World War II."[66]

Other America First leaders also maintained an abiding belief in the noninterventionist cause and the futility of World War II. Burton K. Wheeler asserted more than twenty years after the AFC disbanded that Roosevelt "never tried to keep us out of the war, while deliberately misleading the people into thinking that he was. . . . War simply does not settle anything. . . . The world got dictators and less freedom [as a result of the war]."[67] More than ten years after Wheeler last spoke out Stuart declared that a definitive assessment of the America First position was impossible, but that "as mankind increasingly faces up to the futility and horror of war . . . a position recommending nonintervention will seem wiser and wiser."[68] Speaking a few months after Stuart, Robert Bliss termed his involvement with the AFC "a great experience" and vowed that he would "sure do it again." He was convinced that World War II brutalized American society and led to the looming ascendancy of Russia, but he did maintain that Hitler had to be fought and stopped.[69]

Thirty years after Pearl Harbor some historians also began to turn away from the stridently interventionist texts and monographs that characterized the wartime and the immediate postwar periods.[70] The tensions and national soul-searching brought about by the Vietnam war provided the most powerful impetus for this shift in historical thinking. In a resounding 1972 challenge to the traditional perceptions of World War II, Yale political scientist Bruce M. Russet contended that "most Americans probably would have been no worse off, and possibly a little better, if the United States had never become a belligerent" in the war. Russet reasoned that the basic structure of international politics changed little as a result of World War II, for the Soviet Union replaced Germany as the great threat to European security, and Japan once more became a major power competing for meager world resources. Moreover, asserted Russet, the war set "precedents for our thinking" that led too easily to later interventions in Korea and Vietnam.[71]

Thirty years after the AFC dissolved, however, confirmations of the committee position regarding the futility of World War II itself missed one of the most crucial and valuable points about the American First movement. The AFC significantly contributed to American thought by warning against excessive extension of power in the executive branch of government, official concealment or distortion of information to achieve policy ends not generally understood or approved by the public, campaign speeches for peace followed by warlike actions, inflexible attempts to spread democracy "by the sword," and neglect of pressing domestic concerns because of massive military and financial commitments abroad. Ruth Sarles, an officer in the America First Washington research bureau and later the committee historian, perhaps best expressed this aspect of AFC philosophy when she reacted angrily against undue secrecy in government. "One had only to live in Washington in the months before the country went to war," she fulminated, "to hear the view expressed freely that the tragedy of the times was that the men who knew what to do were handicapped by the slowness of people to recognize 'reality.' " Sarles then went on to pose the vital question: "Does democracy . . . force government into the hands of a cabal of experts who, on the basis of facts available only to them, must scheme to accomplish what the people do not support and must

177

always be propagandizing to make the people catch up with them? ... Is our representative system ... adequate to today?"[72]

The year 1941 was a turning point in the lives of both John Thomas Flynn and the United States of America. In Flynn's case a man fought energetically for a policy that he believed was best for his country. He lost, and he accepted the loss gracefully because he had faith in the democratic tenets of free discussion in peace and national unity in war. However, when he observed the continued vilification of those who disagreed with the administration in power, his anger grew.

The year 1941 also saw the United States go to war. A bitterly divided and somewhat skeptical nation was transformed on December 7 into a unified fighting community. In the drama and excitement of winning the war some of the fundamental reasons for prewar divisions were forgotten. The America First protests against excessive power and secrecy in the executive branch of government were overlooked as the United States pursued the monumental task at hand. The drift away from the traditional constitutional balance of powers continued, and great injury was done to this delicate equilibrium. Perhaps the clearest warning sounded in 1941 against this dangerous new trend was enunciated by New Hampshire senator and AFC spokesman Charles W. Tobey: "In my opinion the greatest menace to this country and to our own form of government, does not come from any enemy abroad, but rather exists right here in our own country ... under the Capitol Dome in Washington, where the people's representatives in the Congress, have apparently lost their sense of responsibility under the Constitution to act as a separate but coordinate branch of the federal government and have yielded to pressure and blandishments of another branch, the executive."[73]

Appendix A

**Persons Present at First Two NYC-AFC
Organizational Luncheons**

DECEMBER 6, 1940—TOWN HALL CLUB, NEW YORK CITY

John T. Flynn

Bruce Barton
Avery Claflin
John Elting
F. Abbott Goodhue
Robert M. Harriss
Randolph Phillips

Allen M. Pope
Harold Sprout
Douglas Stewart
(representing Charles Payson)
H. Dudley Swim
Robert Ralph Young

DECEMBER 12, 1940—BANKERS CLUB, NEW YORK CITY

John T. Flynn
Robert E. Wood

Mrs. J. Howland Auchincloss
W. H. Bennett
Richard E. Berlin
Graham B. Blaine
Thomas W. Bowers

Mr. and Mrs. Cecil J. North
Randolph Phillips
Allen M. Pope
Robert U. Redpath, Jr.
H. Smith Richardson

179

Avery Claflin
Mrs. William Shippen Davis
F. Abbott Goodhue
John P. Grant
Robert M. Harriss
Robert Haydock
Joseph F. Higgins
Hugh Knowlton
William C. Lengel
W. L. Momsen
J. L. Montgomery

Lunsford Richardson
Daniel Rockford
Archibald Roosevelt
C. R. Schaeffer
Willard Simpkins
Benjamin Strong
H. Dudley Swim
Bayard F. Swope
Arthur J. Talley
Robert Ralph Young

Appendix B

Large Contributors to America First from the Northeast

Mr. and Mrs. Berton A. Allen, East Orange, N.J.	$325.00
Mrs. Bruce Barton, NYC	$225.00
Walter J. Black, NYC	$250.00
Graham B. Blaine, NYC	$100.00
John W. Blodgett, Grand Rapids, Mich.	$3,000.00
Mrs. David Boies, Jr., Whitehouse, N.J.	$105.00
Mrs. Sayles Booker, NYC	$200.00
Mr. and Mrs. Frederic E. Camp, East Bluehill, Maine	$200.00
J. H. Carlson, Brooklyn, N.Y.	$100.00
Edward C. Childs, Norfolk, Conn.	$500.00
H. W. Church, Providence, R.I.	$100.00
Marie T. Clausen, NYC	$100.00
Dorothea K. Conrad, Erie, Pa.	$300.00
Mrs. Avery Coonley, Washington, D.C.	$100.00
Mr. and Mrs. J. Sargeant Cram, NYC	$966.00
Nellis M. Crouse, Ithaca, N.Y.	$135.00
Mrs. Pauline Dankelmann, NYC	$100.00
Charles H. Davis, Bass River, Cape Cod, Mass.	$150.00
Miss Helen Davis, NYC	$100.00
George W. Davison, NYC	$100.00

Mrs. M. Hartley Dodge, Madison, N.J. $2,500.00
Mrs. Janet A. Dulles, NYC $950.00
Mrs. William H. Fain, Greenwich, Conn. $170.00
Edward Farley (c/o Christine Gawne),
    Huntington, Long Island, N.Y. $100.00
Mrs. Horace C. Flanigan, Purchase, N.Y. $100.00
F. B. Flood, NYC $100.00
John C. Flynn, Mt. Vernon, N.Y. $225.00
John T. Flynn, Bayside, Long Island, N.Y. $100.00
Dr. Mildred Focht, NYC $110.00
John H. Frey, Brooklyn, N.Y. $100.00
Mr. and Mrs. Childs Frick,
    Roslyn, Long Island, N.Y. $3,000.00
John Hemming Fry, Cos Cob, Conn. $600.00
R. M. Fulle, Montclair, N.J. $100.00
Mrs. Lillian Fuller, NYC $100.00
Charles B. Galvin, NYC $110.00
Mrs. Frederick Geller, NYC $453.00
Bradley Goodyear, Otsego County, N.Y. $125.00
Paul G. Gravenhorst, NYC $105.00
A. G. Gronbeck, Forest Hills, Long Island, N.Y. $125.00
Miss Harjea, NYC $100.00
Robert M. Harriss, NYC $200.00
Mrs. Harold Hatch $100.00
Thomas J. Higgins, Brooklyn, N.Y. $100.00
Otto Hildebrandt, Williston Park,
    Long Island, N.Y. $110.00
Thomas Hitchcock, NYC $150.00
Mrs. E. H. Hooker, Greenwich, Conn. $500.00
Allen S. Hubbard, NYC $100.00
Mrs. Mary Richardson Jackson, New Haven, Conn. $1,000.00
A. M. Joost, Southold, N.Y. $500.00
Thomas H. Kennedy, Bradford, Pa. $500.00
Edward Kracke, Montclair, N.J. $285.00
Mrs. Claude W. Kress, NYC $100.00
Mrs. Cornelius Lane, NYC $400.00
R. G. A. Lesch, NYC $250.00
Mort Lewis, NYC $100.00
Philip Liebman, NYC $250.00
B. A. McAfee, NYC $200.00
David M. McKell, Chillicothe, Ohio $1,200.00

Thomas MacSweeney, NYC $100.00
Cedric A. Major, NYC $100.00
Mrs. A. C. March $100.00
Mrs. Adelaide Hooker Marquand, NYC $750.00
Mrs. Anna H. Matthewson, NYC $240.00
Mrs. Kathleen H. Meeker, Unadilla, N.Y. $120.00
A. Messina, Bronx, N.Y. $250.00
Mrs. Alida K. Milliken, NYC $250.00
Benjamin Franklin Meisner, Millburn, N.J. $100.00
F. J. Muhlfeld, NYC $225.00
C. A. Munn, Jr., NYC $100.00
Mrs. Vanwy Parry Musil, Scarborough, N.Y. $100.00
Kathleen Norris, NYC $103.00
Mrs. Mary O'Donnell, Brooklyn, N.Y. $130.00
Mrs. Evelyn Palmer, Ridgefield, Conn. $375.00
Joseph M. Patterson, NYC $100.00
Mrs. Mary K. Patterson, NYC $250.00
Mr. and Mrs. Walter Piel, NYC $180.00
Mrs. Seton Porter, NYC $100.00
Fred Y. Presley, NYC $1,000.00
Lynn R. Prickett, NYC $120.00
H. Smith Richardson, NYC $3,100.00
H. Smith Richardson, Jr., NYC $1,500.00
Lunsford Richardson, NYC $1,000.00
Miss M. Zorata Richtberg, Richmond Hill, N.Y. $100.00
Mrs. Philip Roosevelt, NYC $170.00
Howell L. Seiple, Chester Springs, Pa. $100.00
Mrs. H. G. Shields, Flemington, N.J. $161.00
Igor Sikorsky, Bridgeport, Conn. $242.00
Mrs. Helen Stauffer, Greenwich, Conn. $100.00
Grace F. Stetson, NYC $1,000.00
C. B. Stuart, NYC $350.00
John R. Surber, NYC $100.00
Eleanor Taylor, NYC $100.00
Mrs. Howell Van Gerbig, NYC $250.00
Ernest T. Walker, East Orange, N.J. $100.00
Eugenie P. Ward, NYC $175.00
Mr. and Mrs. H. E. Ward, NYC $300.00
Edwin S. Webster, Boston, Mass. $1,000.00
Edwin S. Webster, Jr., NYC $5,000.00
Ernest T. Weir, Pittsburgh, Pa. $1,000.00

Mrs. Conkey Whitehead, NYC... $500.00
R. Thornton Wilson, NYC.. $300.00
Mr. and Mrs. William C. S. Wilson, NYC............................ $450.00
Robert R. Young, Newport, R.I. $1,000.00

Contributors of $100 or More to the AFC National Committee from the Northeast

Anonymous (probably Charles Payson), NYC................... $8,000.00
Robert Badenhop, NYC.. $100.00
George F. Baker, Jr., NYC.. $100.00
Francis Bird, East Walpole, Mass... $350.00
Edward Bose, Kearny, N.J. $175.00
Annie J. Bronson, Brookline, Mass...................................... $149.00
Robert W. Byerly, NYC.. $700.00
Mrs. Frederic E. Camp, East Bluehill, Maine...................... $100.00
Mrs. Roscoe A. Carter, Brookline, Mass. $100.00
Mrs. G. Lloyd Cowan, Edgewater Park, N.J. $150.00
Guy W. Cox, Boston, Mass.. $100.00
Henry M. Crane, NYC... $400.00
George D. Crofts, Buffalo, N.Y.. $450.00
Herman Cron, NYC... $125.00
Marquis deCueras, NYC $100.00
Herman H. Doehler, NYC... $1,000.00
Mr. & Mrs. John A. Donahoe, Pittsburgh, Pa. $200.00
James Donahue, NYC.. $300.00
W. P. Draper, NYC $100.00
Mrs. Charles Einsiedler, Stirling, N.J. $250.00
Col. Robert C. Elbert, NYC... $125.00
Mrs. William H. Fain, Greenwich, Conn............................ $105.00
Horace C. Flanigan, Purchase, N.Y. $500.00
Allan W. Gilmore, Philadelphia, Pa. $115.00
William T. Grant, NYC $500.00
Mrs. Frederick Guest, NYC $700.00
Henry Gund, Jr., Cheshire, Conn. $2,200.00
T. C. Haffenreffer, Brookline, Mass.................................... $950.00
Ferdinand Hansen, NYC $100.00
Robert M. Harriss, NYC.. $600.00
Roy W. Heyer, Nazareth, Pa... $325.00
H. W. Huber, NYC $100.00

Frazier Jelke, NYC $1,350.00
James Wood Johnson, NYC $300.00
Mrs. Max Kade, Upper Montclair, N.J. $150.00
F. L. Kennedy, Pelham, N.Y. $100.00
John P. Kennedy, NYC $100.00
Samuel H. Kress Foundation, NYC $100.00
Levingston Lansing, Skaneateles, N.Y. $126.00
Morris E. Leeds, Philadelphia, Pa. $200.00
John E. Leibenderfer, Bronxville, N.Y. $185.00
Nicholas F. Lencsen, NYC $375.00
Charles A. Lindbergh, Huntington, L.I., N.Y. $100.00
Elizabeth D. Lowe, Boston, Mass. $100.00
Mrs. H. C. McEldowney, Pittsburgh, Pa. $100.00
Albert E. McVitty, Princeton, N.J. $210.00
Edward E. Mayer, Montclair, N.J. $105.00
Benjamin Franklin Meisner, Millburn, N.J. $100.00
Mr. & Mrs. David Meyers, St. Davids, Pa. $175.00
Jeremiah Milbank, NYC $5,000.00
E. E. Mueser, Mountain Lakes, N.J. $175.00
C. H. Muhlenberg, Jr., Reading, Pa. $200.00
John B. Paine, Jr., Boston, Mass. $450.00
Robert Treat Paine II, Boston, Mass. $2,200.00
Edgar Palmer, NYC $100.00
Joseph M. Patterson, NYC $4,000.00
Mrs. Edward S. Perot, NYC $100.00
Walter Piel, NYC $500.00
Mrs. Seton Porter, NYC $100.00
William C. Potter, NYC $1,000.00
Wallace E. Pratt, NYC $700.00
Mr. & Mrs. E. Parmelee Prentiss,
    Williamstown, Mass. $1,050.00
Alice L. Priest, Brookline, Mass. $125.00
Col. Latham Reed, Southampton, L.I., N.Y. $250.00
Henry Regnery, East Millsboro, Pa. $1,000.00
Mrs. A. S. Reise, Swansea, Mass. $119.00
J. L. Reiss, NYC $110.00
H. Smith Richardson, NYC $18,000.00
Lunsford Richardson, Greenwich, Conn. $4,000.00
Mrs. Benjamin Rogers, Tuxedo Park, N.Y. $350.00
George S. Rodgers, NYC $190.00
Frederich E. Ryan, NYC $100.00

Mr. & Mrs. Erdman E. Scharg, Rutherford, N.J.................. $305.00
Frederick A. D. Schwarz, NYC $100.00
Howell L. Seiple, Chester Springs, Pa. $100.00
Walter K. Shaw, Jr., Boston, Mass........................ $1,500.00
Igor I. Sikorsky, Bridgeport, Conn. $325.00
H. A. Smith, Bridgeport, Conn. $100.00
F. Stallforth, NYC $100.00
Philip G. Stevens, New Haven, Conn. $150.00
Col. H. H. Stout, Plainfield, N.J........................... $139.00
Charles G. Taylor, Philadelphia, Pa........................ $110.00
Vernon F. Taylor, Indiana, Pa. $950.00
Louis F. Timmerman, NYC $125.00
J. G. Timolat, NYC $410.00
United Cork Company, Kearny, N.J......................... $150.00
Richard H. Waldo, NYC.................................... $125.00
Waterbury, Conn., AFC Chapter........................... $200.00
Edwin S. Webster, Jr., NYC.............................. $2,500.00
Louis A. Wehle, Rochester, N.Y............................ $100.00
E. T. Weir, Pittsburgh, Pa. $500.00
H. K. Weir, Pittsburgh, Pa................................ $1,500.00
E. Schier Welch, Boston, Mass. $100.00
Ernest E. Wheeler, NYC $110.00
Mrs. Geoffrey G. Whitney, Milton, Mass. $110.00
R. Thornton Wilson, NYC................................. $250.00
Mrs. William C. S. Wilson, NYC........................... $250.00
Mary Winsor, Philadelphia, Pa............................. $120.00
Robert R. Young, Newport, R.I. $7,000.00

Appendix C

Final Statement of Receipts and Disbursements of NYC-AFC, Inc., January 23, 1941–May 20, 1941

PREPARED BY ARTHUR YOUNG AND CO., AUDITORS.
SUBMITTED ON MAY 26, 1941

Receipts:

Contributions	$141,865.02
Mass Meetings	$32,248.25
Sale of Tickets ($15,756.60)	
Collections and Misc. Receipts (16,491.65)	
Sale of Literature, Refunds and Misc.	$5,769.93
Sale of Pins	$667.24
Refunds and Advances	$11,311.53
Advances by National Committee (see contra) ($6,584.52)	
Exchanges and Transfers (see contra) ($1,412.50)	
Salaries Refunded by Writers' Committee and	
NYC-AFC Bulletin ($857.53)	
Telephone Deposit Refunds (see contra) ($800.00)	
Bail Bond Refund (see contra) ($490.00)	
Other Advances and Refunds ($1,166.98)	
Sundry Receipts	$80.56
Total Receipts	$191,942.53

187

Disbursements:

Cost of Meetings, Publicity, etc. $94.066.97
    Circularization and Literature for Distribution ($37,736.31)
    Publicity and Publications ($33,550.84)
    Mass Meetings ($22,769.82)

Contributions to Other Chapters and Organizations $13,339.68

Salaries and Wages (inc. Social Security Taxes) $40,787.23

Office and General Expenses $34,410.76
    Telephone, Telegraph and Teletype ($8,613.52)
    Rent ($5,717.51)
    Traveling Expenses ($4,584.00)
    Rental of Office Furniture, Equipment,
    Accounting Services, and Misc. ($15,495.73)

Refunds and Advances $9,287.02
    Repayment of Advances by National Committee
    (see contra) ($6,584.52)
    Exchanges and Transfers (see contra) ($1,412.50)
    Telephone Deposits (see contra) ($800.00)
    Bail Bond Deposit (see contra) ($490.00)

Liquidating Fund, Representing Balance of
    Cash on Hand $50.86

Total Disbursements $191,942.53

NOTE: This included funds received and disbursed by the NYC-AFC chapter committee only; it does not include the funds of any of the subchapters.

Appendix D

AFC Chapters in the Northeast:
Formal and Informal Affiliates of the NYC-AFC.

Connecticut (formal affiliate of NYC-AFC):
Bridgeport—Mrs. Frances Phillips
Hartford—William T. Bissell
New Haven—Kingman Brewster, Jr.; Edwin A. Borchard
Norfolk—Joseph R. Carroll
Stamford, Greenwich, and Norwalk—Gregory Mason
Waterbury—John Fista

Maine (informal affiliate of NYC-AFC):
Lewiston
Portland—Haven Sawyer

Massachusetts (informal affiliate of NYC-AFC):
Boston—Tudor Gardiner, Jr., and Paul Killiam
Cambridge
Greenfield
Northampton
Springfield—Richard Emerson; George Yarrington, and
Mrs. Bradley E. Stafford
Worcester—Mrs. Carl Barnes

189

New Jersey (informal affiliate of NYC-AFC):
  East Orange, Montclair and Paterson—Joseph V. Menegus
  Hackensack (Bergen County)—Mrs. Neal Dow Newby
  Jersey City—Raymond Hanfield
  Newark—Mrs. Mary Henninger
  Trenton—John McGrath

New York
  Bronx (and 17 units)—Vincent A. Giaquinto
  Brooklyn (and 6 units)—William T. Leonard
  Buffalo—Millard Dorntge, and Gilbert Pederson
  Long Island (Five Towns Headquarters, and 8 units)—
    Edgar Treacy
  Manhattan (and 7 branches)—Henry Christ
  Staten Island—Mrs. Lila Jump
  Westchester County (and 6 units)—Allen Campbell

Pennsylvania (informal affiliate of NYC-AFC):
  Philadelphia—Isaac Pennypacker
  Pittsburgh

Vermont (informal affiliate of NYC):
  Bennington
  Burlington

Appendix E

Films, Film Companies and Individuals Scored by Gerald Nye

FILMS NAMED AS PROWAR PROPAGANDA BY NYE AND OTHER NONINTERVENTIONISTS:

1. *After Mein Kampf*
2. *Convoy*
3. *Escape*
4. *Flight Command*
5. *Foreign Correspondent*
6. *Great Dictator, The*
7. *I Married a Nazi*
8. *Man Hunt*
9. *Mortal Storm, The*
10. *Mystery Sea Raider*
11. *Night Train*
12. *Ramparts We Watched*
13. *Sergeant York*
14. *That Hamilton Woman*
15. *They Dare Not Love*
16. *Victory in the West*
17. *World in Flames, The*

COMPANIES AND EXECUTIVES NAMED AS CONSPIRING TO PRODUCE PROWAR PROPAGANDA:

1. Columbia Pictures—Harry and Jack Cohn
2. Goldwyn Inc.—Samuel Goldwyn
3. Loew's Inc.—Samuel Katz, Arthur Loew, Nicholas Schenck, David Bernstein
4. Paramount Pictures—Barney Balaban, Adolph Zukor
5. RKO Radio Pictures Corp.—George J. Scheaffer
6. Twentieth Century-Fox—Darryl F. Zanuck, Joseph Schenk, Sidney R. Kent
7. United Artists—Murray Silverstone, Arthur Kelley
8. Universal Pictures—Nate Blumberg, J. Cheever Cowdin
9. Walter Wanger Productions—Walter Wanger
10. Warner Brothers—Harry M. Warner
11. Motion Picture Producers and Distributors of America (intraindustry regulatory body)—Will H. Hays

Appendix F

Groups Involved in the Great Debate of 1941

NONINTERVENTIONIST GROUPS AND THEIR CHAIRMEN, 1940–41

1. America First Committee—Robert E. Wood
2. America United—Thomas Sully
3. American Destiny Party—Joseph McWilliams
4. American Socialist Party—Norman Thomas
5. Citizens' Keep America Out of War Committee—William J. Grace
6. Citizens' No Foreign War Coalition—Oscar Brumback
7. College Men for Defense First—Richard A. Moore
8. Fellowship of Reconciliation, The—Arthur L. Swift
9. German-American Bund—G. Wilhelm Kunze
10. Keep America Out of War Congress—John T. Flynn, then John F. Finerty
11. Ministers' No War Committee—Albert W. Palmer
12. National Council for the Prevention of War—Frederick Libby
13. No Foreign Wars Committee—Verne Marshall
14. Progressive Students' League, Peace Committee—Nat Lubman
15. Union for Social Justice—Charles Coughlin
16. War Resisters' League—John Haynes Holmes

17. Womens' International League for Peace and Freedom—Dorothy Detzer
18. Writers' Anti-War Bureau—Sidney Hertzberg
19. Youth Committee Against War, The—Fay Bennett

INTERVENTIONIST GROUPS AND THEIR CHAIRMEN, 1940–41

1. All-Chicago Citizens' Rally Committee—?
2. American Committee for Defense of British Homes—C. Suydan Cutting
3. American Communist Party—William Z. Foster
4. American Council on Soviet Relations—?
5. American Friends of German Freedom—Reinhold Niebuhr
6. American Friends of Yugoslavia—Frank L. Polk
7. Anti-Defamation League—Henry Monsky and Sigmund Livingston
8. British War Relief Society of the USA—Winthrop W. Aldrich
9. Bundles for Britain—Mrs. Wales Latham
10. Clearing House for Youth Groups—Dick Brown
11. Committee for American-Irish Defense—Sanford Griffith
12. Committee to Defend America by Aiding the Allies—William Allen White, then Ernest Gibson
13. Council for Democracy—Ernest Angell and Raymond Gram Swing
14. Federal Union (Union Now)—Clarence K. Streit
15. Fight for Freedom—Henry W. Hobson
16. France Forever—Eugene Houdry
17. Free World Association—Mrs. J. Borden Harriman
18. Friends of Democracy—Leo Birkhead
19. Inter-Allied Information Center—M. Hurley
20. League for a Declared War—Harold Von Schmidt
21. Legion for American Unity—?
22. Loyal Americans of German Descent—Robert F. Wagner and George N. Shuster
23. Non-Sectarian Anti-Nazi League to Champion Human Rights —James L. Sheldon and Julius Goldstein
24. Ring of Freedom—Dorothy Thompson
25. Social Democratic Youth—?
26. Student Defenders of Democracy—Dorothy Overlock
27. Union for Democratic Action—Reinhold Niebuhr

Notes

PREFACE

1. Wayne S. Cole, *America First; The Battle Against Interventionism, 1940–41* (Madison: University of Wisconsin Press, 1953), p. 27.
2. Wayne S. Cole, "America First and the South, 1940–41," *Journal of Southern History* 44 (1956): 36–47.
3. Richard Clark Frey, Jr., "John T. Flynn and the United States in Crisis, 1928–50" (unpublished doctor's dissertation, University of Oregon, 1969).
4. Ruth Sarles, "A Story of America First" (unpublished manuscript, Hoover Institution on War, Revolution and Peace, 1942).
5. Morris Burns Stanley, "The America First Committee: A Study in Recent American Non-Interventionism" (unpublished master's thesis, Emory University, 1942); Bart Lanier Stafford III, "The Emergence of Anti-Semitism in the America First Committee, 1940–41" (unpublished master's thesis, New School for Social Research, 1948).

CHAPTER 1

1. Ruth Sarles, "A Story of America First" (unpublished manuscript, Hoover Institution on War, Revolution and Peace, Stanford, Calif., 1942), pp. 42–45.
2. Personal letter from Robert D. Stuart, January 11, 1974.
3. *Ibid.*
4. *Ibid.*
5. Sarles, "A Story of America First," pp. 49–50.
6. *Ibid.*, p. 48.
7. A. N. Marquis, ed., *Who's Who in America, 1942–43* (Chicago: A. N. Marquis Co., 1943), p. 2390.
8. John T. Flynn Papers, University of Oregon, Eugene, File Box 21, Flynn, "Notes on Formation of the New York Chapter," April 1942, p. 3.

9. Personal files of Robert L. Bliss, New York City, William Benton to Richard Ketchum, October 1972.
10. Charles A. Lindbergh, *The Wartime Journals of Charles A. Lindbergh* (New York: Harcourt Brace Jovanovich, 1970), pp. 426, 604.
11. Wayne S. Cole, *America First: The Battle Against Interventionism, 1940–41* (Madison: University of Wisconsin Press, 1953), pp. 19–25.
12. Samuel Grafton, "The Appeasement Tropism," *New Republic,* January 6, 1941, p. 18.
13. For several examples of the transforming power of the liberal minority in the AFC national committee decisions, see chap. 6.
14. America First Committee Papers, Hoover Institution on War, Revolution and Peace, Stanford, Calif. FB64, Flynn to Stuart, January 6, 1941. For a full discussion of the problem of recruiting New York businessmen to the AFC, see chap. 2.
15. AFC Papers, FB32, "Brief Biography of Thomas N. McCarter."
16. AFC Papers, FB32, "Brief Biography of Edward Rickenbacker"; Marquis, *Who's Who, 1942–43,* pp. 2423, 2292; Sarles, "A Story of America First," p. 122; Marquis, *Who's Who, 1942–43,* p. 1358.
17. Sarles, "A Story of America First," pp. 53–54; La Follette later became a frequent speaker for the AFC, however.
18. Flynn Papers, FB21, Flynn, "Notes on Formation," April 1942, p. 1.
19. AFC Papers, FB32, "Brief Biography of Amos Pinchot"; Marquis, *Who's Who, 1942–43,* pp. 365, and 170. Additional AFC national committee members from the New York area who were not members of the conservative business community were George Whipple, professor of pathology and dean of the School of Medicine and Dentistry of the University of Rochester, and joint winner of the Nobel Prize in medicine in 1934; Gregory Mason, anthropologist and chairman of the Department of Journalism at New York University; Adelaide Hooker Marquand, second wife of Pulitzer Prize-winning novelist John Phillips Marquand; and Carl Snavely, head football coach at Cornell University and coach of the 1941 College All-Stars—AFC Papers, FB32, "Brief Biography of George Whipple"; Marquis, *Who's Who, 1942–43,* pp. 1452, 1438; AFC Papers, FB278, AFC Bulletin no. 647, October 23, 1941; Cole, *America First,* pp. 14–15, 21–23.
20. AFC Papers, FB51, clipping from *Chicago Tribune,* September 5, 1940; *New York Times,* October 3, 1940, p. 21.
21. Flynn Papers, FB21, "Notes on Formation," April 1942, pp. 1–3.
22. AFC Papers, FB51, clipping from *Chicago Tribune,* September 5, 1940; see also Cole, *America First,* pp. 15–16.
23. Sarles, "A Story of America First," p. 18. A new set of five principles, drafted by New York advertising executive James P. Selvage, went into effect in March 1941. Although the new principles were more explicit in their condemnation of convoys and other violations of the Neutrality Law, and in their persistence that war would destroy American liberties, the philosophical thrust was similar to that of the original five—AFC Papers, FB183, "New Principles"; AFC Papers, FB67, James P. Selvage to Stuart, March 17, 1941.
24. Flynn Papers, FB16, Flynn, Radio Speech, March 8, 1941; see also AFC Papers, FB183, Stuart to Wood, November 25, 1941.
25. Amos R. E. Pinchot Papers, Library of Congress, Washington, D.C., FB69, Pinchot to Lindbergh, July 14, 1941.
26. AFC Papers, FB218, AFC Press Release, June 28, 1941.
27. AFC Papers, FB163, "Minutes of the National Committee Meeting," October 20, 1941.
28. Wayne S. Cole, "A Tale of Two Isolationists—Told Three Wars Later," *Newsletter,* Society for Historians of American Foreign Relations, vol. 5, no. 1, March 1974, p. 2.

29. U.S. Congress, Senate, Hearings, Senate Foreign Relations Committee, *Modification of the Neutrality Act of 1939,* 77th Cong., 1st sess., Flynn, October 23, 1941 (Washington: Government Printing Office, 1941), p. 206.
30. AFC Papers, FB205, Barbara MacDonald, Speakers' Bureau Folder, March 1941.
31. Edward H. Reisner, "The Case Against Intervention," *Vital Speeches,* 7, August 15, 1941, p. 658.
32. AFC Papers, FB67, James P. Selvage to Stuart, March 17, 1941.
33. Personal letter from Robert D. Stuart, January 11, 1974.
34. AFC Papers, FB57, Wood to Stuart, January 3, 1941.
35. Jerome N. Frank, *Save America First: How to Make Democracy Work* (New York: Harper & Brothers, 1938), pp. 80–89, 159–63.
36. For a full discussion of Lindbergh and his critics, see chap. 7.
37. Lindbergh, *Wartime Journals,* p. 479.
38. AFC Papers, FB205, Barbara MacDonald, Speakers' Bureau Folder, March 1941; see also, U.S. Congress, Senate, Hearings, Foreign Relations Committee, *Further to Promote Defense of the United States,* 77th Cong., 1st sess., Flynn, February 1941 (Washington: Government Printing Office, 1941), pt. I, pp. 10–15, and pt. III, pp. 908–14; Sarles, "A Story of America First," pp. 231–32, citing Gregory Mason, July 1941; AFC Papers, FB92, AFC Washington Research Bureau, "Did You Know: That Elimination of the Neutrality Law Combat Zones Means War?" no. 28, October 25, 1941.
39. Lindbergh, *Wartime Journals,* p. 547.
40. AFC Papers, FB205, Barbara MacDonald, Speakers' Bureau Folder, March 1941.
41. *Ibid.;* see also AFC Papers, FB37, *Uncensored,* no. 94, July 19, 1941; Flynn, "Can Hitler Invade America?" *Reader's Digest,* April 1941, pp. 1–6.
42. Douglas Miller, *You Can't Do Business with Hitler* (Boston: Little, Brown & Co., 1941).
43. Pinchot Papers, FB88 (163), AFC Washington Research Bureau, "Did You Know: That Even If Nazi Germany Conquers Communist Russia the Enlarged Germany May Be Weakened Rather Than Strengthened?" no. 15, August 1, 1941.
44. AFC Papers, FB205, Barbara MacDonald, Speakers' Bureau Folder, March 1941. Synthetic production of rubber in the United States, although technically possible in 1941, was not practical on a massive or useful scale.
45. Pinchot Papers, FB88(163), Pinchot, AFC Pamphlet, p. 13, 1941; AFC Papers, FB163, Bernard Baruch, Raymond Moley, and George N. Peek, "Can Hitler Cripple America's Economy?" 1941; Flynn, "Can Hitler Beat American Business?" *Harper's* magazine, February 1940, pp. 321–28.
46. AFC Papers, FB205, Barbara MacDonald, Speakers' Bureau Folder, March 1941. For more information on AFC beliefs and statements regarding Japan, see chap. 6.
47. AFC Papers, FB297, Stuart to All Chapter Chairmen, July 23, 1941, and Page Hufty to All Chapter Chairmen, October 25, 1941. For a full discussion of Roosevelt's peace pledges and AFC views regarding these, see chap. 4.
48. AFC Papers, FB56, Wood to Mrs. E. Kimbark, May 28, 1941.
49. Walter Johnson, *The Battle Against Isolation* (Chicago: University of Chicago Press, 1944), p. 191, citing Franklin Delano Roosevelt, December 29, 1940.
50. For a full discussion of the AFC's positive plans in late 1941, see chap. 6.
51. Lindbergh, *Wartime Journals,* pp. 526–27. A similar statement was made by Robert L. Bliss, personal interview, March 15, 1974.
52. Flynn Papers, FB21, Flynn to Jessica Forbes, May 3, 1943.
53. Flynn Papers, FB21, Flynn to Hartley Cross, March 4, 1941.
54. Sarles, "A Story of America First," p. 10.
55. Morris Burns Stanley, "The America First Committee: A Study in Recent American Non-Interventionism" (unpublished master's thesis, Emory University,

1942), p. 402, citing Wood to Stanley, February 24, 1942.
56. Flynn Papers, FB21, Hartley Cross to Flynn, February 4, 1941, and Flynn to Cross, March 4, 1941.

CHAPTER 2

1. John T. Flynn Papers, University of Oregon, Eugene, File Box 16, Flynn, Radio Speech, March 8, 1941.
2. Flynn Papers, FB21, Flynn, "Notes on Formation of the New York Chapter of the America First Committee," April 1942, p. 3.
3. America First Committee Papers, Hoover Institution on War, Revolution and Peace, Stanford, Calif. FB205, Mildred H. Dugan to Robert L. Bliss, April 8, 1941.
4. AFC Papers, FB 64, Robert D. Stuart to Robert E. Wood, November 27, 1941.
5. Statement by Rosalie Gordon, personal interview, New York City, April 23, 1973; statement by Thomas D. Flynn, personal interview, New York City, April 25, 1973; statement by Stuart, personal interview, Chicago, August 14, 1973; statement by Burton K. Wheeler, personal letter, March 9, 1973; statement by Walter Trohan, personal letter, March 24, 1973.
6. Statement by Robert L. Bliss, personal interview, New York City, March 15, 1974.
7. Statement by Peter Cusick, personal letter, November 1973.
8. Personal letter from Rosalie M. Gordon, New York City, September 13, 1974, Flynn Papers, FB21, Flynn, statement, 1941.
9. Personal letter from R. M. Gordon, September 13, 1974; Flynn Papers, FB32, Flynn, Diary, date unknown; see also Richard C. Frey, Jr., "John T. Flynn and the United States in Crisis, 1928–50" (unpublished doctor's dissertation, University of Oregon, 1969), pp. 1–2.
10. Personal letter from R. M. Gordon, September 13, 1974. John Flynn, Jr. died in his teenage years. Thomas Flynn, as of this writing, is president of the New York accounting firm of Arthur Young and Company. Information on John Thomas Flynn's early life is extremely sketchy, and almost impossible to obtain.
11. Flynn, *Graft in Business* (New York: Vanguard Press, 1931); *God's Gold: Story of Rockefeller and His Times* (Westport, Conn.: Greenwood Press, 1971); *Country Squire in the White House* (New York: Doubleday, Doran & Company, 1940); *As We Go Marching* (New York: Doubleday, Doran & Company, 1944); *The Roosevelt Myth* (New York: Devin-Adair, 1948); *The Road Ahead* (New York: Devin-Adair, 1949).
12. All biographical material on pages 3–5 is derived from *Who Was Who in America* (Chicago: Marquis–Who's Who, Inc., 1968), IV, 1961–68, p. 319; and from *New York Times*, April 14, 1964, p. 37.
13. Flynn Papers, FB20, Flynn to Oswald G. Villard, July 12, 1940.
14. Flynn, *Country Squire in the White House*, p. v; Flynn, "Why a Liberal Party?" *Forum and Century*, March 1932, pp. 158–63; see also Frey, "John T. Flynn," p. 45.
15. Flynn, "Other People's Money," *New Republic*, July 29, 1940, p. 141.
16. Samuel Crafton, "The Appeasement Tropism," *New Republic*, January 6, 1941, p. 18; Flynn Papers, FB19, Flynn to Bruce Bliven, January 8, 1941.
17. Statement by Thomas D. Flynn, personal interview, April 23, 1973; Flynn, "That Post-War Federal Debt," *Harper's* magazine, July 1942, pp. 183–88; Flynn Papers, FB20, Flynn to Dagobert Runes, December 16, 1931; see also Frey, "John T. Flynn," pp. 44–47, 351.

18. Frey, "John T. Flynn," p. 356.
19. Flynn Papers, FB20, Flynn to Jerome N. Frank, September 18, 1940.
20. Flynn Papers, FB19, Flynn to Burt MacBride, April 28, 1950.
21. Flynn Papers, FB32, Flynn, Diary, January 6, 1940.
22. Flynn Papers, FB20, Flynn to Hiram Johnson, October 15, 1932, and Flynn to Senator Fletcher, May 17, 1933; see also Flynn, "Inside the RFC," *Harper's* magazine, January 1933, pp. 161–69.
23. Flynn Papers, FB20, Flynn to Hiram Johnson, October 15, 1931; Flynn Papers, FB18, Flynn to Frank Hogan, November 7, 1931; see also Frey, "John T. Flynn," p. 48.
24. Flynn, "Other People's Money," *New Republic,* December 6, 1933, and July 11, 1934, and July 18, 1934, and October 9, 1935; see also Frey, "John T. Flynn," pp. 62, 85–94.
25. Flynn, "Other People's Money," *New Republic,* June 28, 1933, and November 6, 1933; Flynn, "American Revolution: 1933," *Scribner's Commentator,* July 1933, p. 1–6; Flynn Papers, FB16, Flynn, Radio Speech, "Consumer Under the New Deal," December 1933; see also Frey, "John T. Flynn," pp. 95–101.
26. Flynn, "Other People's Money," *New Republic,* March 28, 1934; Flynn, "An Approach to the Problem of War Finance," *Annals of the American Academy of Political and Social Science* 186 (January 1936): 217–22. For similar reasons, Flynn also disapproved of the Gold Reserve Act and the Silver Purchase Act of 1934, as well as many other New Deal measures.
27. Flynn, "The Social Security Reserve Swindle," *Harper's* magazine, February 1939, pp. 238–48; see also Frey, "John T. Flynn," pp. 105–6.
28. Flynn, "Other People's Money," *New Republic,* December 11, 1935, and January 1, 1936.
29. Flynn, "That Post-War Federal Debt," *Harper's* magazine, July 1942, pp. 183–88.
30. Flynn, *Country Squire in the White House,* p. 57.
31. Flynn, *The Decline of the American Republic,* p. 137.
32. Flynn Papers, FB32, Flynn, Diary, January 6, 1940.
33. Flynn Papers, FB19, Flynn to Henry Smith Richardson, November 18, 1943.
34. Frey, "John T. Flynn," p. 119.
35. Flynn, *As We Go Marching,* p. 207; Flynn, "Other People's Money," *New Republic,* November 2, 1938.
36. Flynn, "Other People's Money," *New Republic,* November 2, 1938.
37. Flynn Papers, FB16, Flynn, Radio Speech, "America Looks at Europe's War," September 12, 1939.
38. Flynn, "Plain Economics," *New York World-Telegram,* April 19, 1940, and December 30, 1940.
39. Flynn Papers, FB20, Flynn to Homer Bone, November 6, 1939.
40. Flynn Papers, FB32, Flynn, Diary, January 6, 1940.
41. Wayne S. Cole, *An Interpretive History of American Foreign Relations* (Homewood, Ill.: Dorsey Press, 1968), p. 448.
42. Kathryn D. T. Bartimo, "American Opinion Toward the European War" (unpublished doctor's dissertation, Clark University, June 1941), p. 241.
43. Flynn Papers, FB20, Flynn to Homer Bone, July 5, 1940.
44. Norman Thomas Papers, New York City Public Library, FB35, Flynn to Thomas, August 6, 1940.
45. Flynn, *Country Squire in the White House,* p. 101.
46. Flynn, "Other People's Money," *New Republic,* June 24, 1940, and July 15, 1940.
47. Flynn, "Other People's Money," *New Repbulic,* September 6, 1940.
48. Flynn, *As We Go Marching,* pp. 153–54, 250–53; see also U.S. Congress, Senate, Committee on Foreign Relations, *Modification of the Neutrality Act of 1939,* Hearings, 77th Cong., 1st sess., Flynn, October 23, 1941 (Washington: Government Printing Office, 1941), pp. 201–16.

49. AFC Papers, FB51, clipping from *Chicago Tribune*, September 5, 1940. For a complete listing of the AFC principles, see chap. 1.
50. AFC Papers, FB205, Barbara MacDonald, Speakers' Bureau Folder, March 1941.
51. Flynn Papers, FB16, Flynn, Radio Speech, "Aid to Russia," September 27, 1941; see also Flynn Papers, FB21, Flynn, "Would the Fall of England Mean the End of Democracy in Europe?" August 1941; Flynn Papers, FB16, Flynn, "Opening Remarks for NYC-AFC Rally," April 23, 1941.
52. Flynn Papers, FB21, Flynn, Interview with Lawrence Gould, October 10, 1941.
53. For a full discussion of Flynn's opposition to extension of the power of the executive branch of government, see chap. 4 (Lend-Lease Bill discussion), and chaps. 5, 6, 9.
54. Flynn, *As We Go Marching*, pp. 11–27, 161–62; see also Flynn, "Coming: A Totalitarian America," *American Mercury*, February 1941, pp. 156–57.
55. Flynn, *As We Go Marching*, pp. 2–3.
56. Flynn Papers, FB16, Flynn, Speech to Washington (D.C.) AFC, February 2, 1941; see also Flynn, "Other People's Money," *New Republic*, September 9, 1940, p. 352.
57. Flynn, *As We Go Marching*, pp. 57, 75–77.
58. *Ibid.*, p. 75.
59. It can be argued that Arthur M. Schlesinger, Jr.'s work, *The Imperial Presidency* (Boston: Houghton Mifflin Co., 1973), confirms Flynn's opinion that well-meaning leaders can set precedent and conditions that then allow future leaders to abuse power in a way that threatens American democracy.
60. Thomas Papers, FB40, Thomas to Jerry Voorhis, November 14, 1941, and Thomas to Ernest Wheeler, October 8, 1941, and Thomas to the editor of the *New York Times*, December 6, 1941; Thomas Papers, FB36, Thomas to M. Johns, December 2, 1940; Thomas Papers, FB37, Thomas to M. Dewirtz, January 24, 1941.
61. Raymond Gram Swing, *Forerunners of American Fascism* (New York: Julian Messner, 1935), pp. 13–22.
62. Flynn Papers, FB16, Flynn, Radio Speech, "America Looks at Europe's War," September 12, 1939; Flynn Papers, FB21, Flynn, statement, 1941.
63. Flynn Papers, FB32, Flynn, Diary, June 29, 1941.
64. *Ibid.*, August 30, 1941.
65. Flynn Papers, FB21, Flynn, "Memo for Mr. Cudahy," October 15, 1941; see also AFC Papers, FB284, Flynn to Wood, June 5, 1941; Flynn Papers, FB21, Flynn to Paul Palmer, August 15, 1941, and Flynn, statement, 1941. Flynn did call for a negotiated peace from KAOWC platforms, however: *New York Times*, May 31, 1941, p. 9.
66. Thomas Papers, FB37, Thomas, "Statement for Union Labor News," February 14, 1941.
67. Flynn, "Can Hitler Invade America?" *Reader's Digest*, April 1941, pp. 1–6.
68. Flynn Papers, FB21, Flynn to Mrs. Janet Fairbank, December 1, 1941.
69. Flynn Papers, FB21, Flynn to Hartley Cross, March 4, 1941.
70. Flynn, "Nazi Economy a Threat?" *Scribner's Commentator*, August 1941, pp. 19–26.
71. Flynn, "Can Hitler Beat American Business?" *Harper's* magazine, February 1940, pp. 321–28.
72. Flynn Papers, FB21, Flynn, "Notes on Formation," April 1942, p. 2; AFC Papers, FB29, KAOWC folder; Bernard K. Johnpoll, *Pacifist's Progress: Norman Thomas and the Decline of American Socialism* (Chicago: Quadrangle Books, 1970), pp. 205–11.
73. Among the groups included in the KAOWC were: National Council for the Prevention of War (Frederick J. Libby, Chairman), Women's International League for Peace and Freedom (Dorothy Detzer, Executive Secretary for the United

States; Mrs. Burton K. Wheeler, Treasurer), Youth Committee Against War (Fay Bennett, Executive Secretary), Fellowship of Reconciliation (Arthur L. Swift, Chairman), Ministers' No-War Committee (Albert W. Palmer, Director; New York's most prominent member was Harry Emerson Fosdick, pastor of the Riverside Church); War Resisters' League (John Haynes Holmes, Chairman; this last group was a conscientious objectors' organization that counted among its prominent members Dr. Evan Thomas, professor of medicine at New York University and brother of Norman Thomas. Evan Thomas had been jailed as a conscientious objector in World War I).

74. Johnpoll, *Pacifist's Progress*, pp. 205–11; AFC Papers, FB29, "Chicago KAOWC Bulletin," October 1940.
75. Thomas Papers, FB38, Thomas to Flynn, May 10, 1941; AFC Papers, FB61, Stuart to Mary Hillyer, May 8, 1941; AFC Papers, FB29, "Anti-War News Service," no. 20, January 20, 1941.
76. Flynn Papers, FB16, Flynn, Radio Speech, "America Looks at Europe's War," September 12, 1939.
77. AFC Papers, FB29, KAOWC Press Release, September 4, 1940.
78. Flynn Papers, FB20, Flynn to Oswald G. Villard, July 12, 1940; Flynn Papers, FB32, Flynn, Diary, September 1940.
79. Flynn Papers FB16, Flynn, Radio Speech, November 3, 1940; see also Flynn, "Other People's Money," *New Republic,* November 11, 1940.
80. Flynn Papers, FB20, Flynn to Oswald G. Villard, August 6, 1940.
81. Flynn Papers, FB18, Flynn to Alf Landon, November 22, 1940; Flynn Papers, FB32, Flynn, Diary, September 1940.
82. AFC Papers, FB39, Barbara MacDonald to Gilbert Pederson, November 18, 1940; Flynn, *Men Of Wealth* (New York: Simon & Schuster, 1941).
83. Flynn Papers, FB21, Flynn, "Notes on Formation," April 1942, p. 1.
84. Ruth Sarles, "A Story of America First" (unpublished manuscript, Hoover Institution, Stanford, Calif., 1942), pp. 67–70.
85. AFC Papers, FB212, Flynn, *NYC-AFC Bulletin,* vol. 1, no. 11, August 9, 1941.
86. Flynn Papers, FB21, Harry Schnibbe to Flynn, "Schnibbe History," April 1942, p. 79.
87. Flynn Papers, FB21, Flynn, "Notes on Formation," April 1942, pp. 1–3; AFC Papers, FB205, Mildred H. Dugan to Robert L. Bliss, April 8, 1941.
88. AFC Papers, FB285, William Potter to Wood, September 9, 1940.
89. AFC Papers, FB291, Wallace Pratt to Wood, August 30, 1941.
90. Charles A. Lindbergh, *The Wartime Journals of Charles A. Lindbergh* (New York: Harcourt Brace Jovanovich, 1970), p. 529.
91. AFC Papers, FB3, Robert Harriss to Wood, October 15, 1940.
92. Flynn Papers, FB21, "Schnibbe History," p. 82, citing Stuart to Lindbergh, September 30, 1940.
93. AFC Papers, FB59, Bowles to Stuart, January 23, 1941.
94. AFC Papers, FB35, Bowles to Sidney Hertzberg, January 16, 1941. For a similar attitude expressed by another New York noninterventionist advertising executive, see AFC Papers, FB67, James Selvage to H. Smith Richardson, May 6, 1941. Throughout 1941 Bowles's guilt feelings over the crippling effects of his business upon his beliefs increased. In August, after spending a sleepless night, he informed Stuart that he was going to make a strong radio speech against intervention. The recalcitrant New Yorker had decided, he said, "that if we were really going to get into a long war, it was more important to me to be on speaking terms with myself even though I become highly unpopular in most other quarters [the business community]"—see AFC Papers, FB59, Bowles to Stuart, August 8, 1941; for a further indication of Bowles's guilt feelings, see Chester Bowles, *Promises to Keep: My Years in Public Life, 1941–1969* (New York: Harper &

201

Row, 1971), p. 10. Nonetheless, Bowles never made a strong statement in behalf of the AFC. He did publish a diluted statement in a magazine article in December 1941 (for a discussion of this article, see chap. 3).

95. AFC Papers, FB16, NY Chapter Correspondence. These individuals were Mrs. Robert P. Breckinridge, Timothy F. Bannon, and Ralph L. Stephenson.
96. AFC Papers, FB16, Marie Luhrs to Robert Bliss, December 13, 1940.
97. AFC Papers, FB58, Stuart to Stanley Burke, December 8, 1940; Richard Polenberg, "The National Committee to Uphold Constitutional Government," *Journal of American History* 52 (1965): 582–98.
98. For more information on *Scribner's Commentator*, see chap. 8.
99. Flynn Papers, FB21, "Schnibbe History," p. 84, citing Stuart to Lindbergh, September 30, 1940.
100. AFC Papers, FB285, Sidney Hertzberg to Stuart, September 28, 1940.
101. After being refused by the AFC, Hart helped to organize an unsuccessful, anti-Semitic and profascist group known as the No Foreign Wars Committee. For a full discussion of this group, see chap. 7.
102. Flynn Papers, FB21, "Schnibbe History," p. 85.
103. AFC Papers, FB285, Stuart to Flynn, December 2, 1940; Flynn Papers, FB21, Flynn, "Notes on Formation," pp. 3–4. For a complete listing of those attending both luncheons, see Appendix A.
104. For a description of General Robert E. Wood and the power of his reputation in aiding and establishing the national AFC, see chap. 1.
105. Flynn Papers, FB21, Flynn, "Notes on Formation," pp. 4–6; AFC Papers, FB64, Flynn to Stuart, January 6, 1941.
106. *Ibid.* (both sources).
107. AFC Papers, FB55, Wood to Flynn, January 16, 1941.
108. AFC Papers, FB58, Stuart to Flynn, January 18, 1941; AFC Papers, FB60, Stuart to F. Abbott Goodhue, January 17, 1941.
109. Lindbergh, *Wartime Journals*, p. 439.
110. Statement by Robert L. Bliss, personal interview, March 15, 1974. For a full discussion of the Flynn-Webster feud, see chap. 7.
111. AFC Papers, FB64, Flynn to Stuart, January 6, 1941; see also Sarles, "A Story of America First," p. 68.
112. Flynn Papers, FB21, "Schnibbe History," pp. 85–87.
113. Flynn Papers, FB18, Flynn to Lindbergh, December 29, 1941.
114. Flynn Papers, FB21, "Schnibbe History," pp. 89–90; Lindbergh, *Wartime Journals,* pp. 500–501; AFC Papers, FB62, Allen Pope to Wood, March 10, 1941. In the fall of 1941 a feud split Flynn and Webster irreparably. For a full discussion of this argument, see chap. 7.

CHAPTER 3

1. America First Committee Papers, Hoover Institution on War, Revolution and Peace, Stanford, Calif., File Box 65, AFC Circular, October 16, 1941; John T. Flynn Papers, University of Oregon, Eugene, File Box 21, Harry Schnibbe to Flynn, "Schnibbe History," April 1942, pp. 89–90.
2. AFC Papers, FB179, Flynn to All NYC-AFC Chapter Chairmen, "Procedures on Direction of Chapter Affairs," October 8, 1941.
3. Flynn Papers, FB21, "Minutes of the NYC-AFC Chapter Committee Meeting," June 4, 1941.
4. Flynn Papers, FB21, "Minutes of the NYC-AFC Executive Committee Meetings," January 1941–March 1942.

5. Amos Pinchot, *History of the Progressive Party, 1912–16* (New York: New York University Press, 1958), Helen Maxwell Hooker, Introduction, pp. 10–13. The two books on which Pinchot worked were the above book (published posthumously in incomplete form) and *Big Business in America* (never published or completed).
6. Amos Pinchot, "The American Liberal and His Program," *Churchman*, April 1, 1933, p. 14.
7. Pinchot, *History of the Progressive Party*, Hooker, Introduction, pp. 17–30, 61, citing Pinchot to Henry Lane Eno, July 20, 1914.
8. *Ibid.*, pp. 32–49, 68–69.
9. *Ibid.*, pp. 70–71.
10. *Ibid.*, p. 80, citing Pinchot to David K. Niles, September 23, 1932.
11. George L. Record, *How to Abolish Poverty* (Jersey City: George L. Record Memorial Association, 1936), Pinchot, Introduction, pp. 11–18.
12. Pinchot, *History of the Progressive Party*, Hooker, Introduction, p. 82, citing Pinchot to John L. Lewis, September 3, 1938.
13. *Ibid.*, Hooker, Introduction, pp. 82–83, citing Pinchot to Hiram Johnson, August 31, 1940.
14. Pinchot, "Roosevelt—Laski Scheme," *Scribner's Commentator*, October 1941, pp. 62–68.
15. Richard Polenberg, "The National Committee to Uphold Constitutional Government," *Journal of American History* 52 (1965): 582–98. In late 1940 this group split irrevocably over foreign policy, and Pinchot then decided to join the America First Committee.
16. Amos Pinchot Papers, Library of Congress, Washington, D.C., FB69, Pinchot to Joseph M. Patterson, November 27, 1941.
17. AFC Papers, FB284, Pinchot to Stuart, December 3, 1941.
18. Pinchot Papers, FB69, Pinchot to Flynn, August 8, 1941.
19. Pinchot Papers, FB70, Pinchot to Robert A. Taft, March 4, 1941.
20. Pinchot Papers, FB69, Huntington Wilson to Pinchot, June 16, 1941, and Pinchot to Wilson, June 18, 1941; see also Pinchot Papers, FB70, Pinchot to Rembert Smith, July 1, 1941.
21. AFC Papers, FB201, Pinchot to S. Stanwood Menken, October 4, 1941.
22. AFC Papers, FB64, Webster to Stuart, February 13, 1941.
23. AFC Papers, FB64, H. Dudley Swim to Wood, November 17, 1941.
24. Flynn Papers, FB21, H. Dudley Swim to Flynn, November 24, 1941.
25. Flynn Papers, FB21, H. Dudley Swim to Flynn, December 9, 1940.
26. Statement by Robert L. Bliss, personal interview, New York City, March 15, 1974.
27. AFC Papers, FB64, "Minutes of the NYC-AFC Executive Committee Meetings," January 1941–March 1942.
28. AFC Papers, FB64, Adelaide Marquand to Flynn, November 24, 1941, and Flynn to Marquand, November 27, 1941. Adelaide Marquand was replaced on the chapter executive committee because she had a baby in November 1941.
29. Flynn Papers, FB21, "Schnibbe History," p. 87.
30. All data on NYC-AFC membership and composition can be found in the AFC Papers, FB180–200 and 328–35. Additional sponsoring committee members were businessmen Colonel Allen Pope, Randolph Phillips, Louis Timmerman, Ernest E. Wheeler, Stanley Burke, and Robert Ralph Young; society women Mrs. Graham B. Blaine, Mrs. William Shippen Davis, Mrs. Seth Milliken, Mrs. William H. Fain, and Mrs. Paul Palmer; clergymen Father James M. Gillis (editor of *Catholic World*), Rev. Frank O. Hall, and Rev. Frederick K. Stamm; medical doctors George Whipple and Charles Fleischer; educators Alan Valentine, Edward Reisner, and Philip Jessup; liberal journalist Dorothy Dunbar Bromley; and Daniel A. Lindley and Philip Liebman, whose professions are unknown.

31. Norman Thomas Papers, New York City Public Library, FB36, Thomas to Stuart, November 19, 1940.
32. Thomas Papers, FB40, Thomas to Maynard Kreuger, December 11, 1941.
33. Thomas Papers, FB40, Thomas to Eunice Armstrong, November 24, 1941.
34. Thomas Papers, FB38, Thomas to Wood, May 12, 1941.
35. Bernard K. Johnpoll, *Pacifist's Progress: Norman Thomas and the Decline of American Socialism* (Chicago: Quadrangle Books, 1970), p. 211, citing Thomas.
36. Thomas Papers, FB40, Thomas to the Editor of the *New York Times,* December 6, 1941.
37. Thomas, "The War on Hitler," *Vital Speeches,* vol. 7, no. 18, July 1, 1941, pp. 561–62; see also Thomas Papers, FB40, Thomas to Ernest E. Wheeler, October 8, 1941.
38. Thomas Papers, FB35, Thomas to Franklin D. Roosevelt, July 24, 1940; Johnpoll, *Pacifist's Progress,* p. 13, citing Thomas.
39. Thomas Papers, FB35, Thomas to Porter Sargent, October 2, 1940.
40. Thomas Papers, FB38, Thomas to Burton K. Wheeler, December 5, 1940.
41. Thomas Papers, FB39, Thomas to James Lipsig, July 1941.
42. Chester Bowles, *Promises to Keep: My Years in Public Life, 1941–1969* (New York: Harper & Row, 1971), p. 9; AFC Papers, FB285, Bowles to Stuart, October 22, 1940.
43. AFC Papers, FB43, Harry Elmer Barnes to Robert Bliss, May 22, 1941; Flynn Papers, FB21, Harry Emerson Fosdick to Flynn, January 10, 1941; AFC Papers, FB65, Charles A. Beard to Stuart, August 5, 1940; AFC Papers, FB35, Stuart Chase to Stuart, November 12, 1940; AFC Papers, FB35, FB17, Joseph Boldt to Robert Bliss, April 18, 1941; Sinclair Lewis, *It Can't Happen Here* (New York: New American Library, 1970). Villard resigned official membership in the AFC shortly after joining, because of differences of opinion regarding pacifism and national defense: Ruth Sarles, "A Story of America First" (unpublished manuscript, Hoover Institution, Stanford, Calif., pp. 61, 125. Another New York liberal who cooperated unofficially with, and often spoke for, the NYC-AFC was Henry Noble MacCracken, president of Vassar College since 1915.
44. Flynn Papers, FB32, Flynn, Diary, June 29, 1941; Herbert Hoover, "Call to Reason," *Vital Speeches,* vol. 7, no. 19, July 15, 1941, pp. 580–84.
45. AFC Papers, FB55, Hoover to Wood, July 11, 1941, and June 20, 1941.
46. Thomas Papers, FB40, Thomas to Chester Bowles, December 5, 1941; Charles Lindbergh, *The Wartime Journals of Charles A. Lindbergh* (New York: Harcourt Brace Jovanovich, 1970), p. 538.
47. AFC Papers, FB17, and FB201; Flynn Papers, FB20, and 21; Sarles, "A Story of America First," pp. 86, 607–29; Charles Lindbergh is discussed at length in chap. 7. Another New York conservative who aided the chapter unofficially was Bruce Barton, author, advertising executive, and former Republican congressman.
48. Flynn Papers, FB21, "NYC-AFC Donors List, $100. or More," 1942; AFC Papers, FB338, "Contributions of Larger Amounts Received Through November 29, 1941," December 1941.
49. Flynn Papers, FB21, Wood to Flynn, December 16, 1940; AFC Papers, FB68, H. Smith Richardson to Wood, February 25, 1941, and May 16, 1941, and Stuart to H. Smith Richardson, November 6, 1941. For a complete list of NYC-AFC donors of $100 or more, as well as the larger donors from the Northeast to the national committee, see Appendix B. Full confidence cannot be placed in these lists, however, as Flynn was quite sure that the chapter's financial records were altered by Swim and Webster to camouflage donors who might "embarrass" the committee: AFC Papers, FB285, Flynn to Wood, May 11, 18, 25 and July 17, 1942.
50. Lindbergh, *Wartime Journals,* pp. 428–29.
51. AFC Papers, FB17, and 201; Flynn Papers, FB21.

52. Sarles, "A Story of America First," p. 297.
53. AFC Papers, FB285, Ralph P. De Swarte, "Final Audit of the Chicago Chapter, AFC," April 24, 1942; AFC Papers, FB284, Wood to Henry Christ, May 9, 1942. The final auditor's report of the NYC-AFC, prepared in May 1942, shows that the chapter received and disbursed a total of slightly less than $190,000. This figure includes only money collected by the Manhattan central office; the much smaller revenues of the various branches were listed separately by the committee. For a complete copy of the final auditor's report, see Appendix C. All financial reports of the NYC-AFC can be found in the AFC Papers, FB172.
54. AFC Papers, FB17, Robert Bliss to Webster, April 11, 1941, and Lee Swanson to Fred Horner, October 2, 1941; AFC Papers, FB172, "NYC-AFC Auditor's Reports," 1941–42.
55. Personal files of Robert L. Bliss, New York City, William Benton to Richard Ketchum, October 1972.
56. Morris Burns Stanley, "The America First Committee: A Study in Recent American Non-Interventionism" (unpublished master's thesis, Emory University, 1942), p. 269, citing Flynn, personal interview, March 20, 1941; see also AFC Papers, FB55, Stuart to Flynn, May 21, 1941.
57. Lindbergh, Wartime Journals, p. 500.
58. John Roy Carlson (in reality Avedis Derounian), UnderCover (New York: E. P. Dutton & Co., 1943), pp. 248–49.
59. AFC Papers, FB172, "NYC-AFC Auditor's Reports," 1941–42. In February 1941 the highest-paid NYC-AFC staff member was the publicity director, who received $100 per week. Typist and file clerks, the lowest paid, received $20–$25 per week. By September 1941 the publicity director was receiving $75 per week, and typists and clerks $15.00–$17.50 per week. After June 1, 1941, a special publicity assistant from the national committee, Robert L. Bliss, was stationed in New York and became the highest-paid member of the NYC-AFC staff. He received $125 per week, but his salary was provided as a stipend by wealthy, private donor H. Smith Richardson.
60. AFC Papers, FB3, Robert L. Bliss folder.
61. AFC Papers, FB56, Bliss to Stuart, May 16, 1941.
62. AFC Papers, FB64, Joseph Boldt to Bliss, January 8, 1941.
63. AFC Papers, FB3, Joseph R. Boldt folder; see also Sarles, "A Story of America First," pp. 78–79.
64. AFC Papers, FB185, Bliss to Boldt, March 5, 1941, and Boldt to Bliss, March 9, 1941.
65. AFC Papers, FB179, Flynn to All NYC-AFC Chapter Chairmen, "Procedures on Direction of Chapter Affairs," October 8, 1941.
66. AFC Papers, FB201, Boldt to R. W. Croxdale, February 1941; Flynn Papers, FB21, "Minutes of the NYC-AFC Chapter Committee Meeting," January 23, 1941; AFC Papers, FB181, Bliss to NYC-AFC Staff, September 23, 1941; AFC Papers, FB173, "Minutes of the AFC National Committee Meetings," October 20, and November 28, 1941.
67. AFC Papers, FB284, Flynn to Wood, June 5, and December 22, 1941; Flynn Papers, FB21, Flynn to Wood, October 13, 1941, and Flynn to Page Hufty, September 4, 1941. For a complete discussion of the question of subversive elements within the NYC-AFC, see chap. 7.
68. AFC Papers, FB64, Stuart to Wood, November 27, 1941. There is ample evidence that other respectable chapters also resented Flynn's tight dictatorial control: AFC Papers, FB3, Florence Seifried to Wood, September 28, 1941; AFC Papers, FB284, Mary Henninger to Wood, February 18, 1942, and Midtown (Manhattan) Branch Executive Committee to Wood, November 26, 1941, and Otto Durholz and Russell Palmer to Stuart, December 9, 1941; AFC Papers, FB203, Tudor

Gardiner, Jr. and Paul Killiam to Stuart, December 8, 1941.

69. AFC Papers, FB179, Flynn to All NYC-AFC Chapter Chairmen, "Procedures on Direction of Chapter Affairs," October 8, 1941.

70. AFC Papers, FB181, National Committee, "How to Organize Your Chapter," February 1941; AFC Papers, FB17, R. W. Croxdale to Bliss, March 14, 1941; AFC Papers, FB284, Flynn to Wood, January 2, 1941; AFC Papers, FB163, "Lists of Chapters by State"; see also Sarles, "A Story of America First," pp. 321–22. For a complete list of AFC chapters in the Northeast, see Appendix D.

71. AFC Papers, FB286, Boldt to Harry Schnibbe, September 23, 1941, and Harold Tucker to Boldt, September 22, 1941.

72. AFC Papers, FB55, Flynn to Wood, September 24, 1941. For a complete discussion of anti-Semitism and the NYC-AFC, see chap. 7.

73. AFC Papers, FB65, Stuart to Webster, March 10, 1941; AFC Papers, FB209, Bliss to Gerald Nye, September 27, 1941.

74. AFC Papers, FB17, Bliss to Richard A. Moore, December 5, 1941.

75. AFC Papers, FB200, Charles Wiley, Jr. to Flynn, November 7, 1941, and Richards H. Emerson (for Flynn) to Wiley, November 17, 1941; Flynn Papers, FB21, "Minutes of the NYC-AFC Executive Committee Meeting," March 3, 1941, and National Committee to Brooklyn Chapter, December 2, 1941; see also Thomas Papers, FB38, Thomas to Flynn, June 25, 1941.

76. New York Times, July 25, 1941, p. 1.

77. AFC Papers, FB201, Julian Garrett (for NYC-AFC) to Pvt. Frederick W. Michaelson, August 1941.

78. AFC Papers, FB206, Flynn to Col. Early Duncan, November 7, 1941.

79. Figures concerning Flynn's speaking engagements were compiled from various sources among the AFC Papers and the Flynn Papers, by keeping lists of Flynn's activities throughout the period.

80. Sarles, "A Story of America First," p. 300.

81. Flynn, "Can Hitler Invade America?" Reader's Digest, April 1941, pp. 1–6; Flynn, "Nazi Economy a Threat?" Scribner's Commentator, August 1941, pp. 19–26; Flynn, "Radio: Intervention's Trump," Scribner's Commentator, April 1941, pp. 45–49; Flynn, "Coming—A Totalitarian America," American Mercury, February 1941, pp. 151–57; AFC Papers, FB67, Flynn, "Wake Up, America!" June 1941; AFC Papers, FB28, Flynn, "The Effect of the Lend-Lease Bill on the American Merchant Marine," and "War, What Is It?" February 1941, and others; AFC Papers, FB 288, William T. Leonard to Richard A. Moore, September 6, 1941; AFC Papers, FB212, Flynn, Statement, 1941.

82. New York Times, February–September 8, 1941.

83. Flynn Papers, FB21, Flynn to Ambrose J. McCall, July 9, 1941; see also AFC Papers, FB181; and Sarles, "A Story of America First," p. 76. The AFC Bulletin was completely separate and different from the "AFC Bulletins" published on a daily basis by the national committee.

84. Flynn Papers, FB20, Flynn to Norman Levy, June 20, 1940. The KAOWC, throughout 1941, maintained a separate, weekly newspaper titled The Anti-War News Service: AFC Papers, FB29.

85. Nancy Schoonmaker and Doris F. Reid, We Testify (New York: Smith & Durrell, 1941).

86. Charles Lindbergh, magazine articles: "Lindbergh for the Record," Scribner's Commentator, August 1941, pp. 8–13; "Impregnable America," Scribner's Commentator, January 1941, pp. 3–6; "Letter to Americans," Collier's, March 29, 1941, pp. 14–15; "Time Lies with Us," Scribner's Commentator, November 1941, pp. 88–93. Lindbergh, speeches: "Our Air Defense," Vital Speeches, 7, February 1, 1941, pp. 241–42; "We Are Not Prepared for War," ibid., February 15, 1941, pp. 266–67; "We Cannot Win This War for England," ibid., May 1, 1941, pp. 424–26; "Election Promises Should Be Kept," ibid., June 1, 1941, pp. 482–83. Nor-

man Thomas, articles and speeches: "War on Hitler," *ibid.,* July 1, 1941, p. 561; "How to Fight for Democracy," *Annals of the American Academy,* 216, July 1941, pp. 58–64; "Is the Extension of the Draft Necessary?" *Vital Speeches,* 7, August 15, 1941, pp. 671–72; "Lindbergh Speech," *Commonweal,* October 10, 1941. Amos Pinchot, articles: "To the President; Poem," *Scribner's Commentator,* July 1941, p. 6; "Roosevelt-Laski Scheme," *ibid.,* October 1941, pp. 62–68.

87. Herbert Hoover, speeches: "Problems That Confront Us," *Vital Speeches,* 7, January 1, 1941, pp. 181–83; "Question of Peace," *ibid.,* April 15, 1941, pp. 405–8; "We Are Not Prpared for War," *ibid.,* May 15, 1941, pp. 457–60; "Call to Reason," *ibid.,* July 15, 1941, pp. 580–84; "Crisis," *ibid.,* October 1, 1941, pp. 745–48; "Shall We Send Armies to Europe?" *Vital Speeches,* 8, December 1, 1941. Chester Bowles, "What's Wrong with the Isolationists by a Non-Interventionist," *Common Sense,* December 1941, pp. 374–77.

88. AFC Papers, FB215, Bliss to H. Dudley Swim, February 4, 1942.

89. AFC Papers, FB209, Flynn to William Orton, September 15, 1941; AFC Papers, FB212, William Orton, Speech, September 24, 1941.

90. AFC Papers, FB205, Mildred H. Dugan to Bliss, April 18, 1941; see also Lindbergh, *Wartime Journals,* p. 534.

91. AFC Papers, FB285, Boldt to Bliss, April 18, 1941.

92. Sarles, "A Story of America First," p. 17; see also AFC Papers, FB183.

93. AFC Papers, FB5, National Committee Bulletin, no. 267, May 20, 1941.

94. AFC Papers, FB181, Richards H. Emerson (for Flynn) to All NYC-AFC Chapter Chairmen, August 25, 1941. Following the outbreak of war, Flynn launched his own drive against the cost-plus method; see U.S. *Congressional Record,* 77th Cong., 2nd sess. (1942), 88, app. 3507, citing Flynn, "'Cost-Plus,' A World War Evil, Returns," *Barron's National Business and Financial Weekly,* August 31, 1941; Flynn, "Cost-Plus and Red Tape Hamper War Production," *Reader's Digest,* October 1941, pp. 108–11.

95. AFC Papers, FB55, Flynn to Wood, November 16, 1941; see also AFC Papers, FB212, Flynn, *AFC Bulletin,* vol. 1, no. 11, August 9, 1941.

96. Bruce Barton, "How to Write to Your Congressman," *Reader's Digest,* September 1940, pp. 87–90. The AFC national committee also regarded mail as a high priority. In October 1941 it organized a secret "mail brigade" network in chapters nationwide. This network theoretically could have flooded any Washington official very quickly with mail against a particular speech, vote or action, but the system never had time to develop (see AFC Papers, FB3, Earl C. Jeffrey [for national committee] to Bliss, October 22, 1941).

97. AFC Papers, FB191, Helen Ganong to Flynn, November 3, 1941; see also Flynn Papers, FB21, Dr. Horace Greeley, Jr. to Flynn, August 8, 1941.

98. AFC Papers, FB200, Marie Luhrs to Eunice Armstrong, May 8, 1941; see also, AFC Papers FB16, Luhrs to Bliss, December 13, 1940; AFC Papers, FB17, Miles Grover to Flynn, November 26, 1941, and Mrs. William Cornell to Flynn, November 12, 1941.

99. AFC Papers, FB285, Boldt to Bliss, April 18, 1941.

100. AFC Papers, FB17, Bliss to Page Hufty, August 30, 1941.

101. *New York Times,* October 31, 1941, p. 1. For more information on each of the six individual rallies, see chaps. 4–6, 8–9. AFC Papers, FB55, Flynn to Wood, November 16, 1941; AFC Papers, FB284, Flynn to Wood, December 3, 1941. For further information on Flynn's plans for the committee, see chap. 6.

102. Thomas Papers, FB37, Flynn to Thomas, March 17, 1941.

103. For a complete discussion of Flynn's investigation of interventionism, see chaps. 8, 9. For a complete discussion of the NYC-AFC's special polls, see chap. 4.

104. Flynn Papers, FB21, Flynn to Peter Vischer, September 1941.

105. AFC Papers, FB4, Boldt to Stuart, May 8, 1941.

106. AFC Papers, FB5, Kathryn Holmes to John Broeksmit, July 30, 1941. For similar sentiments, see AFC Papers, FB5, Howard Smith to Wood, July 25, 1941.
107. Flynn Papers, FB21, Flynn to Henry Christ, December 4, 1941. Flynn did feel that contingency plans for a march on Washington should be developed to be used "as a trump card to be played in a big way" if Roosevelt attempted to force a premature war declaration through Congress (see Flynn Papers, FB21, Flynn to Stuart, August 13, 1941).
108. AFC Papers, FB17, Fred Burdick to Bliss, October 15, 1941; AFC Papers, FB56, Bliss to Wood, March 13, 1941; Flynn Papers, FB21, Samuel Adams to Flynn, April 1, 1941; AFC Papers, FB5, Wood to Bliss, July 14, 1941.

CHAPTER 4

1. Wayne S. Cole, *An Interpretive History of American Foreign Relations* (Homewood, Ill.: Dorsey Press, 1968), p. 449.
2. Henry L. Stimson and McGeorge Bundy, *On Active Service in Peace and War* (New York: Harper & Row, 1948), p. 367, citing Stimson, Diary, December 19, 1940.
3. Walter Johnson, *The Battle Against Isolation* (Chicago: University of Chicago Press, 1944), p. 191, citing Franklin D. Roosevelt, December 29, 1940.
4. Cole, *Interpretive History*, p. 449.
5. *New York Times*, December 30, 1940, p. 1.
6. Philip La Follette, "The Doctrine of Fear," *Vital Speeches*, 7, February 15, 1941, pp. 264–65, citing F. D. Roosevelt, January 6, 1941.
7. Charles A. Lindbergh, *The Wartime Journals of Charles A. Lindbergh* (New York: Harcourt Brace Jovanovich, 1970), p. 453.
8. Ruth Sarles, "A Story of America First" (unpublished manuscript, Hoover Institution on War, Revolution and Peace, Stanford, Calif., 1942), p. 152, citing Stimson, February 1941.
9. John T. Flynn Papers, University of Oregon Library, Eugene, File Box 21, AFC Washington Research Bureau; "A Factual Analysis of H.R. 1776" (Lend-Lease Bill), February 1941; America First Committee Papers, Hoover Institution, Stanford, Calif., FB95, National Committee, Press Release, January 11, 1941; see also Sarles, "A Story of America First," p. 136.
10. AFC Papers, FB28, John T. Flynn folder, clipping from *Progressive*, January 18, 1941.
11. Flynn Papers, FB21, AFC Washington Research Bureau, "A Factual Analysis of H.R. 1776," February 1941.
12. For a full report on Flynn's decision to become NYC-AFC chairman on January 6, 1941, see chap. 2.
13. Scores of letters that Flynn received from sympathetic New Yorkers immediately following January 6, 1941, are preserved in the AFC Papers, FB16.
14. P. La Follette, "The Doctrine of Fear," pp. 264–65.
15. AFC Papers, FB17, Webster to Stuart, January 17, 1941; AFC Papers, FB185, Joseph Boldt to Robert Bliss, January 18, 1941.
16. AFC Papers, FB185, Boldt to Bliss, January 20, 1941.
17. AFC Papers, FB69, Bliss to R. E. Wood, January 29, 1941.
18. U.S. Congress, Senate, Committee on Foreign Relations, *Further to Promote Defense of the United States*, Hearings, 77th Cong., 1st sess., January 27–February 10, 1941 (Washington: Government Printing Office, 1941), pt. 2, p. 309.
19. *Ibid.*, pt. 3, pp. 49, 914. Flynn did not actually present these figures in person.

Instead, he pleaded illness, submitted the figures and a statement in writing, and spoke at a rally of the Milwaukee chapter of the AFC.

20. *Ibid.*, pt. 3, p. 908.
21. AFC Papers, FB28, Flynn, "The Effect of the Lend-Lease Bill on the American Merchant Marine," February 1941.
22. *New York Times,* January 28, 1941, p. 10; AFC Papers, FB28, Flynn, "War, What Is It?" February 1941; AFC Papers, FB29, *Anti-War News Service,* no. 19, January 17, 1941.
23. AFC Papers, FB29, Flynn, KAOWC Press Release, February 28, 1941.
24. *New York Times,* January 13, 1941, p. 1.
25. *New York Times,* January 15, 1941, p. 1.
26. AFC Papers, FB33, Amos Pinchot to F. D. Roosevelt, February 9, 1941. This letter can also be found in the Amos Pinchot Papers, Library of Congress, Washington, D.C., FB69.
27. *New York Times,* February 21, 1941, p. 7.
28. AFC Papers, FB62, Joseph Patterson to R. E. Wood, January 24, 1941.
29. Lindbergh, *Wartime Journals,* p. 437.
30. *Ibid.*
31. AFC Papers, FB64, Flynn to Stuart, February 3, 1941.
32. Sarles, "A Story of America First," p. 140.
33. Flynn Papers, FB21, Flynn, Memo to Self, January 29, 1941.
34. AFC Papers, FB37, *Uncensored,* no. 72, February 15, 1941, citing Wendell Willkie, February 1941; see also Sarles, "A Story of America First," p. 154.
35. AFC Papers, FB29, *Anti-War News Service,* no. 21, February 8, 1941.
36. *Public Opinion Quarterly* 5, no. 2 (summer 1941): 321–25.
37. *Ibid.*, p. 323.
38. Sarles, "A Story of America First," p. 165.
39. *Ibid.*, p. 508.
40. AFC Papers, FB68, H. S. Richardson to Wood, February 25, 1941.
41. AFC Papers, FB59, William Benton to Chester Bowles, February 26, 1941.
42. AFC Papers, FB64, Webster to Stuart, February 13, 1941; AFC Papers, FB185, Boldt to R. Bliss, February 16, 1941.
43. Flynn Papers, FB16, "Speech to Springfield, Mass., AFC," April 21, 1941, citing Herbert Agar, March 13, 1941.
44. AFC Papers, FB185, Boldt to Bliss, February 16, 1941.
45. AFC Papers, FB200, Webster to NYC-AFC Staff, February 10, 1941.
46. AFC Papers, FB59, Stuart to C. Bowles, March 12, 1941.
47. Flynn Papers, FB16, Flynn, Radio Speech, March 8, 1941.
48. AFC Papers, FB4, Boldt to Eastern Chapter Chairmen, March 9, 1941.
49. AFC Papers, FB61, Stuart to Charles Payson, April 30, 1941.
50. Flynn Papers, FB16, Flynn "Speech to Springfield, Mass., AFC," April 21, 1941.
51. *New York Times,* March 30, 1941, pp. 1, 42.
52. AFC Papers, FB32, Flynn, *Anti-War News Service,* no. 23, March 8, 1941, p. 1.
53. Pinchot Papers, FB87(162), Flynn, *AFC Bulletin,* vol. 1, no. 20, October 11, 1941.
54. Wayne Cole, *America First: The Battle Against Interventionism, 1940–41* (Madison: University of Wisconsin Press, 1953), pp. 65–67.
55. Pinchot Papers, FB87(162), Flynn, *AFC Bulletin,* vol. 1, no. 18, September 27, 1941.
56. *New York Times,* October 31, 1940, p. 1.
57. AFC Papers, FB17, Flynn, NYC-AFC leaflet, no date; AFC Papers, FB218, Barbara MacDonald, AFC Speakers' Bureau folder, no date.
58. Pinchot Papers, FB69, Pinchot, Memo, May 9, 1941.
59. Pinchot Papers, FB69, Pinchot to Gerald Nye, April 2, 1941.

60. Pinchot Papers, FB69, Pinchot to Lindbergh, April 30, 1941.
61. Pinchot Papers, FB69, Pinchot, Speech, July 1, 1941.
62. Lindbergh, *Wartime Journals,* p. 497.
63. AFC Papers, FB212, clipping from *New York Daily News,* November 4, 1941.
64. *New York Times,* March 30, 1941, pp. 1, 42.
65. AFC Papers, FB65, Stuart to Flynn, July 29, 1941.
66. Lindbergh, *Wartime Journals,* p. 485.
67. AFC Papers, FB55, Flynn to Wood, April 17, 1941.
68. Flynn Papers, FB21, "Minutes of the NYC-AFC Chapter Committee Meeting," April 8, 1941.
69. AFC Papers, FB68, Stuart to H. S. Richardson, April 23, 1941.
70. AFC Papers, FB67, Stuart to James Selvage, April 23, 1941.
71. AFC Papers, FB285, Stuart to Bowles, April 29, 1941.
72. Flynn Papers, FB21, Flynn to Wood, January 14, 1941.
73. Sarles, "A Story of America First," p. 476. Forty-eight questions out of the fifty-five "dubious" cases were judged to be biased in favor of interventionism.
74. *Public Opinion Quarterly* 5, no. 1 (March 1941): 159; no. 2 (summer 1941): 326; no. 3 (fall 1941): 482; no. 4 (winter 1941): 680; 6, no.1 (spring 1942): 164. It is impossible to analyze the opinions of the Northeast as distinct from the rest of the United States because separate results from geographical sections are given only sporadically in the Gallup and Roper polls. However, in those cases where discrete results are given, the correspondence of the Northeast to the national average is extremely close. Breakdowns for the South and the Midwest, where given, confirm the AFC belief that the South was more interventionist, and the Midwest less so, than the country as a whole. The Northeast struck a balance.
75. *Public Opinion Quarterly* 5, no. 1 (March 1941): 156; no. 3 (fall 1941): 476; 6. no. 1 (spring 1942): 149.
76. *Public Opinion Quarterly* 5, no. 1 (March 1941): 159; no. 2 (summer 1941): 325–26; no. 3 (fall 1941): 481; 6, no. 1 (spring 1942): 151; 5, no. 3 (fall 1941): 483.
77. Lindbergh, *Wartime Journals,* p. 437.
78. *Public Opinion Quarterly* 5, no. 3 (fall 1941): 485–86; see also *ibid.* 5, no. 1 (March 1941): 158.
79. Sarles, "A Story of America First," p. 478.
80. Flynn Papers, FB21, Flynn, "Opening Remarks, Rally," April 23, May 23, 1941; see also Sarles, "A Story of America First," pp. 479–80.
81. Sarles, "A Story of America First," p. 476.
82. AFC Papers, FB65, Stuart to Bliss, June 11, 1941; AFC Papers, FB62, Wood to Joseph Patterson, June 23, 1941; see also, Sarles, "A Story of America First," p. 208.
83. AFC Papers, FB62, Bliss to Richard A. Moore, July 15, 1941.
84. AFC Papers, FB62, Stuart to Joseph Patterson, July 7, 1941.
85. Flynn Papers, FB21, Catholic Laymen's Committee for Peace, Press Release, October 15, 1941.
86. Sarles, "A Story of America First," pp. 495–96.
87. AFC Papers, FB62, Stuart to H. S. Richardson, June 27, 1941.
88. AFC Papers, FB291, George Yarrington to Wood, July 30, 1941.
89. AFC Papers, FB212, Flynn, *AFC Bulletin,* vol. 1, no. 11, August 9, 1941.

CHAPTER 5

1. Wayne S. Cole, *An Interpretive History of American Foreign Relations* (Homewood, Ill.: Dorsey Press, 1968), p. 449.

2. Amos R. E. Pinchot Papers, Library of Congress, Washington, D.C., File Box 69, Pinchot to Lindbergh, April 30, 1941.
3. *New York Times,* February 21, 1941, p. 7.
4. For a discussion of the no-convoy amendment to the Lend-Lease Act, see chap. 4.
5. John T. Flynn Papers, University of Oregon Library, Eugene, FB16, Flynn, Speech to Springfield (Mass.) AFC, April 21, 1941, citing Walter George, March 1941.
6. *New York Times,* January 21, 1941, p. 1.
7. Ruth Sarles, "A Story of America First" (unpublished manuscript, Hoover Institution on War, Revolution and Peace, Stanford, Calif., 1942), p. 187, citing Joseph Alsop and Robert Kintner, in the *Washington Post,* April 7, 1941. Public opinion in regard to convoys in early April was running approximately forty-one percent in favor of the transports (*Public Opinion Quarterly* 5, no. 3 [fall 1941]: 485).
8. Sarles, "A Story of America First," p. 187.
9. For a full discussion of the Committee to Defend America by Aiding the Allies and its involvement with the Roosevelt Administration and with the America First Committee, see chap. 8.
10. Sarles, "A Story of America First," p. 194.
11. *New York Times,* April 26, 1941, p. 1.
12. America First Committee Papers, Hoover Institution, Stanford, Calif., FB37, *Uncensored,* no. 87, May 31, 1941.
13. Norman Thomas Papers, New York City Public Library, FB38, Thomas to Franklin D. Roosevelt, May 12, 1941.
14. Hamilton Fish, "We Should Not Convoy Materials to Europe," *Vital Speeches,* April 15, 1941, pp. 414–15.
15. AFC Papers, FB28, Flynn, "Record of the Speeches and Debate on America's Town Meeting of the Air, May 8, 1941" (New York, Columbia University Press), vol. 6, no. 26, May 12, 1941.
16. Pinchot Papers, FB69, Pinchot to Charles Tobey, April 7, 1941.
17. Charles Lindbergh, *The Wartime Journals of Charles A. Lindbergh* (New York: Harcourt Brace Jovanovich, 1970), pp. 476–77.
18. AFC Papers, FB17, Flynn to Robert L. Bliss, April 24, 1941; AFC Papers, FB291, Miss Janet Fairbank to Mrs. Janet Fairbank, May 1941.
19. AFC Papers, FB69, Robert D. Stuart to Robert E. Wood, April 26, 1941.
20. *New York Times,* June 8, 1941, p. 24.
21. AFC Papers, FB68, Wood to several wealthy donors, April 24, 1941; Burton K. Wheeler, "The American People Want No War," *Vital Speeches,* June 1, 1941, p. 489.
22. AFC Papers, FB69, Stuart to Wood, April 26, 1941.
23. *New York Times,* April 27, 1941, p. 27.
24. *New York Times,* April 25, 1941, p. 1. "Copperheads" were Northerners who sympathized with the South during the Civil War. Roosevelt specifically compared Lindbergh to Clement L. Vallandigham, an Ohio congressman who was convicted of treason and banished to the Confederacy in 1863.
25. *New York Times,* April 24, 1941, p. 12.
26. Lindbergh, *Wartime Journals,* p. 480. Lindbergh also seriously considered resigning from the AFC to shield the committee from further insults directed at him: personal interview with R. L. Bliss, New York City, March 15, 1974.
27. *New York Times,* April 29, 1941, p. 10; Pinchot Papers, FB69, Pinchot to Lindbergh, April 28, 1941, and Pinchot to John F. Sinclair, May 2, 1941, and Pinchot, Press Release, April 28, 1941.
28. Henry L. Stimson and McGeorge Bundy, *On Active Service in Peace and War* (New York: Harper & Row, 1948), p. 370.

211

29. AFC Papers, NYC-AFC Chapter Committee to Stuart, April 26, 1941; Sarles, "A Story of America First," pp. 410–11.
30. AFC Papers, FB59, Stuart to Chester Bowles, May 10, 1941; AFC Papers, FB68, H. S. Richardson to Wood, May 16, 1941.
31. Amos Pinchot, *History of the Progressive Party, 1912–16* (New York: New York University Press, 1958), Appendix 1, pp. 235–43, citing Pinchot to Hiram Johnson, January 19, 1932.
32. AFC Papers, FB62, Pinchot to Henry L. Stimson, May 8, 1941; also found in Pinchot Papers, FB69.
33. Lindbergh, *Wartime Journals,* p. 488.
34. Sarles, "A Story of America First," p. 198.
35. Lindbergh, *Wartime Journals,* p. 488.
36. Pinchot Papers, FB70, Pinchot to Lincoln Colcord, May 13, 1941; see also AFC Papers, FB62, Pinchot to Stuart, May 15, 1941; Pinchot Papers, FB70, Pinchot to R. D. Williamson, May 13, 1941.
37. AFC Papers, FB37, *Uncensored,* no. 85, May 17, 1941.
38. AFC Papers, FB69, Bowles to Wood, May 29, 1941; AFC Papers, FB285, Wood, Press Release, May 28, 1941; *New York Times,* May 28, 1941, p. 20, citing KAOWC Press Release, and May 29, 1941, p. 2, citing Robert M. La Follette, Jr., and Hamilton Fish; AFC Papers, FB37, *Uncensored,* no. 87, May 31, 1941; AFC Papers, FB212, Flynn, *AFC Bulletin,* vol. 1, no. 11, August 9, 1941.
39. *New York Times,* May 28, 1941, p. 1, and May 29, 1941, p. 1; see also Sarles, "A Story of America First," pp. 198–99. A limited national emergency, declared by Roosevelt, had been in effect since September 8, 1939.
40. AFC Papers, FB62, Pinchot to Wood, May 28, 1941; Pinchot Papers, FB69, Pinchot to Lindbergh, May 28, 1941.
41. AFC Papers, FB212, Flynn, *AFC Bulletin,* vol. 1, no. 11, August 9, 1941.
42. Lindbergh, *Wartime Journals,* pp. 497–98.
43. Flynn Papers, FB21, Flynn, "Minutes of the NYC-AFC Chapter Committee Meeting," June 4, 1941.
44. Lindbergh, *Wartime Journals,* pp. 496–97.
45. Pinchot Papers, FB87(162), Flynn, *AFC Bulletin,* vol. 1, no. 1, May 30, 1941. The *New York Times* concurred in Flynn's opinion regarding the powers granted in the emergency proclamation (*Times,* May 28, 1941, p. 7).
46. AFC Papers, FB62, Pinchot to Wood, May 28, 1941.
47. Pinchot Papers, FB87(162), Flynn, *AFC Bulletin,* vol. 1, no. 3, June 14, 1941; Flynn Papers, FB21, Flynn to Wood, June 5, 1941. Flynn knew of a special report from Burton K. Wheeler to Wood. According to Wheeler, Roosevelt's top Senate supporters had cautioned the President to proceed slowly, and had told him that sentiment in both houses of Congress had swung noticeably to the noninterventionist side (Sarles, "A Story of America First," p. 207; Lindbergh, *Wartime Journals,* 1941, p. 502). Also, rumors of a negotiated peace between England and Germany were rampant in the world in late May and early June (Lindbergh, *Wartime Journals,* p. 498).
48. *Public Opionion Quarterly* 5, no. 3 (fall 1941): 485.
49. *Ibid.,* pp. 477–78.
50. *Ibid.,* p. 480.
51. *Ibid.,* pp. 479, 477.
52. Stimson and Bundy, *On Active Service,* p. 368, citing Stimson, Diary, April 10, 1941.
53. *New York Times,* July 10, 1941, p. 1; see also Sarles, "A Story of America First," p. 212.
54. *New York Times,* June 23, 1941, p. 1.
55. Flynn Papers, FB32, Flynn, Diary, June 27, 1941; Flynn Papers, FB16, Flynn,

"Understudy for Russia" (Radio Speech), June 26, 1941; AFC Papers, FB288, Flynn, Press Release, June 23, 1941.

56. Flynn Papers, FB21, Norman Thomas, in "Uncle Sam a Fellow Traveler?" (AFC National Committee pamphlet), July 1941; see also *New York Times*, June 23, 1941, p. 2.

57. Pinchot Papers, FB69, Igor Sikorsky, "The Nature and Objectives of the Soviet Communist Government," July 11, 1941.

58. Flynn Papers, FB21, Flynn, in "Uncle Sam a Fellow Traveler?" July 1941; see also, *New York Times*, June 23, 1941, p. 2.

59. Flynn Papers, FB32, Flynn, Diary, June 27, 1941.

60. Pinchot Papers, FB69, Igor Sikorsky, "Soviet Communist Government," July 11, 1941.

61. Burton K. Wheeler, *Yankee from the West* (Garden City, N.Y.: Doubleday & Co., 1962), p. 31.

62. Robert D. Stuart, personal letter to the author, January 11, 1974.

63. *New York Times*, July 2, 1941, p. 2. This statement by Lindbergh brought a charge from Secretary of the Interior Harold Ickes that the aviator was "a cheerer-on of Hitler . . . a mouthpiece of the Nazi party line" (*New York Times*, July 15, 1941, p. 1). Lindbergh wrote to Roosevelt and demanded either a public apology or the firing of Ickes (Lindbergh, *Wartime Journals*, p. 518). Roosevelt took no action, but the NYC-AFC used the incident to galvanize support for the claim that the administration's arguments were "getting more and more desperate and more and more phoney, day by day" (Pinchot Papers, FB87[162], Flynn, *AFC Bulletin*, vol. 1, no. 10, August 2, 1941; see also, AFC Papers, FB37, *Uncensored*, no. 96, August 2, 1941).

64. Flynn Papers, FB21, Richards H. Emerson, in "Uncle Sam a Fellow Traveler?" July 1941; see also *New York Times*, June 23, 1941, p. 2.

65. Herbert Hoover, "Call to Reason," *Vital Speeches*, 7, July 15, 1941, pp. 580–84; Pinchot Papers, FB69, Igor Sikorsky, "Soviet Communist Government," July 11, 1941.

66. Pinchot Papers, FB 69, Pinchot to Sikorsky, August 5, 1941.

67. *New York Times*, June 26, 1941, p. 8; see also, *New York Herald-Tribune*, June 26, 1941; Flynn Papers, FB21, Flynn, "No Red Allies for the U.S.," June 26, 1941.

68. *New York Times*, October 3, 1941, p. 10; see also, AFC Papers, FB209, Bliss to Bailey Stortz, October 3, 1941. NYC-AFC executive secretary Edwin Webster reported that this advertisement produced a "very noticeable effect" in New York: AFC Papers, FB284, Webster to Wood, October 7, 1941.

69. Flynn Papers, FB21, Catholic Laymen's Committee for Peace, Press Release, October 15, 1941.

70. *Public Opinion Quarterly* 5, no. 4 (winter 1941): 675–79.

71. *Ibid.*, 6, no. 1 (spring 1941): 152.

72. AFC Papers, FB200, Richards Emerson to Flynn, Memo, July 11, 1941.

73. Flynn Papers, FB16, Flynn, Speech to Springfield (Mass.) AFC, April 21, 1941.

74. *New York Times*, July 8, 1941, p. 1, and July 9, 1941, p. 1; see also Sarles, "A Story of America First," p. 212.

75. Thomas Papers, FB40, John A. Danaher to Thomas, July 8, 1941; Sarles, "A Story of America First," p. 204.

76. Thomas Papers, FB40, Danaher to Thomas, July 8, 1941.

77. Thomas Papers, FB40, Thomas to Jerry Voorhis, November 14, 1941.

78. Flynn Papers, FB21, Flynn, Press Release, July 7, 1941.

79. Lindbergh, *Wartime Journals*, pp. 515–16, and July 10, 1941, p. 516.

80. AFC Papers, FB62, Pinchot to F. D. Roosevelt, July 11, 1941.

81. Thomas Papers, FB35, Flynn to Thomas, August 6, 1940; AFC Papers, FB212,

Flynn, "Memo on Marshall's Report," July 3, 1941, and Flynn, Press Release, July 3, 1941.

82. *Public Opinion Quarterly* 5, no. 4 (winter 1941): 680; Sarles, "A Story of America First," pp. 222–23: The two resolutions that eventually comprised the draft-extension bill were Senate Joint Resolutions no. 92 and no. 93.

83. AFC Papers, FB200, NYC-AFC Executive Committee to all NYC-AFC Members, circular, July 23, 1941.

84. AFC Papers, FB65, Stuart to Flynn, July 31, 1941.

85. AFC Papers, FB65, Flynn to Page Hufty, July 30, 1941.

86. Norman Thomas, "Is the Extension of the Draft Necessary?" *Vital Speeches*, 7, August 15, 1941, pp. 671–72.

87. Sarles, "A Story of America First," pp. 231–32, citing Gregory Mason.

88. Pinchot Papers, FB87(162), Flynn, *AFC Bulletin*, vol. 1, no. 9, July 26, 1941.

89. *Ibid.*

90. Sarles, "A Story of America First," pp. 222–24.

91. Pinchot Papers, FB87(162), Flynn, *AFC Bulletin*, vol. 1, no. 10, August 2, 1941; see also AFC Papers, FB37, *Uncensored*, no. 96, August 2, 1941.

92. Thomas Papers, FB39, Adelaide Marquand to Thomas, August 5, 1941; Pinchot Papers, FB69, Pinchot to Sikorsky, August 5, 1941.

93. *Public Opinion Quarterly* 5, no. 4 (winter 1941): 682.

94. Edward H. Reisner, "The Case Against Intervention," *Vital Speeches*, 7, August 15, 1941, p. 655.

95. U.S., *Congressional Record*, 77th Cong., 1st sess., 1941, p. 6965.

96. AFC Papers, FB288, Flynn to NYC-AFC Staff, Memo, August 13, 1941.

97. *Ibid.*

98. U.S., *Congressional Record*, 77th Cong., 1st sess., 1941, pp. 2097, 7074.

99. Flynn Papers, FB21, Flynn to Henry Christ, December 4, 1941.

100. Sarles, "A Story of America First," p. 233.

101. Flynn Papers, FB16, Flynn, Radio Speech, September 27, 1941.

102. Henry Noble MacCracken, "An Examination of the Eight Points," *Vital Speeches*, 7, September 1, 1941, pp. 679–80.

103. AFC Papers, FB172, Bliss to Geraldine Farrar, September 2, 1941; Flynn Papers, FB32, Flynn, Diary, August 27, 1941.

104. Lindbergh, *Wartime Journals*, p. 532.

105. *New York Times*, August 22, 1941, p. 1; see also Sarles, "A Story of America First," p. 234, citing Roosevelt.

106. *Public Opinion Quarterly* 5, no. 4 (winter 1941): 675, 677, 680.

CHAPTER 6

1. America First Committee Papers, Hoover Institution on War, Revolution and Peach, Stanford, Calif., File Box 284, Amos Pinchot to Robert D. Stuart, December 3, 1941; see also AFC Papers, FB64, Pinchot and Edwin Webster to Robert E. Wood, November 10, 1941.

2. *New York Times*, June 21, 1941, p. 1.

3. Wayne S. Cole, *America First: The Battle Against Intervention, 1940–41* (Madison: University of Wisconsin Press, 1953), p. 160.

4. John T. Flynn Papers, University of Oregon Library, Eugene, FB21, Flynn to Sidney Hertzberg, no date.

5. *Public Opinion Quarterly* 5, no. 2, (summer 1941): 327.

6. AFC Papers, FB54, Samuel Gill, Inc., "Results of Robert M. Hutchins Poll,"

June 1941. Sixty-two percent of the people, according to an early October Gallup poll, approved of the shoot-on-sight order itself: *Public Opinion Quarterly* 6, no. 1 (spring 1942): 163.

7. AFC Papers, FB60, Stuart to All Chapter Chairmen, June 4, 1941, citing Joseph Alsop and Robert Kintner, in the *Washington Post*, June 4, 1941.
8. AFC Papers, FB33, AFC Washington Research Bureau, "Did You Know: That the *Robin Moor*'s Cargo Was 70% Contraband?" June 1941.
9. Flynn Papers, FB21, Flynn, Press Release, September 12, 1941.
10. Amos R. E. Pinchot Papers, Library of Congress, Washington, D.C., FB87(162), Flynn, *AFC Bulletin*, vol. 1, no. 17, September 20, 1941.
11. *Ibid.*, and AFC Papers, FB62, Pinchot to Stuart, September 26, 1941; AFC Papers, FB200, "Plans for Constitution Day Rally"; AFC Papers, FB215, "Statement of Receipts and Expenses for Constitution Day Rally."
12. Ruth Sarles, "A Story of America First" (unpublished manuscript, Hoover Institution, Stanford, Calif., 1942), pp. 242–44, 257.
13. Charles Lindbergh, *The Wartime Journals of Charles A. Lindbergh* (New York: Harcourt Brace Jovanovich, 1970), p. 540.
14. AFC Papers, FB201, Flynn to NYC-AFC Staff and Chapter Chairmen, September 12, 1941; see also AFC Papers, FB 55, Flynn to Wood and Stuart, October 20, 1941.
15. Lindbergh, *Wartime Journals*, pp. 544–45.
16. Cole, *America First*, p. 160.
17. *New York Times*, October 2, 1941, p. 1.
18. Pinchot Papers, FB70, Pinchot to John F. Sinclair, October 2, 1941.
19. Flynn Papers, FB21, AFC Washington Research Bureau, "Did You Know: That Elimination of the Neutrality Law Combat Zones Means War?" October 25, 1941; German Admiral Erich Rader's "wolfpack" technique made the second quarter of 1941 the worst period of the war for British shipping losses.
20. AFC Papers, FB33, Pinchot to Franklin D. Roosevelt, October 24, 1941.
21. Flynn Papers, FB21, Flynn, Press Release, October 17, 1941.
22. Flynn Papers, FB21, Flynn, Press Release, October 21, 1941; AFC Papers, FB183, Richard A Moore (for national committee) to All Chapter Chairmen, Bulletin, October 18, 1941; Flynn Papers, FB32, Flynn, Diary, October 17, 1941.
23. AFC Papers, FB33, Pinchot to F. D. Roosevelt, October 24, 1941. In this letter Pinchot also compared Roosevelt's "misinterpretations of an 'enemy's' provocations" to former German Chancellor Otto von Bismarck's deliberate and deceitful editing of the Ems (Abeken) telegram in 1870. Bismarck's duplicity at that time precipitated the Franco-Prussian War.
24. *New York Times*, October 28, 1941, p. 1.
25. Pinchot Papers, FB87(162), Flynn, *AFC Bulletin*, vol. 1, no. 27, November 29, 1941.
26. Flynn Papers, FB21, F. D. Roosevelt, "Address to Congress" (copy), September 21, 1941.
27. Sarles, "A Story of America First," p. 239.
28. AFC Papers, FB59, Stuart to Chester Bowles, October 11, 1941; see also Flynn Papers, FB32, Flynn, Diary, October 10, 1941; AFC Papers, FB209, Flynn to NYC-AFC Chapter Chairmen, November 4, 1941.
29. Norman Thomas Papers, New York City Public Library, FB40, Wood to Thomas, October 31, 1941; Flynn Papers, FB21, Wood to Flynn, October 28, 1941.
30. Thomas Papers, FB40, Thomas to Stuart, October 30. 1941.
31. Flynn Papers, FB21, Flynn to Wood and Stuart, October 21, 1941; see also AFC Papers, FB55, Flynn to Wood and Stuart, October 20, 1941.
32. AFC Papers, FB285, Sarles to Wood, October 20, 1941, and Wood to Sarles, October 22, 1941, and Wood to F. D. Roosevelt, October 23, 1941.

33. "America First Roughouse," *Life*, October 20, 1941, p. 41.
34. U.S. Congress, Senate, Hearings, Senate Foreign Relations Committee, *Modification of the Neutrality Act of 1939*, 77th Cong., 1st sess., October 23, 1941 (Washington: Government Printing Office, 1941), Flynn, p. 201. Neither Flynn nor any other America Firsters were able to appear before the House Foreign Relations Committee hearings on neutrality repeal. Their requests to testify were not approved until a few hours before they were to be allowed to speak. Flynn protested this "gag" technique to committee chairman Sol Bloom (Flynn Papers, FB21, Flynn to Sol Bloom, October 13, 1941; see also AFC Papers, FB29, *Anti-War News Service*, no. 39, October 22, 1941).
35. Lindbergh, *Wartime Journals*, p. 551.
36. AFC Papers, FB181, Flynn to NYC-AFC Staff, October 31, 1941.
37. AFC Papers, FB209, Flynn to several persons in Binghamton, Endicott, and Johnson City, New York, November 4, 1941; see also AFC Papers, FB3, Earl Jeffrey (for national committee) to Robert Bliss, October 22, 1941.
38. *Public Opinion Quarterly* 6, no. 1 (spring 1942): 162.
39. Sarles, "A Story of America First," pp. 495–96.
40. AFC Papers, FB55, Flynn to Wood, November 11, 1941.
41. Thomas Papers, FB40, Thomas to Stuart, October 30, 1941.
42. AFC Papers, FB55, Flynn to Wood, October 20, 1941, and Wood to Flynn, October 30, 1941.
43. AFC Papers, FB55, Flynn to Wood, November 16, 1941; see also AFC Papers, FB62, Stuart to Pinchot, November 21, 1941.
44. Pinchot Papers, FB87(162), Flynn, Press Release, November 14, 1941.
45. AFC Papers, FB55, Flynn to Wood, November 16, 1941; see also Pinchot Papers, FB87(162), Flynn, *AFC Bulletin*, vol. 1, no. 26, November 22, 1941, and no. 27, November 29, 1941.
46. *Ibid.* (all three sources); AFC Papers, FB291, William F. Turner to Wood, November 14, 1941; Flynn Papers, FB21, Wood to All Chapter Chairman, November 18, 1941, and Walter Reynolds (for Hamilton Fish) to Bliss, November 19, 1941, and Francis Case, "Report to the Second Congressional District of South Dakota," November 17, 1941. Flynn received from Fish's office a private list of those congressmen allegedly bribed by the administration into voting for repeal. Among those listed was Joseph Casey of Massachusetts, who was said to have been offered a judgeship for his vote.
47. Thomas Papers, FB40, Burton K. Wheeler to Thomas, November 25, 1941.
48. AFC Papers, FB17, Marie Hennessey to Harry Schnibbe, November 18, 1941.
49. Sarles, "A Story of America First," p. 276.
50. All information concerning voting records was found in U.S. *Congressional Record*, 77th Cong., 1st sess., 1941, pp. 2097, 7074; and in Flynn Papers, FB21.
51. AFC Papers, FB198, G. Bogart Blakely to NYC-AFC, November 14, 1941. Many more of these late-1941 letters of resignation from NYC-AFC members are preserved in the AFC Papers, FB198. No figures are available, however, on the rate or total number of the resignations.
52. Flynn Papers, FB21, Joseph Boldt to Flynn, November 18, 1941.
53. Flynn Papers, FB21, National Committee Memo, "Situation in the Field," December 2, 1941.
54. Thomas Papers, FB40, Thomas to B. K. Wheeler, November 21, 1941.
55. Flynn Papers, FB21, "Minutes of the NYC-AFC Executive Committee Meeting," November 25, 1941.
56. AFC Papers, FB284, Pinchot to Wood, November 27, 1941, and Pinchot to Stuart, December 3, 1941; Pinchot Papers, FB69, Pinchot to Karl Mundt, November 21, 1941, and Pinchot to Joseph M. Patterson, November 27, 1941.
57. Thomas Papers, FB40, Thomas to B. K. Wheeler, November 21, 1941; AFC Papers, FB284, Pinchot to Stuart, December 3, 1941; AFC Papers, FB55, Flynn

to Wood, November 16, 1941; Lindbergh, *Wartime Journals*, pp. 556–57.

58. AFC Papers, FB55, Flynn to Wood, November 11, 16, 1941. The idea for the AFC to keep silent following neutrality repeal came to Flynn originally from an old noninterventionist friend, Lincoln Colcord of Maine. Colcord counseled Flynn that "there are times when the opposition only damages its case by carrying on the opposition" (Flynn Papers, FB21, L. Colcord to Flynn, November 2, 1941).

59. AFC Papers, FB55, Flynn to Wood, November 16, 1941; AFC Papers, FB64, Stuart to Wood, November 27, 1941, and Wood to Flynn, December 3, 1941.

60. Flynn Papers, FB32, Flynn, Diary, August 2, 1941; Flynn Papers, FB21; Sarles, "A Story of America First," p. 258; Pinchot Papers, FB87(162), Flynn, *AFC Bulletin*, vol. 1, no. 25, November 15, 1941, and no. 28, December 6, 1941.

61. Flynn Papers, FB21. There is no definitive evidence that these advertisements ever found their way into print.

62. Pinchot Papers, FB87(162), Flynn, *AFC Bulletin*, no. 28, December 6, 1941. For additional examples of Flynn's beliefs and actions in his "economic offensive," see Flynn Papers, FB21, Flynn to Pinchot, September 8, 1941, and Mrs. Janet A. Fairbank to Flynn, November 25, 1941, and Flynn to Mrs. Fairbank, November 1941; Pinchot Papers, FB87(162), Flynn, *AFC Bulletin*, vol. 1, no. 19, October 4, 1941.

63. Flynn Papers, FB21, C. B. Yorke to Flynn, November 25, 1941; *Public Opinion Quarterly* 6, no. 1 (spring 1942): 153–54.

64. AFC Papers, FB42, "Minutes of the National Committee Meeting," November 28, 1941.

65. AFC Papers, FB284, Webster to Wood, March 10, 1941.

66. For examples of directives demanding a strictly nonpolitical AFC, see AFC Papers, FB42, "Minutes of the AFC National Committee Meeting," November 1, 1940; AFC Papers, FB181, Bliss (for Flynn) to NYC-AFC Staff, July 11, 1941.

67. AFC Papers, FB5, "Minutes of the AFC Chapter Chairmen Meeting," July 12, 1941.

68. AFC Papers, FB284, Wood to Webster, August 8, 1941.

69. AFC Papers, FB64, Webster to Stuart, February 13, 1941.

70. AFC Papers, FB59, Bowles to Stuart, July 15, 1941. By late November Bowles had changed his mind and believed that the AFC was too diverse to become an effective third political party (AFC Papers, FB55, Bowles to Stuart, November 28, 1941).

71. Pinchot Papers, FB87(162), Flynn, *AFC Bulletin*, vol. 1, no. 20, October 11, 1941.

72. AFC Papers, FB181, Bliss to Doris F. Reid, September 15, 1941.

73. Lindbergh, *Wartime Journals*, p. 557; AFC Papers, FB55, Flynn to Wood, November 16, 1941; Flynn Papers, FB21, Flynn to William T. Pheiffer, November 29, 1941, and "Minutes of the NYC-AFC Executive Committee Meeting," November 25, 1941; AFC Papers, FB200, Richards Emerson to Mrs. James Kennedy, November 24, 1941.

74. Flynn Papers, FB21, National Committee Statement, December 1, 1941; also found in AFC Papers, FB55 and FB62.

75. AFC Papers, FB207, Stuart to All Chapter Chairmen, November 6, 1941.

76. AFC Papers, FB55, Clay Judson to Wood, November 29, 1941, and Wood to Herbert Hoover, December 2, 1941, and Hoover to Wood, December 4, 1941; see also AFC Papers, FB163, Judson to Wood, December 4, 1941; AFC Papers, FB57, Robert M. Harriss to Wood, November 26, 1941; AFC Papers, FB60, Stuart to Hoover, December 5, 1941.

77. Many of the letters of approval from Northeastern chapter chairmen are preserved in the AFC Papers, FB5.

78. Thomas Papers, FB40, Thomas to Bowles, December 5, 1941.

79. AFC Papers, FB284, Pinchot to Stuart, December 3, 1941.
80. Sarles, "A Story of America First," p. 122.
81. AFC Papers, FB284, Flynn to Wood, December 3, 1941.
82. John Roy Carlson (in reality Avedis Derounian), *UnderCover* (New York: E. P. Dutton & Co., 1943), pp. 481–84, citing Edward Atwell.
83. Flynn Papers, FB21, Flynn to Wood and Stuart, December 4, 1941.
84. AFC Papers, FB284, Flynn to Wood, December 3, 1941.
85. AFC Papers, FB205, Barbara MacDonald, "Manual for Speakers," March 1941. One prophetic NYC-AFC staff member, Joseph Boldt, did predict as early as February 1941 that America's "real war crisis" would come in the Far East. The administration was "willfully" directing public attention toward Europe, Boldt stated, so that "when the 'emergency' comes, the people will be taken so un-awares that they will really believe it is an emergency, and before they know what is happening, will be acquiescing" in war (AFC Papers, FB185, Boldt to Bliss, February 16, 1941).
86. Thomas Papers, FB39, B. K. Wheeler to Thomas, August 27, 1941; Flynn, "Plain Economics," *Washington Daily News*, February 24, 1941.
87. AFC Papers, FB163, AFC National Committee Resolution, August 11, 1941.
88. Pinchot Papers, FB87(162), Flynn, *AFC Bulletin*, vol. 1. no. 10, August 2, 1941, citing NYC-AFC Executive Committee Telegram to Sumner Welles.
89. Thomas Papers, FB39, Thomas to George Fitch, August 9, 1941, and Thomas to B. K. Wheeler, August 25, 1941. Thomas, however, had long advocated economic sanctions involving little or no risk of war against Japan. An example of such sanctions, American refusal to buy Japanese gold, was rejected by Roosevelt.
90. Flynn Papers, FB32, Flynn, Diary, August 30, 1941.
91. Flynn Papers, FB32, Flynn, Diary, October 17, 1941.
92. Some of these telegrams are preserved in the AFC Papers, FB85. One example, from a Baldwin, New York, man, is Howard Sheaff to Wood, November 28, 1941.
93. Thomas Papers, FB40, Thomas to B. K. Wheeler, November 21, 1941; AFC Papers, FB284, Pinchot to Wood, November 16, 1941; Pinchot Papers, FB87(162), Flynn, *AFC Bulletin*, vol. 1, no. 28, December 6, 1941.
94. *Public Opinion Quarterly* 5, no. 2 (summer 1941): 333–34.
95. *Ibid.* 6, no. 1 (spring 1942): 149, 151, 163.
96. B. K. Wheeler, *Yankee from the West* (Garden City, N.Y.: Doubleday & Co., 1962), p. 32.
97. *Ibid.*, pp. 32–35.
98. Lindbergh, *Wartime Journals*, pp. 560–61.
99. H. Montgomery Hyde, *Room 3603: The Story of the British Intelligence Center in New York During WWII* (New York: Farrar & Straus, 1962), p. 74, citing Gerald P. Nye.
100. B. K. Wheeler, *Yankee from the West*, p. 36.
101. Lindbergh, *Wartime Journals*, pp. 654, 923.
102. B. K. Wheeler, *Yankee from the West*, p. 31.
103. Sarles, "A Story of America First," p. 7.
104. Flynn Papers, FB21, Flynn, "The Truth About Pearl Harbor," 1944, and "The Final Secret of Pearl Harbor," 1945; Flynn Papers, FB9, Flynn to E. V. Gold-smith, October 16, 1945; Flynn, *New York Journal-American*, July 26, 1946; see also Richard C. Frey, "John T. Flynn and the United States in Crisis" (unpub-lished doctoral dissertation, University of Oregon, 1969), chap. 8.
105. Personal interview, Page Hufty, March 3, 1974.
106. Flynn did not begin to entertain thoughts of presidential culpability in the raid for at least three months: personal interview, Thomas D. Flynn, April 25, 1973.
107. AFC Papers, FB201, NYC-AFC Executive Committee Press Release, December 8, 1941, and Flynn to NYC-AFC Chapter Chairmen and Staff, December 10, 1941; also found in AFC Papers, FB162.

108. *Ibid.* (both sources); AFC Papers, FB215, Flynn, Radio Speech, December 17, 1941.
109. Sarles, "A Story of America First," p. 82, citing early AFC Organizational Manual.
110. Morris Burns Stanley, "The America First Committee: A Study in Recent American Noninterventionism" (unpublished master's thesis, Emory University, 1942), p. 398, citing a personal interview with Flynn, March 20, 1942.
111. *Ibid.*; AFC Papers, Flynn to Wood, June 5, 1941, and William T. Leonard to Wood, December 9, 1941; see also AFC Papers, FB201, Flynn to NYC-AFC Chapter Chairmen and Staff, December 10, 1941.
112. AFC Papers, FB284, Flynn to Wood, June 5, 1941. For a complete discussion of Flynn's fears regarding profascist elements in and around the NYC-AFC, see chap. 7.
113. AFC Papers, FB284, Stuart to All Chapter Chairmen, December 8, 1941.
114. AFC Papers, FB284, Edith O. Newby to Stuart, December 9, 1941, and several telegrams to Wood and Stuart, December 9, 10, 1941.
115. AFC Papers, FB55, Wood to Flynn, November 12, 1941; AFC Papers, FB284, Wood Proposal, December 11, 1941.
116. AFC Papers, FB5, A. Venti to Wood, and Horace J. Haase to Wood, December 7, 1941.
117. AFC Papers, FB284, "Minutes of the AFC National Committee Meeting," December 11, 1941.
118. AFC Papers, FB215, Wood to All Chapter Chairmen and Staff, December 15, 1941.
119. AFC Papers, FB285, Bowles to Wood, December 22, 1941.
120. Thomas Papers, FB40, Thomas to Maynard Kreuger, December 11, 1941; AFC Papers, FB284, Mary Hillyer, KAOWC Press Release, January 2, 1942.
121. AFC Papers, FB4, Page Hufty to Boldt, December 14, 1941.
122. *Ibid.*
123. AFC Papers, FB285, Flynn to Wood, July 17, 1942.
124. AFC Papers, FB162, Flynn to Wood, December 22, 1941.
125. AFC Papers, FB285, D. Richards to Wood, December 19, 1941, and Wood to Webster, July 13, 1942.
126. AFC Papers, FB162, Flynn to Wood, December 22, 1941; see also AFC Papers, FB284, Flynn to Wood, January 7, 1942; Flynn Papers, FB17, Flynn to John Cudahy, January 13, 1942.

CHAPTER 7

1. John T. Flynn Papers, University of Oregon Library, Eugene, File Box 21, Harry Schnibbe to Flynn, April 1942, p. 89.
2. Ruth Sarles, "A Story of America First" (Hoover Institution on War, Revolution and Peace, Stanford, Calif., 1942), pp. 70, 332.
3. Flynn Papers, FB21, Flynn, "Notes on Formation of the NYC-AFC," April 1942, p. 11.
4. For a full discussion of Flynn's defenses of the AFC, his conspiracy theory, and his bitterness in later years, see further in chap. 7, and in chaps. 8, and 9.
5. Sarles, "A Story of America First," pp. 119, 331.
6. America First Committee Papers, Hoover Institution, Stanford, Calif. FB69, John E. F. Wood to Robert E. Wood, November 9, 1940; see also AFC Papers, FB59, Page Hufty to William Biggs, July 3, 1941.
7. For a complete discussion of Flynn's tight personal control over the NYC-AFC,

see chap. 3. Examples of potential NYC-AFC members who turned away because of affiliation with undesirable groups follow: AFC Papers, FB194, Evelyn Palmer to Karl Marx, May 5, 1941, and NYC-AFC to Helen Milas, June 11, 1941; AFC Papers, FB201, Eunice Armstrong to Mary Kipling, March 26, 1941.

8. Leland Virgil Bell, "Anatomy of a Hate Movement: The German-American Bund, 1936–41" (unpublished doctor's dissertation, West Virginia University, 1968), pp. 249–59; Flynn Papers, FB21, Flynn, "Notes on Formation," p. 10.

9. Personal letter from Wayne S. Cole, February 25, 1973, citing Flynn to Cole, August 6, 1947.

10. AFC Papers, FB264, Flynn to Wood, June 5, 1941; Flynn Papers, FB21, Flynn, "Notes on Formation," pp. 8–16, and Schnibbe to Flynn, April 1942, p. 89.

11. Burton K. Wheeler, *Yankee from the West* (Garden City, N.Y.: Doubleday & Co., 1962), p. 29; Sarles, "A Story of America First," p. 334.

12. Personal interview with Robert L. Bliss, New York City, March 15, 1973; John Roy Carlson (Avedis Derounian), *UnderCover* (New York: E. P. Dutton, 1943), pp. 481–82, citing Edward Atwell; AFC Papers, FB17, Joseph Boldt to V. A. Cusack, April 21, 1941; Morris Burns Stanley, "The America First Committee: A Study in Recent American Non-Interventionism" (unpublished master's thesis, Emory University, 1941), p. 320, citing personal interview with Paul Killiam, March 20, 1942.

13. Stanley, "The America First Committee," p. 321, citing personal interview with Norman Thomas, March 20, 1942.

14. *Ibid.*, pp. 320–21, citing personal interview with Edwin Webster, March 23, 1942.

15. "Crash Landing," *Newsweek*, February 23, 1942, pp. 28–29; Flynn Papers, FB21, Flynn, "Notes on Formation," pp. 15–16; "The Trial of Laura Ingalls," *Nation*, Febrary 21, 1942, p. 206; see also Michael Sayers and Albert Kahn, *Sabotage! The Secret War Against America* (New York: Harper & Brothers, 1942), pp. 209–15; *New York Times*, February 11, 1942.

16. H. Montgomery Hyde, *Room 3603: The Story of the British Intelligence Center in New York During WWII* (New York: Farrar & Straus, 1962), pp. 89–91.

17. *New York Times*, May 22, 1941, p. 10; AFC Papers, FB287, Boldt to Bliss, May 1941; Sarles, "A Story of America First," p. 334.

18. AFC Papers, FB17, Boldt to V. A. Cusack, April 21, 1941; AFC Papers, FB286, Boldt to Schnibbe, September 23, 1941.

19. Wayne S. Cole, *America First: The Battle Against Intervention, 1940–41* (Madison: University of Wisconsin Press, 1953), p. 135.

20. AFC Papers, FB59, Chester Bowles to Robert D. Stuart, and Stuart to Bowles, May 13, 1941, and Dorothy D. Bromley to Stuart, May 14, 1941.

21. William Benton to Richard Ketchum, October 1972 (files of Robert L. Bliss, New York City).

22. Sarles, "A Story of America First," p. 335.

23. Flynn Papers, FB21, Flynn, "Notes on Formation," p. 9.

24. AFC Papers, FB285, Stuart to Flynn, December 11, 1940; Sarles, "A Story of America First," p. 119; Charles Lindbergh, *The Wartime Journals of Charles Lindbergh* (New York: Harcourt Brace Jovanovich, 1970), pp. 487–92.

25. Geoffrey Smith, *To Save a Nation: American Countersubversives, The New Deal, and the Coming of WWII* (New York: Basic Books, 1973), pp. 163–80.

26. Flynn Papers, FB21, Flynn to Lawrence Gould, interview, October 10, 1941, and Flynn, "Notes on Formation," p. 8; Norman Thomas Papers, New York City Public Library, FB37, Thomas to Dorothy Thompson, February 24, 1941; see also AFC Papers, FB29, Keep America Out of War Congress Press Release, February 26, 1941.

27. Flynn Papers, FB21, Sidney Hertzberg to Wood and Stuart, February 18, 1941;

AFC Papers, FB65, Nathan Alexander to Stuart, March 8, 1941; AFC Papers, FB17, Fice Mork to Bliss, March 13, 1941; Flynn Papers, FB21, Flynn to Hertzberg, March 5, 1941.

28. *New York Times,* February 21, 1941, p. 7.
29. Thomas Papers, FB 37, Thomas to D. Thompson, February 24, 1941; see also AFC Papers, FB29, KAOWC Press Release, February 26, 1941.
30. Flynn Papers, FB21, Flynn, "Notes on Formation," pp. 8–9; AFC Papers, FB291, Webster to Stuart, June 18, 1941; see also Sarles, "A Story of America First," p. 333.
31. For additional examples of criticisms of NYC-AFC rally crowds, see: Flynn Papers, FB21, Kenneth Birkhead to Flynn, April 25, 1941; *New York Times,* May 25, 1941, III, p. 3, and May 26, 1941, p. 12.
32. Lindbergh, *Wartime Journals,* pp. 476–77, 493–94, 532, 538, 551–52.
33. AFC Papers, FB55, Wood to Flynn, May 20, 1941; Lindbergh, *Wartime Journals,* pp. 493–94; Carlson, *UnderCover,* pp. 251–53; see also AFC Papers, FB291, Miss Janet Fairbank to Mrs. Janet Fairbank, May 1941; Sarles, "A Story of America First," p. 333.
34. AFC Papers, FB284, Stuart to Archibald Naugle, January 30, 1941.
35. Sarles, "A Story of America First," pp. 363–64. For a complete discussion of the strong and unique interventionist pressures in New York, see chap. 2.
36. AFC Papers, FB55, Flynn to Wood, March 5, 1941.
37. *New York Times,* March 3, 1941, p. 8.
38. *Ibid.,* March 17, 1941, p. 16.
39. *Ibid.,* March 24, 1941, p. 16.
40. AFC Papers, FB285, Hertzberg to Lester Markel, March 31, 1941.
41. AFC Papers, FB212, clipping from *New York Daily News,* October 22, 1941.
42. *New York Times,* March 12, 1941, p. 15.
43. AFC Papers, FB291, Wood to Louis J. Taber, March 29, 1941.
44. Amos R. E. Pinchot Papers, Library of Congress, Washington, D.C., FB69, Arthur H. Sulzberger to Pinchot, April 28, 1941; *New York Times,* March 12, 1941, p. 15; see also Sarles, "A Story of America First," pp. 339–40.
45. Flynn Papers, FB17, John Dewey to Flynn, March 17, 1941, and Flynn to Dewey, March 19, 1941.
46. Flynn Papers, FB17, Dewey to Flynn, March 21, 1941.
47. *New York Times,* May 9, 1941, p. 12; see also AFC Papers, FB55, AFC National Committee Bulletin, no. 257, May 15, 1941; Bell, "The German-American Bund," pp. 249–50.
48. Flynn Papers, FB21, S. H. Hauck to Flynn, July 25, 1941, and Flynn to Hauck, September 4, 1941; see also Sarles, "A Story of America First," p. 343.
49. Flynn Papers, FB21, Dorothy D. Bromley to Flynn, August 2, 1941, citing Wood to *Social Justice* and Lulu Wheeler to *Social Justice,* July 1941.
50. AFC Papers, FB297, clipping from the *Call,* August 16, 1941.
51. Thomas Papers, FB39, Thomas to Stuart, August 8, and 18, 1941.
52. Flynn Papers, FB21, D. D. Bromley to Flynn, August 2, 1941, and Flynn to Bromley, August 15, 1941.
53. *New York Times,* July 11, 1941, p. 3; AFC Papers, FB281, clipping from *Chicago Tribune,* August 20, 1941; *New York Times,* June 23, 1941, p. 2; see also Lindbergh, *Wartime Journals,* p. 538; Flynn Papers, FB21, "Notes on Formation," p. 11.
54. *New York Times,* April 14, 1941, p. 19.
55. Pinchot Papers, FB87(162), *AFC Bulletin,* vol. 1, no. 15, September 6, 1941.
56. *New York Times,* May 11, 1941, p. 34; Thomas Papers, FB38, Thomas to Wood, June 10, 1941; *New York Times,* June 18, 1941, p. 16. For an additional example of unpleasant action against the NYC-AFC in the summer of 1941, see AFC

Papers, FB212, "Island Park AFC Press Release," September 7, 1941; Flynn Papers, FB21, "Notes on Formation," p. 10.
57. *New York Times,* June 18, 1941, p. 16.
58. Pinchot Papers, FB87(162), *AFC Bulletin,* vol. 1, no. 15, September 6, 1941.
59. Flynn Papers, FB32, Flynn, Diary, August 30, 1941.
60. Flynn Papers, FB21, Flynn to Wood, October 22, 1941, and Flynn to Mrs. D. B. Armstrong, January 6, 1942; see also Richard C. Frey, "John T. Flynn and the United States in Crisis, 1928–50" (unpublished doctor's dissertation, University of Oregon, 1969), chap. 8.
61. AFC Papers, FB1, A. G. Keeler to Wood, September 16, 1941.
62. For a complete discussion of Flynn's investigation, see chap. 8.
63. Lindbergh, *Wartime Journals,* pp. 437, 537, 554.
64. *Ibid.,* Lindbergh to William Jovanovich, December 18, 1969, Introduction, p. xiii.
65. Lowell R. Fleischer, "Charles A. Lindbergh and Isolationism, 1939–41" (unpublished doctor's dissertation, University of Connecticut, 1963), pp. 109–14, citing Lindbergh, Speech, September 14, 1939; "Lindbergh for the Record," *Scribner's Commentator,* August 1941, pp. 8–13.
66. "Lindbergh for the Record," *Scribner's Commentator,* August 1941, pp. 8–13.
67. Lindbergh, *Wartime Journals,* pp. 478–79.
68. *Ibid.,* 478–79, 599.
69. *New York Times,* April 24, 1941, p. 1, and May 24, 1941, p. 1; Lindbergh, *Wartime Journals,* pp. 498–99.
70. Lindbergh, "We Cannot Win This War for England," *Vital Speeches,* 7, May 1, 1941, pp. 424–26.
71. Lindbergh, *Wartime Journals,* p. 452, and several other entries regarding the press.
72. Thomas Papers, FB35, Thomas to Lindbergh, August 9, 1940, and FB38, Thomas to Wood, May 12, 1941, and FB39, Thomas to Wood, September 11, 1941; see also Bernard Johnpoll, *Pacifist's Progress: Norman Thomas and the Decline of American Socialism* (Chicago: Quadrangle Books, 1970), pp. 230–31.
73. Flynn Papers, FB18, Lindbergh to Flynn, May 2, 1941.
74. AFC Papers, FB285, Hertzberg to Stuart, September 28, 1940.
75. Sarles, "A Story of America First," pp. 507–10; William Benton to Richard Ketchum, October 1972, files of Robert L. Bliss, New York City; Lindbergh, *Wartime Journals,* pp. 471–73.
76. AFC Papers, FB1, Mrs. Thornton K. Brown (for NYC-AFC) to Harry Himmel, June 26, 1941; Lindbergh, *Wartime Journals,* p. 440.
77. Dale Kramer, "Verne Marshall of Iowa," *New Republic,* January 13, 1941, pp. 50–51; Justus Doenecke, "Verne Marshall's Leadership of the No Foreign War Committee," *Annals of Iowa* 40 (winter 1973): 1153–72; Flynn Papers, FB21, Schnibbe to Flynn, April 1942, p. 68; personal interview with Robert D. Stuart, Chicago, August 14, 1973.
78. Flynn Papers, FB21, Schnibbe to Flynn, April 1942, pp. 69–71.
79. *Ibid.,* pp. 72–73.
80. AFC Papers, FB285, Stuart to Flynn, December 2, 1940, and Flynn to Stuart, December 1940; for more information on Payson's and Milbank's contributions to the AFC, see chap. 3.
81. AFC Papers, FB59, Stuart to Dorothy Detzer, February 10, 1941; AFC Papers, FB285, Stuart, Memo, February 25, 1941; Sarles, "A Story of America First," p. 106.
82. Flynn Papers, FB21, Schnibbe to Flynn, April 1942, p. 66, citing Lindbergh to Stuart, October 1940; Lindbergh, *Wartime Journals,* pp. 426–28; *New York Times,* December 19, 1940; see also Doenecke, "Verne Marshall's Leadership," p. 1167.

83. Lindbergh, *Wartime Journals*, pp. 428–32, 440; Flynn Papers, FB21, Schnibbe to Flynn, April 1942, pp. 72–73; Doenecke, "Verne Marshall's Leadership," pp. 1166–67; *New York Times*, December 31, 1940; see also AFC Papers, FB33, clippings from *PM*, December 31, 1940, and January 6, 1941, and *St. Louis Post-Dispatch*, December 31, 1940.

84. In reality, a stronger link than Lindbergh existed between the NYC-AFC and the NFWC. At the time of the NFWC's dissolution in April 1941, the NYC-AFC quietly acquired the former group's mailing lists and its director of mailings and money receipts, John Springer (AFC Papers, FB284, Webster to Wood, April 19, 1941, and Wood to Webster, April 30, 1941). However, Springer was young, idealistic, and not personally anti-Semitic or profascist (Flynn Papers, FB21, Flynn to Herbert Peele, April 6, 1941). Also, the names garnered from the NFWC mailing lists were carefully screened by the NYC-AFC to prevent subversive elements from being circularized or invited into the America First movement.

85. Lindbergh, *Wartime Journals*, pp. 486–92, 536–38.

86. *Public Opinion Quarterly* 5, no. 3 (fall 1941): 496.

87. AFC Papers, FB57, Lindbergh, "Who Are the War Agitators?" September 11, 1941; see also AFC Papers, FB285.

88. *Ibid.*

89. AFC Papers, FB1, D. D. Bromley to Wood, September 14, 1941.

90. Mark Lincoln Chadwin, *The Warhawks* (Chapel Hill: University of North Carolina Press, 1968), p. 211, citing Wendell Willkie, September 1941; Sarles, "A Story of America First," p. 353, citing Stephen Early; for more negative comments from interventionists regarding the Des Moines speech, see *New York Times*, September 15, 1941; AFC Papers, FB1, Reinhold Niebuhr to Flynn, and Niebuhr to Wood, September 15, 1941, and Raymond G. Swing and Ernest Angell to Wood, September 25, 1941, and editorial clipping from *New York Journal-American*, September 14, 1941; Flynn Papers, FB21, Joseph Goldstein to Fiorello La Guardia, September 29, 1941, and William Schneur to Flynn, October 13, 1941; AFC Papers, FB200, Andrew Leredu to Flynn, September 26, 1941, and many other examples.

91. Frey, "John T. Flynn," chap. 7; Flynn Papers, FB21, Ernest Wheeler to Flynn, September 24, 1941, and Charles Fleischer to Flynn, October 10, and 17, 1941; AFC Papers, FB163, Thomas McCarter to Wood, September 29, 1941, and Kathryn Lewis to Stuart, October 10, 1941; AFC Papers, FB42, "Minutes of the AFC National Committee Meeting," September 18, 1941.

92. Thomas Papers, FB39, Thomas to Emanual Muravchik, September 16, 1941, and Thomas to Stuart, September 12, and 23, 1941.

93. For further repudiations of the Des Moines speech by noninterventionists, see AFC Papers, FB61, Mary Hillyer to Stuart, September 17, 1941; Thomas Papers, FB39, Frederick Libby to Stuart, September 22, 1941; Flynn Papers, several references.

94. AFC Papers, FB284, Flynn to Wood, June 5, 1941.

95. Flynn Papers, FB21, Flynn to Lindbergh, September 15, 1941.

96. AFC Papers, FB284, Flynn to Wood, and Flynn to Stuart, September 12, 1941; see also Flynn Papers, FB21.

97. Lindbergh, *Wartime Journals*, p. 540.

98. AFC Papers, FB5, Marie Hennessey to Wood, September 16, 1941.

99. AFC Papers, FB201, Pinchot to S. Stanwood Menken, October 4, 1941.

100. Lindbergh, *Wartime Journals*, pp. 539, 541–42. For further praise of the Des Moines speech by America Firsters, see Flynn Papers, FB21, Gregory Mason to Flynn, September 18, 1941, and several other references; AFC Papers, FB5, Swim to Wood, September 17, 1941, and several other references; William Benton to Richard Ketchum, October 1972, citing Wood, September 1941, personal files of Robert L. Bliss, New York City.

101. Flynn Papers, FB21, Flynn to Mort Lewis, September 17, 1941.
102. Flynn Papers, FB32, Flynn, Diary, September 19, 1941; Thomas Papers, FB39, Mrs. Janet Fairbank, to Thomas, September 24, 1941.
103. AFC Papers, FB291, Chester Bowles to Wood, September 16, 1941, and Bowles to Stuart, September 19, 1941; Thomas Papers, FB39, Thomas to Mrs. Janet Fairbank, September 27, 1941; AFC Papers, FB291, Thomas to Stuart, September 29, 1941.
104. Flynn Papers, FB21, clipping from *PM*, September 19, 1941, p. 1.
105. Flynn Papers, FB32, Flynn, Diary, October 8, 1941; see also Flynn Papers, FB21, Flynn, "Notes on Formation," p. 14.
106. AFC Papers, FB286, Boldt to Schnibbe, September 23, 1941.
107. Cole, *America First*, p. 117.
108. Flynn Papers, FB21, Flynn to Wood, October 13, 1941; personal interview with Robert L. Bliss, March 15, 1974; Sarles, "A Story of America First," p. 70.
109. AFC Papers, FB64, Flynn to Stuart, August 4, 1941.
110. Flynn Papers, FB21, Flynn, "Notes on Formation," p. 14.
111. AFC Papers, FB5, Richards H. Emerson to Wood, September 17, 1941; see also Flynn Papers, FB21, William S. Thomas to Charles Fleischer, October 23, 1941.
112. Flynn Papers, FB21, Flynn to Wood, October 13, 1941; personal interview with Robert Bliss, March 15, 1974; Lindbergh, *Wartime Journals*, p. 543; AFC Papers, FB62, Pinchot to Stuart, October 3, 1941.
113. Flynn Papers, FB21, Flynn to Wood, October 13, 1941.
114. AFC Papers, FB64, Stuart to Wood, "Miscellaneous Problems Concerning Friday's Meeting," November 27, 1941.
115. Lindbergh, *Wartime Journals*, pp. 568, 597–600.
116. *Ibid.*, pp. 587, 597–600.
117. AFC Papers, FB284, Flynn to Wood, January 7, 1942, and February 25, 1942, and Swim to Wood, March 20, 1942, and June 12, 1942, and Webster to Wood, May 20, 1942.
118. AFC Papers, FB285, Flynn to Wood, May 11, 1942.
119. AFC Papers, FB285, Flynn to Wood, May 18, and 25, 1942, and June 1, 1942, and Wood to Flynn, June 3, 1942, and Webster to Wood, June 12, 1942. For a complete discussion of the charges and rumors against the AFC that circulated during World War II, see chap. 9.
120. For a complete discussion of Flynn's conspiracy theory, see chap. 8.

CHAPTER 8

1. John T. Flynn Papers, University of Oregon Library, Eugene, FB16, Flynn, Speech, December 18, 1940.
2. America First Committee Papers, Hoover Institution on War, Revolution and Peace, Stanford, Calif., FB28, clipping from *Chicago Daily News*, December 20, 1940.
3. Flynn Papers, FB16, Flynn, Speech to Washington, D.C., AFC, February 2, 1941.
4. Philip H. Gibbs, *Now It Can Be Told* (Garden City, N.Y.: Garden City Press, 1920), pts. 7, 8; Harry E. Barnes, *Genesis of the World War* (New York: Alfred A. Knopf, 1926), p. 645.
5. Richard C. Frey, Jr., "John T. Flynn and the United States in Crisis, 1928–50" (unpublished doctor's dissertation, University of Oregon, 1969), chap. 5.
6. Flynn, "Radio, Intervention's Trump," *Scribner's Commentator*, April 1941, p.

48, partially citing Sidney Rogerson and Liddell Hart, *Propaganda in the Next War* (New York: Garland Publishing Co., 1972).

7. Flynn, *The Roosevelt Myth*, rev. ed. (New York: Devin-Adair, 1956), p. 137. For a complete discussion of Flynn's views of Roosevelt's and Wall Street's motives for war, see chap. 2 of the current study.

8. Flynn, "Plain Economics: The Multi-Million Dollar British War Propaganda Budget," *Washington Daily News*, June 17, 1940; see also Flynn, "Other People's Money," *New Republic*, May 27, 1940, p. 728; AFC Papers, FB37, *Uncensored*, no. 92 and no. 93, July 5 and 12, 1941.

9. Flynn Papers, FB16, Flynn, Speech, April 21, 1941.

10. Flynn Papers, FB16, Flynn, Speech, February 1, 1941, partially citing Winston Churchill.

11. AFC Papers, FB59, Chester Bowles to Robert D. Stuart, July 15, 1941.

12. Amos R. E. Pinchot Papers, Library of Congress, Washington, D.C., FB70, Pinchot to Mrs. Charles Whalen, July 1, 1941.

13. Norman Thomas Papers, New York City Public Library, FB40, Thomas to Morris Cohen, November 4, 1941; Bernard Johnpoll, *Pacifist's Progress: Norman Thomas and the Decline of American Socialism* (Chicago: Quadrangle Books, 1970), p. 231; *New York Times*, April 24, 1941, p. 1; William Langer and S. Everett Gleason, *The Undeclared War, 1940–41* (New York: Harper & Brothers, 1953), p. 747.

14. AFC Papers, FB291, Miss Janet Fairbank to Mrs. Janet Fairbank, May 1941.

15. AFC Papers, FB286, Sidney Hertzberg to Stuart, November 12, 1940.

16. AFC Papers, FB16, Park Chamberlain to Robert E. Wood, December 16, 1940, and Robert Bliss (for Wood) to Chamberlain, December 28, 1940.

17. Flynn Papers, FB21, Harry C. Schnibbe to Flynn, April 14, 1942, p. 84, citing Stuart to Charles A. Lindbergh, September 30, 1940.

18. AFC Papers, FB65, Flynn to Page Hufty, July 30, 1941.

19. Charles A. Lindbergh, *The Wartime Journals of Charles A. Lindbergh* (New York: Harcourt Brace Jovanovich, 1970), p. 517; Flynn Papers, FB21, Flynn to R. K. Hines, August 5, 1941, and Flynn to Wood, August 8, 1941, and Flynn to NYC-AFC Executive Committee, September 16, 1941; AFC Papers, FB64, Flynn to Stuart, August 4, 1941; Flynn Papers, FB21, Flynn to Burton K. Wheeler, August 6, 1941, and Flynn to Nye, August 29, 1941.

20. Flynn Papers, FB21, Flynn to Wood, August 8, 1941, and Flynn to Miss Bettinger, July 1941, and Flynn to Nye, July 1941.

21. Ruth Sarles, "A Story of America First" (unpublished manuscript, Hoover Institution, Stanford, Calif., 1942), p. 377.

22. AFC Papers, FB61, David Munro to Stuart, May 16, 1941; Flynn Papers, FB21, Flynn, Opening Statement to Testimony Before Senate Subcommittee Investigating the Motion Picture Industry, September 11, 1941, and "Mike" to Flynn, September 25, 1941.

23. Flynn Papers, FB21, Flynn to Wood, August 8, 1941; see also Flynn Papers, FB21, Flynn to Wheeler, August 6, 1941, and Flynn to Nye, August 29, 1941; Lindbergh, *Wartime Journals*, p. 524.

24. Gerald Nye (written by Flynn), "War Propaganda," *Vital Speeches*, 7, September 15, 1941, pp. 720–23; AFC Papers, FB53, clipping from *Chicago Tribune*, September 10, 1941. For a complete list of the movies scored by Nye, see Appendix E.

25. Nye, "War Propaganda," pp. 722–23.

26. Flynn Papers, FB32, Flynn, Diary, August 1, 1941; Flynn Papers, FB21, Flynn to R. K. Hines, August 5, 1941; AFC Papers, FB53, clipping from *Chicago Tribune*, September 2, 1941; see also AFC Papers, FB37, *Uncensored*, no. 76, March 15, 1941. Previous requests for investigatory funds by Senators Wheeler, Bennett C. Clark, and Harry Truman were either denied or, in the case of Truman, cut substantially. Noninterventionists interpreted these denials as deliberate sup-

pression of their views by administration stalwarts on the Senate Rules, and Audit and Control Committees.

27. Flynn Papers, FB21, Flynn to D. Worth Clark, September 17, 1941.
28. AFC Papers, FB89, AFC National Committee Bulletin no. 453, July 30, 1941; see also Sarles, "A Story of America First," p. 235; AFC Papers, FB285, Wood to Stanton Griffis, October 31, 1941.
29. AFC Papers, FB53, clippings from the *Chicago Tribune,* September 9, 10, 1941.
30. Flynn Papers, FB21, Flynn, Opening Statement to Testimony Before Senate Subcommittee Investigating the Motion Picture Industry, September 11, 1941.
31. Flynn Papers, FB21, Flynn to D. Worth Clark, September 17, 1941; AFC Papers, FB284, Flynn to Stuart, September 12, 1941.
32. AFC Papers, FB53, clipping from *Washington Times-Herald,* September 17, 1941.
33. AFC Papers, FB53, clippings from *Chicago Tribune,* September 24–27, 1941, partially citing Darryl F. Zanuck.
34. AFC Papers, FB89, AFC National Committee Bulletin no. 627, October 14, 1941; AFC Papers, FB53, clipping from *Chicago Tribune,* September 29, 1941, citing Nye; "America First Roughhouse," *Life,* October 20, 1941, p. 41, citing Wheeler.
35. Lowell Mellett, "Government Propaganda," *Atlantic Monthly,* September 1941, pp. 311–13; see also "Censorship in the Offing," *Time,* February 17, 1941, pp. 52 –57.
36. Flynn Papers, FB21, clipping from *New York World-Telegram,* October 19, 1940, citing Charlie Chaplin.
37. AFC Papers, FB53, clipping from *Chicago Tribune,* September 10, 1941, citing Louis de Rochemont. Henry Luce, strong interventionist, was dominant in the "March of Time" company.
38. AFC Papers, FB53, clipping from *Chicago Tribune,* September 10, 1941.
39. AFC Papers, FB287, Richard A. Moore, Confidential Memo, August 28, 1941.
40. Douglas Waples, "Press, Radio and Film in the National Emergency," *Public Opinion Quarterly* 5, no. 3 (fall 1941): 463–69.
41. Flynn Papers, FB21, Rosalie Gordon, Confidential Memo, January 20, 1941.
42. Flynn Papers, FB21, Memo, no date. One such radio drama, a serial titled "Helen Holden, Government Girl," portrayed a dedicated, patriotic interventionist in her daily battles with antiwar "obstructionists." Flynn deeply resented this program, carried unsponsored by WOR.
43. AFC Papers, FB65, Flynn to Stuart, July 18, 1941. In June Flynn refused to participate in a radio debate on "Round Table" because he believed that "the Round Table's conducting its own private little war" (AFC Papers, FB65, Benson Inge [for Flynn] to Sherman Dryer, June 1941).
44. Harold N. Graves, Jr., "Propaganda by Short-Wave: London Calling America," *Public Opinion Quarterly* 5, no. 1 (March 1941): 38–51, partially citing Leslie Howard.
45. Flynn Papers, FB21, Flynn to David Sarnoff, March 3, 1941.
46. Flynn Papers, FB21, Flynn to George Feld, March 17, 1941; AFC Papers, FB5, March Richelson, NYC-AFC Report, March 6, 1941. Other prowar radio commentators that especially bothered Flynn were Raymond Gram Swing, Alexander Wollcott, and Gabriel Heatter.
47. Sarles, "A Story of America First," p. 112.
48. Flynn Papers, FB20, Thomas to Flynn and Stuart, November 27, 1941; see also Thomas Papers, FB88, Thomas to Gerald L. K. Smith, May 9, 1941.
49. AFC Papers, FB29, clipping from *Washington Daily Star,* February 22, 1941.
50. Flynn, "Radio: Intervention's Trump," *Scribner's Commentator,* April 1941, pp. 45–49.
51. AFC Papers, FB65, Stuart to Flynn, May 30, 1941, and Flynn to Stuart, June 30, 1941, and Stuart to Flynn, July 2, 1941.

52. AFC Papers, FB53, clipping from *Chicago Tribune,* September 10, 1941.
53. AFC Papers, FB288, Flynn, Press Release, October 29, 1941; see also Sarles, "A Story of America First," p. 113.
54. Flynn Papers, FB21, NYC-AFC Executive Committee to James Lawrence, October 29, 1941.
55. Flynn Papers, FB21, Niles Trammell to Flynn, October 27, 1941.
56. Sarles, "A Story of America First," p. 131; see also Flynn Papers, FB21, Flynn to Hulbert Taft, November 5, 1941.
57. Vernon McKenzie, "Treatment of War Themes in Magazine Fiction," *Public Opinion Quarterly* 5, no. 2 (summer 1941): 227–32.
58. James S. Twohey, "An Analysis of Newspaper Opinion and War Issues," *Public Opinion Quarterly* 5, no. 3 (fall 1941): 448–55.
59. Flynn Papers, FB21.
60. Lindbergh, *Wartime Journals,* 429; AFC Papers, FB 67, Memo regarding *Saturday Evening Post,* May 28, 1941.
61. Lindbergh, *Wartime Journals,* pp. 511, 547; Flynn Papers, FB32, Flynn, Diary, June 27, 1941; see also Lindbergh, *Wartime Journals,* pp. 513, 544–45.
62. Flynn Papers, FB32, Flynn, Diary, June 27, and August 3, and 30, and October 8, and 17, 1941. Even Stuart had doubts about the accuracy of newspaper reports on the Russo-German war (AFC Papers, FB59, Stuart to Bowles, October 11, 1941).
63. Lindbergh, *Wartime Journals,* pp. 511, 513, 547.
64. *Ibid.,* p. 560.
65. *Ibid.,* p. 526.
66. AFC Papers, FB17, Wood to Flynn, February 26, 1941.
67. Personal interview with Robert L. Bliss, New York City, March 15, 1974; AFC Papers, FB291, Wood to *PM,* May 28, 1941; AFC Papers, FB3, Bliss to Kenneth Crawford, June 14, 1941.
68. Flynn Papers, FB21, Flynn to Stuart, September 12, 1941.
69. AFC Papers, FB185, Flynn to All NYC-AFC Chapter Committee Members, September 15, 1941.
70. AFC Papers, FB163, Stuart to Thomas N. McCarter, October 4, 1941.
71. Flynn Papers, FB21, Flynn to Lawrence Gould, October 15, 1941.
72. James J. Martin, *American Liberalism and World Politics, 1931–41* (New York: Devin-Adair, 1964), p. 1271, citing *New Republic,* June 2, 1941, p. 744.
73. "America First Roughhouse," *Life,* October 20, 1941, p. 41.
74. AFC Papers, FB185, Bowles to Flynn, October 25, 1941; Flynn Papers, FB17, John Haynes Holmes to Flynn, December 11, 1940.
75. Martin, *American Liberalism,* p. 1156, citing Oswald Garrison Villard, "Valedictory," *Nation,* June 29, 1940.
76. "Editor's Note," *New Republic,* November 18, 1940, p. 677; see also Martin, *American Liberalism,* pp. 10, 1157–58, 1232.
77. "Editorial," *New Republic,* October 21, 1940, p. 541; "Editor's Note," *New Republic,* November 11, 1940, p. 660. For further examples, see "Editor's Note," *New Republic,* August 5, 1940, p. 188; "Editorial," *New Republic,* September 9, 1940, p. 335.
78. Flynn Papers, FB19, Flynn to Bruce Bliven, November 8, 1940.
79. Flynn, "Mr. Flynn Speaks for Himself," *New Republic,* February 3, 1941, pp. 148–49.
80. Frey, "John T. Flynn," chap. 8; Flynn Papers, FB32, Flynn, Diary, October 8, 1941. The Scripps-Howard newspapers also dropped antiwar professor and KAOWC leader Harry Elmer Barnes during this period (Flynn Papers, FB17, John Haynes Holmes to Flynn, December 11, 1940).
81. Wayne Cole, *America First: The Battle Against Interventionism, 1940–41* (Madison: University of Wisconsin Press, 1953), p. 133; Leland V. Bell, *In Hitler's Shadow* (Port Washington, N.Y.: Kennikat Press, 1973).

82. Personal letter from Professor Justus D. Doenecke (New College, Sarasota, Florida), September 24, 1973; Thomas Papers, FB40, Thomas to Harriet Connor Brown, October 27, 1941.
83. Flynn Papers, FB21, Flynn to Wood, October 13, 1941; see also Flynn to Dorothy D. Bromley, August 15, 1941; Frey, "John T. Flynn," chap. 8; Flynn, *The Road Ahead* (New York: Devin-Adair, 1949). For a complete discussion of the later changes in Flynn's writing career, see chap. 9 of the current study.
84. Elliott Roosevelt, ed., *F.D.R., His Personal Letters, 1928–45* (New York: Duell, Sloane, & Pearce, 1950), vol. 2, p. 904, citing Franklin D. Roosevelt to Wilbur Cross, July 7, 1939. The Flynn article that angered Roosevelt at the time of this letter was "Mr. Hopkins and Mr. Roosevelt" (*Yale Review* 28, no. 4 [June 1939]: 667–79).
85. Sarles, "A Story of America First," pp. 424–25, citing Flynn; see also Flynn Papers, FB21, Flynn, Memo: "On Overall Planning for Interventionist Organizations," April 1942.
86. For a complete listing of the committees on both sides of the Great Debate, see Appendix F.
87. Morris Burns Stanley, "The America First Committee: A Study in Recent American Non-Interventionism" (unpublished master's thesis, Emory University, 1942), p. 31, citing Gallup poll, November 1941.
88. Sarles, "A Story of America First," chap. 10.
89. Walter Johnson, *The Battle Against Isolation* (Chicago: University of Chicago Press, 1944), pp. 39–52.
90. *Ibid.,* p. 181.
91. *Ibid.,* pp. 181–82, citing William Allen White to Roy Howard, December 20, 1940.
92. Flynn Papers, FB16, Flynn, Speech to Washington, D.C., AFC, February 2, 1941.
93. Johnson, *The Battle Against Isolation,* pp. 187–91; see also AFC Papers, FB29, *Anti-War News Service,* no. 17, January 3, 1941.
94. Mark Lincoln Chadwin, *The Warhawks* (Chapel Hill: University of North Carolina Press, 1968), pp. 156–58; Sarles, "A Story of America First," p. 190; AFC Papers, FB284, AFC *Washington Newsletter,* no. 19, April 15, 1941.
95. Johnson, *The Battle Against Isolation,* p. 91, partially citing William Allen White.
96. Chadwin, *The Warhawks,* pp. 201–6; see also pp. 54, 110, 113, 126, 129–31.
97. Sarles, "A Story of America First," pp. 379, 410–11; Langer and Gleason, *The Undeclared War,* p. 443.
98. AFC Papers, FB65, Flynn to Stuart, May 1941, and Stuart to Flynn, May 19, 1941.
99. Sarles, "A Story of America First," p. 411.
100. AFC Papers, FB37, *Uncensored,* no. 76, March 15, 1941.
101. Sarles, "A Story of America First," pp. 424–25, citing Flynn; see also Flynn Papers, FB21, Flynn, Memo: "On Overall Planning for Interventionist Organizations," April 1942.
102. *New York Times,* February 23, 1941, p. 24.
103. Personal interviews with Rosalie M. Gordon (New York City), April 23, 1973, and Robert L. Bliss (New York City), March 15, 1974.
104. Flynn Papers, FB21, Flynn to Leo Birkhead, April 23, 1941.
105. AFC Papers, FB37, *Uncensored,* no. 94, July 19, 1941.
106. Lindbergh, *Wartime Journals,* pp. 551–52.
107. H. Montgomery Hyde, *Room 3603: The Story of the British Intelligence Center in New York During WWII* (New York: Farrar & Straus, 1962), pp. 72–74.
108. *Ibid.*
109. AFC Papers, FB184, NYC-AFC Staff Memo: "October 30 Rally Plans," October 1941.

110. Sarles, "A Story of America First," pp. 424–25, citing Flynn; see also Flynn Papers, FB21, Flynn, Memo: "On Overall Planning for Interventionist Organizations," April 1942.
111. For a complete discussion of Flynn's later years, see chap. 9.

CHAPTER 9

1. America First Committee Papers, Hoover Institution on War, Revolution and Peace, Stanford, Calif., File Box 284, John T. Flynn to Robert E. Wood, January 7, 1942; see also John T. Flynn Papers, University of Oregon, Eugene, FB20, Flynn to Bailey Stortz, October 19, 1942.
2. John Roy Carlson (in reality Avedis Derounian), *UnderCover* (New York: E. P. Dutton & Co., 1943).
3. AFC Papers, FB28, Flynn, "Record of the Speeches and Debate Between John T. Flynn and Dr. Reinhold Niebuhr on America's Town Meeting of the Air," May 8, 1941.
4. AFC Papers, FB215, Flynn, Radio Speech, December 17, 1941.
5. Flynn Papers, FB18, Flynn to Clarence Buddington Kelland, January 6, 1942; see also Richard C. Frey, "John T. Flynn and the United States in Crisis, 1928–50" (unpublished doctor's dissertation, University of Oregon, 1969), chap. 8.
6. Flynn Papers, FB19, Flynn to Bessie Simon, November 18, 1943.
7. Flynn Papers, FB18, Flynn to C. B. Kelland, January 6, 1942; see also Frey, "John T. Flynn," chap. 8.
8. Flynn Papers, FB21, Thomas Connolly (in collaboration with Flynn), "Keep the Elections Free," May 1942.
9. Flynn, "That Post-War Federal Debt," *Harper's* magazine, July 1942, pp. 180–88. For a complete explanation of Flynn's definition of fascism, see chap. 2.
10. Flynn Papers, FB32, Flynn, "Kidding the People on Paying for the War," October 1943, and Harry Byrd (in reality Flynn), "We Owe It to Ourselves," February 17, 1944; Flynn Papers, FB24, Flynn, "Government Debt," 1945; Ralph Owen Brewster (in reality Flynn), "Let's Not Be Suckers Again," *American* magazine, January 1945, pp. 24–25, 96–98.
11. Flynn, *As We Go Marching* (New York: Doubleday & Co., 1944).
12. For an example of the type of human-interest story that *Reader's Digest* accepted from Flynn, see Flynn, "Detroit's Fighting Milkman," *Reader's Digest*, September 1942, pp. 57–60.
13. Frey, "John T. Flynn," chap. 8.
14. Flynn Papers, FB32, Flynn, "What Is Back of the Ball Resolution?" March 6, 1943; *New York Herald-Tribune*, November 2, 1943.
15. Flynn Papers, FB32, Flynn, "The Moscow Pact," November 1943.
16. Flynn Papers, FB25, Flynn to Paul Palmer, Memo: "What Is the President's Foreign Policy and What Is Wrong with It?" June 12, 1944; see also Flynn Papers, FB32, Flynn, "A Memo on Dumbarton Oaks," and "My Dear Friend" (form letter), April 1945; Flynn Papers, FB29, Flynn, "San Fiasco Charter," summer 1945.
17. Flynn Papers, FB29, Flynn, "Testimony Before the Senate Foreign Relations Committee in Opposition to Confirmation of the San Francisco Charter," July 13, 1945.
18. Carlson, *UnderCover*, pp. 248–60.
19. John Roy Carlson (Avedis Derounian), "Inside the America First Movement," *American Mercury*, January 1942, pp. 7–25; Albert Kahn and Michael Sayers, *Sabotage! The Secret War Against America* (New York: Harper & Brothers, 1942),

pp. 191–92.
20. Flynn Papers, FB 21, Flynn to Wood, May 4, 1942.
21. Flynn Papers, FB23, Friends of Democracy, "The Propaganda Battlefront," vol. 2, no. 17, May 31, 1944.
22. Flynn Papers, FB20, Flynn to Robert Young, November 18, 1943.
23. Flynn Papers, FB24, Flynn to Wood, January 3, 1944, and Flynn, Memo to Ike McAnally, early 1944; see also Flynn Papers, FB24, Flynn to Burton K. Wheeler, January 3, 1944; Flynn Papers, FB20, Flynn to R. Young, December 20, 1943.
24. Flynn Papers, FB24, Flynn to Wheeler, December 30, 1943.
25. For many letters pertaining to fundraising and research for the investigation of *UnderCover,* see Flynn Papers, FB24.
26. Flynn Papers, FB24, Flynn, Memo to McAnally, early 1944.
27. Flynn Papers, FB24, clipping from *Washington Times-Herald,* April 23, 1944; Flynn, "Uncovering *UnderCover:* The True Facts About the Smear Book's Odd Author."
28. Flynn Papers, FB23, Flynn to J. H. McKnight, February 29, 1944.
29. Flynn Papers, FB24, Flynn, Radio Speech, February 13, 1944, and Flynn, "Plan II," March 1944.
30. Flynn Papers, FB24, Flynn, "Plan II," March 1944.
31. Flynn Papers, FB24, clipping from *Washington Times-Herald,* April 23, 1944: Flynn, "Uncovering *UnderCover.*"
32. Frey, "John T. Flynn," chap. 8, pp.276–81.
33. Flynn Papers, FB20, Flynn to Bailey Stortz, October 19, 1942.
34. Flynn Papers, FB28, Flynn to DeWitt Wallace, October 14, 1944.
35. Flynn Papers, FB26, Flynn, Confidential Memo on Foundation for Foreign Affairs, December 1944.
36. Flynn Papers, FB26, Flynn, Memo on Foundation for Foreign Affairs, December 6, 1944.
37. Flynn Papers, FB26, Flynn, Confidential Memo on Foundation for Foreign Affairs, early 1945.
38. *Ibid.*
39. Flynn Papers, FB16, Flynn, "Government Domination of Radio," no date (sometime late wartime); Flynn Papers, FB17, Flynn, Memo on American Writers' Association, late 1946; see also James M. Cain, "Do Writers Need an AAA?" *Saturday Review of Literature,* November 16, 1946, p. 9.
40. Flynn Papers, FB29, Flynn, "Smear—A Recent Incident," January 1945.
41. Flynn Papers, FB29, Flynn, "The Smear Terror," 1947.
42. Flynn, *The Roosevelt Myth* (New York: Devin-Adair, 1948).
43. *Ibid.,* pp. 77, 286–89.
44. *Ibid.,* pp. 444–45, 426, 153.
45. *Ibid.,* pp. 82–84, 77.
46. *Ibid.,* pp. 310, 413, 319.
47. Flynn Papers, FB23, Flynn, "Why the Americans Did Not Take Berlin," May 1948.
48. Flynn Papers, FB23, Flynn to DeWitt Wallace, May 12, 1948.
49. Flynn Papers, FB32, Flynn, Diary, May 6, 1948.
50. Frey, "John T. Flynn," chap. 9.
51. Flynn, *The Road Ahead* (New York: Devin-Adair, 1949); *The Decline of the American Republic and How to Rebuild It* (New York: Devin-Adair, 1955); *While You Slept—Our Tragedy in Asia and Who Made It* (New York: Devin-Adair, 1951); *The Lattimore Story* (New York: Devin-Adair, 1953).
52. Flynn, *The Decline of the American Republic,* p. 137.
53. Frey, "John T. Flynn," chap. 9.
54. Personal interview with Thomas D. Flynn, New York City, April 25, 1973; Flynn, *The Roosevelt Myth,* rev. ed. (New York: Devin-Adair, 1956), p. 297.

55. Flynn Papers, FB21, Flynn, Statement, 1941; personal interview with T. D. Flynn, April 25, 1973; Flynn, *The Roosevelt Myth*, rev. ed., pp. 430–40.
56. *New York Times*, May 22, 1941, p. 10.
57. AFC Papers, FB285, Wood to Alice Roundy, April 16, 1942; Charles Lindbergh, *The Wartime Journals of Charles A. Lindbergh* (New York: Harcourt Brace Jovanovich, 1970), p. 869; personal interview with Robert L. Bliss, New York City, March 15, 1974.
58. AFC Papers, FB285, Wood to A. Roundy, April 16, 1942.
59. Ruth Sarles, "A Story of America First" (unpublished manuscript, Hoover Institution, Stanford, Calif., 1942), p. 535, citing Lindbergh to Wood, December 26, 1941.
60. Lindbergh, *Wartime Journals*, pp. 579–84; Henry Harley Arnold, *Global Missions* (New York: Harper & Brothers, 1949), p. 189. Lindbergh had resigned his U.S. Army Air Corps commission in April 1941 after being accused by the President of disloyalty. For a complete discussion of this incident, see chap. 5 herein.
61. Lindbergh, *Wartime Journals*, pp. 590, 600.
62. *Ibid.*, p. 593.
63. *Ibid.*, p. 597.
64. *Ibid.*, pp. 608–610, 612; *New York Times*, August 27, 1974, p. 1.
65. *Ibid.*, July 8, 1944, p. 869.
66. *Ibid.*, Lindbergh to William Jovanovich, December 18, 1969, Introduction, pp. xiii–xv.
67. Burton K. Wheeler, *Yankee from the West* (Garden City, N.Y.: Doubleday & Co., 1962), pp. 29–31.
68. Personal letter from Robert D. Stuart, January 11, 1974.
69. Personal interview with R. L. Bliss, March 15, 1974. For further reaffirmations of the AFC position and criticisms of World War II by former noninterventionists, see personal interview with Page Hufty (telephone), March 3, 1974; William Henry Chamberlin, *America's Second Crusade* (Chicago: Henry Regnery, 1950), pp. 337–39.
70. Three of the most militant of the early postwar studies were: Walter Johnson, *The Battle Against Isolation* (Chicago: University of Chicago Press, 1944), p. 234; Selig Adler, *The Isolationist Impulse* (New York: Abelard-Schuman, 1957), pp. 280, 393; Thomas Bailey, *The Man in the Street* (New York: Macmillan Press, 1948), p. 13.
71. Bruce M. Russet, *No Clear and Present Danger: A Skeptical View of the United States Entry into WWII* (New York: Harper & Row, 1972), pp. 19–21. For a viewpoint similar to that of Russet, see Robert Tucker, *A New Isolationism: Threat or Promise?* (New York: Universe Books, 1972), pp. 11–13. For some earlier, preliminary challenges to the strongly interventionist histories of American involvement in World War II, see Charles A. Beard, *President Roosevelt and the Coming of the War, 1941: A Study in Appearances and Reality* (New Haven: Yale University Press, 1948); Charles C. Tansill, *Back Door to War: The Roosevelt Foreign Policy, 1933–41* (Chicago: Henry Regnery, 1952); Albert Coady Wedemeyer, *Wedemeyer Reports!* (New York: Devin-Adair, 1958); Paul Shroeder, *The Axis Alliance and Japanese-American Relations, 1941* (Ithaca, N.Y.: Cornell University Press, 1958), pp. 177–78, 215; William Appleman Williams, *The Tragedy of American Diplomacy* (Cleveland: World, 1959), pp. 183–84; Lloyd Gardner, *Economic Aspects of New Deal Diplomacy* (Madison: University of Wisconsin Press, 1964); Manfred Jonas, *Isolationism* (Ithaca, N.Y.: Cornell University Press, 1966); Otis Graham, *An Encore for Reform* (New York: Oxford University Press, 1967); Gabriel Kolko, *The Politics of War* (New York: Random House, 1968); Noam Chomsky, *American Power and the New Mandarins* (New York: Pantheon Books, 1969); Basil Henry Liddell Hart, *A History of the Second World War* (New York: Putnam, 1971). Even James M. Burns, Roosevelt's rather

sympathetic biographer, stated in 1970 that the President's 1940–45 rhetoric and expedential diplomacy led to skepticism within the United States and "sowed the seeds of the Cold War" (*Roosevelt, Soldier of Freedom* [New York: Harcourt Brace Jovanovich, 1970], p. 609).

72. Sarles, "A Story of America First," pp. 9–10.
73. Charles W. Tobey, "Wake Up, America! The Hour Is Late," *Vital Speeches*, 7, October 1, 1941, pp. 748–51.

Bibliography

I. Primary Sources

A. Manuscripts and Manuscript Collections

America First Committee Papers (Hoover Institution on War, Revolution and Peace, Stanford, Calif.).

Flynn, John Thomas Papers (University of Oregon Library, Eugene, Oreg.).

Pinchot, Amos Richards Eno Papers (Library of Congress, Washington, D.C.).

Sarles, Ruth, "A Story of America First" (unpublished manuscript, Hoover Institution on War, Revolution and Peace, Stanford, Calif., 1942).

Thomas, Norman Mattoon Papers (New York City Public Library, New York).

B. Personal Correspondence

Benton, William, to Ketchum, Richard (personal files of Robert L. Bliss, New York City), October 1972.

Bliss, Robert L., to the author, January 31, 1974, and April 25, 1974.

Cole, Wayne S., to the author, March 9, 1973.

Cusick, Peter, to the author, November 1973.

Doenecke, Justus D., to the author, September 24, 1973.

Fish, Hamilton, Jr., to the author, August 21, 1974.

Flynn, Thomas D., to the author, June 28, 1972, and March 14, 1973.

Gordon, Rosalie M., to the author, April 11, 1973, and September 13, 1974.

Stuart, Robert D., Jr., to the author, March 23, 1974, and January 11, 1974, and April 23, 1974.

Swim, Katherine, to the author, March 10, 1974.

Trohan, Walter, to the author, March 24, 1973.

Wheeler, Burton K., to the author, March 9, 1973.

C. Personal Interviews

Bliss, Robert L., New York City, March 15, 1974.
Flynn, Thomas D., New York City, April 25, 1973.
Gordon, Rosalie M., New York City, April 23, 1973.
Hufty, Page, by telephone from Palm Beach, Florida, March 3, 1974.
Stuart, Robert D., Chicago, August 14, 1973.

D. Published Writings of John T. Flynn

Books:

Investment Trusts Gone Wrong (New York: New Republic, Inc., 1930).
Graft in Business (New York: Vanguard Press, 1931).
God's Gold: Story of Rockefeller and His Times (New York: Harcourt, Brace & Co., 1932).
Country Squire in the White House (New York: Doubleday, Doran & Co., 1940).
Men of Wealth (New York: Simon & Schuster, 1941).
As We Go Marching (New York: Doubleday, Doran & Co., 1944).
Meet Your Congress (New York: Doubleday, Doran & Co., 1944).
The Epic of Freedom (Philadelphia: Fireside Press, 1947).
The Roosevelt Myth (New York: Devin-Adair, 1948; rev. ed., 1956).
The Road Ahead (New York: Devin-Adair, 1949).
While You Slept: Our Tragedy in Asia and Who Made It (New York: Devin-Adair, 1951).
The Lattimore Story (New York: Devin-Adair, 1953).
The Decline of the American Republic and How to Rebuild It (New York: Devin-Adair, 1955).

Articles:

"Why Liberal Party?" *Forum and Century* 87 (March 1932): 158–63.
"Inside the RFC," *Harper's* magazine, January 1933, pp. 161–69.
"Other People's Money," *New Republic,* May 10, 1933–November 4, 1940.
"American Revolution: 1933," *Scribner's Commentator,* July 1933, pp. 1–6.
"An Approach to the Problem of War Finance," *Annals of the American Academy of Political and Social Science* 186 (January 1936): 217–22.
"The Social Security Reserve Swindle," *Harper's* magazine, February 1939, pp. 238–48.
"Mr. Hopkins and Mr. Roosevelt," *Yale Review* 28, no. 4 (June 1939): 667–79.
"President's Demand for More Funds for National Defense Merely Confuses Budget Issue," *Congressional Digest* 19 (January 1940): 32.
"Can Hitler Beat American Business?" *Harper's* magazine, February 1940, pp. 321–28.
"New Deal Spending Policies," *Congressional Digest* 19 (February 1940): 48–53.

"Coming: A Totalitarian America," *American Mercury* 52 (February 1941): 156–57.

"Mr. Flynn Speaks for Himself," *New Republic*, February 3, 1941, pp. 148–49.

"Can Hitler Invade America?" *Reader's Digest*, April 1941, pp. 1–6.

"Radio: Intervention's Trump," *Scribner's Commentator*, April 1941, pp. 45–49.

"Nazi Economy a Threat?" *Scribner's Commentator*, August 1941, pp. 19–26.

"That Post-War Federal Debt," *Harper's* magazine, July 1942, pp. 183–88.

"Detroit's Fighting Milkman," *Reader's Digest*, September 1942, pp. 57–60.

"Cost-Plus and Red Tape Hamper War Production," *Reader's Digest*, October 1942, pp. 108–11.

E. Books (by other than John T. Flynn)

Arnold, Henry H., *Global Missions* (New York: Harper & Brothers, 1949).

Barnes, Harry E., *Genesis of the World War* (New York: Alfred A. Knopf, 1926).

Bowles, Chester, *Promises to Keep: My Years in Public Life, 1941–69* (New York: Harper & Row, 1971).

Carlson, John Roy (in reality Avedis Derounian), *The Plotters* (New York: E. P. Dutton & Co., 1946).

—— (Avedis Derounian), *UnderCover* (New York: E. P. Dutton & Co., 1943).

Churchill, Winston S., *The Grand Alliance* (Boston: Houghton Mifflin Co., 1950).

Frank, Jerome N., *Save America First: How to Make Democracy Work* (New York: Harper & Brothers, 1938).

Gibbs, Philip H., *Now It Can Be Told* (Garden City, N.Y.: Garden City Press, 1920).

Hyde, H. Montgomery, *Room 3603: The Story of the British Intelligence Center in New York During WWII* (New York: Farrar & Straus, 1962).

Lewis, Sinclair, *It Can't Happen Here* (Garden City, N.Y.: Doubleday, Doran & Co., 1935).

Libby, Frederick J., *To End War: The Story of the National Council for Prevention of War* (Nyack, N.Y.: Fellowship Publications, 1969).

Lindbergh, Charles A., *The Wartime Journals of Charles A. Lindbergh* (New York: Harcourt Brace Jovanovich, 1970).

Miller, Douglas, *You Can't Do Business with Hitler* (Boston: Little, Brown & Co., 1941).

Pinchot, Amos R. E., *History of the Progressive Party, 1912–1916* (New York: New York University Press, 1958).

Record, George L., *How to Abolish Poverty* (Jersey City: George L. Record Memorial Association, 1936).

Rogerson, Sidney, and Liddell Hart, B. H. *Propaganda in the Next War* (New York: Garland Publishing Co., 1938).

Roosevelt, Elliott, ed., *F.D.R., His Personal Letters, 1928–1945* (New York: Duell, Sloane & Pearce, 1950), vol. 2.

Sayers, Michael, and Kahn, Albert, *Sabotage! The Secret War Against America* (New York: Harper & Brothers, 1941).

Schoonmaker, Nancy, and Reid, Doris F., *We Testify* (New York: Smith & Durrell, 1941).

Stimson, Henry L., and Bundy, McGeorge, *On Active Service in Peace and War* (New York: Harper & Row, 1948).

Swing, Raymond Gram, *Forerunners of American Fascism* (New York: Julian Messner, 1935).

Wedemeyer, Albert C., *Wedemeyer Reports!* (New York: Devin-Adair, 1958).

Wheeler, Burton K., *Yankee from the West* (Garden City, N.Y.: Doubleday & Co., 1962).

F.   Articles (by other than John T. Flynn)

"America First Roughhouse," *Life,* October 20, 1941, p. 41.

Bagley, C. R., "War and the Socialists," *New Republic,* September 29, 1941, pp. 407–8.

Barton, Bruce, "How to Write Your Congressman," *Reader's Digest,* September 1940, pp. 87–90.

Bowles, Chester, "What's Wrong with the Isolationists by a Non-Interventionist," *Common Sense,* December 1941, pp. 374–77.

Brewster, Ralph Owen, "Let's Not Be Suckers Again," *American* magazine, January 1945, pp. 24–25, 96–98.

Cain, James M., "Do Writers Need an AAA?" *Saturday Review of Literature,* November 16, 1946, p. 9.

Carlson, John Roy (Avedis Derounian), "Inside the America First Movement," *American Mercury* 54 (January 1942): 7–25.

"Censorship in the Offing," *Time,* February 17, 1941, pp. 52–57.

"Crash Landing," *Newsweek,* February 23, 1942, pp. 28–29.

"Editorial," *New Republic,* September 9, 1940, p. 335, and October 21, 1940, p. 541.

"Editor's Note," *New Republic,* August 5, 1940, p. 188, and November 11, 1940, p. 660, and November 18, 1940, p. 677.

Grafton, Samuel, "The Appeasement Tropism," *New Republic,* January 6, 1941, p. 18.

Graves, Harold N., Jr., "Propaganda by Short-Wave: London Calling America," *Public Opinion Quarterly* 5, no. 1 (March 1941): 38–51.

Kramer, Dale, "Verne Marshall of Iowa," *New Republic,* January 13, 1941, pp. 50–51.

Lindbergh, Charles A., "Impregnable America," *Scribner's Commentator,* January 1941, pp. 3–6.

———, "Letter to Americans," *Collier's,* March 29, 1941, pp. 14–15.

———, "Lindbergh for the Record," *Scribner's Commentator,* August 1941, pp. 8–13.

———, "Time Lies with Us," *Scribner's Commentator,* November 1941, pp. 88–93.

McKenzie, Vernon, "Treatment of War Themes in Magazine Fiction," *Public Opinion Quarterly* 5, no. 2: 227–32.

Masland, John W., "Pressure Groups and American Foreign Policy," *Public Opinion Quarterly* 6, no. 1 (spring 1942): 113–22.

Mellett, Lowell, "Government Propaganda," *Atlantic Monthly ,* September 1941, pp. 311–13.

"Mr. Flynn and the New Republic," *New Republic,* December 9, 1940, pp. 792–94.

Pinchot, Amos R. E., "The American Liberal and His Program," *Churchman,* April 1, 1933, p. 14.

———, "To the President; Poem," *Scribner's Commentator,* July 1941, p. 6.

———, "Roosevelt-Laski Scheme," *Scribner's Commentator,* October 1941, pp. 62–68.

"Portrait," *Saturday Review of Literature,* May 31, 1941, p. 6.

Thomas, Norman, "How to Fight for Democracy," *Annals of the American Academy* 216 (July 1941): 58–64.

———, "Lindbergh Speech," *Commonweal,* October 10, 1941, p. 509.

"Trial of Laura Ingalls," *Nation,* February 21, 1941, p. 206.

Twohey, James S., "An Analysis of Newspaper Opinion and War Issues," *Public Opinion Quarterly* 5, no. 3 (fall 1941): 448–55.

Villard, Oswald G., "Valedictory," *Nation,* June 29, 1940, p. 782.

Waples, Douglas, "Press, Radio and Film in the National Emergency," *Public Opinion Quarterly* 5, no. 3 (fall 1941): 463–69.

G. Speeches (by other than John T. Flynn—Flynn's speeches are found in the Flynn Papers, University of Oregon Library)

Fish, Hamilton, "We Should Not Convoy Materials to Europe," *Vital Speeches,* 7, April 15, 1941, pp. 414–15.

Hoover, Herbert C., "Problems That Confront Us," *Vital Speeches,* 7, January 1, 1941, pp. 181–83.

———, "Question of Peace," *Vital Speeches,* 7, April 15, 1941, pp. 405–8.

———, "We Are Not Prepared for War," *Vital Speeches,* 7, May 15, 1941, pp. 457–60.

———, "Call to Reason," *Vital Speeches,* 7, July 15, 1941, pp. 580–84.

———, "Shall We Send Armies to Europe?" *Vital Speeches,* 8, December 1, 1941, pp. 117–20.

La Follette, Philip F., "The Doctrine of Fear," *Vital Speeches,* 7, February 15, 1941, pp. 264–65.

Lindbergh, Charles A., "Our Air Defense," *Vital Speeches,* 7, February 1, 1941, pp. 241–42.

———, "We Are Not Prepared for War," *Vital Speeches,* 7, February 15, 1941, pp. 266–67.

———, "We Cannot Win This War for England," *Vital Speeches,* 7, May 1, 1941, pp. 424–26.

———, "Election Promises Should Be Kept," *Vital Speeches,* 7, June 1, 1941, pp. 482–83.

MacCracken, Henry N., "An Examination of the Eight Points," *Vital Speeches,* 7, September 1, 1941, pp. 679–80.

Nye, Gerald, "War Propaganda," *Vital Speeches,* 7, September 15, 1941, pp. 720–23.

Reisner, Edward H., "The Case Against Intervention," *Vital Speeches,* 7, August 15, 1941, p. 655.

Thomas, Norman M., "War on Hitler," *Vital Speeches,* 7, July 1, 1941, pp. 561–62.

———, "Is the Extension of the Draft Necessary?" *Vital Speeches,* 7, August 15, 1941, pp. 671–72.

Tobey, Charles W., "Wake Up, America! The Hour Is Late," *Vital Speeches,* 7, October 1, 1941, pp. 748–51.

Villard, Oswald G., "Behind the Scenes in Fighting Europe," *Vital Speeches,* 7, March 1, 1941, pp. 357–58.

Wheeler, Burton K., "The American People Want No War," *Vital Speeches,* 7, June 1, 1941, p. 489.

H. Government Documents

U.S., *Congressional Record,* 76th Cong., 3rd sess. (1940), LXXXVI, and 77th Cong., 1st sess. (1941), LXXXVII.

U.S., Congress, House, Committee on Foreign Affairs, *Further to Promote Defense of the United States,* Hearings, 77th Cong., 1st sess., January 15–29, 1941 (Washington: Government Printing Office, 1941).

U.S., Congress, Senate, Committee on Foreign Relations, *Further to Promote Defense of the United States,* Hearings, 77th Cong., 1st sess., January 27–February 11, 1941 (Washington: Government Printing Office, 1941).

U.S., Congress, House, Committee on Military Affairs, *Providing for National Defense by Removing Restrictions on Numbers and Length of Service of Draftees,* Hearings, 77th Cong., 1st sess., July 15, 1941 (Washington: Government Printing Office, 1941).

U.S., Congress, Senate, Committee on Military Affairs, *Reserve and Selective Service Extension Beyond Twelve Months,* Hearings, 77th Cong., 1st sess., July 17–24, 1941 (Washington: Government Printing Office, 1941).

U.S., Congress, House, Committee on Foreign Affairs, *Arming Merchant Vessels,* Hearings, 77th Cong., 1st sess., October 13–14, 1941 (Washington: Government Printing Office, 1941).

U.S., Congress, Senate, Committee on Foreign Relations, *Modification of the Neutrality Act of 1939*, Hearings, 77th Cong., 1st sess., October 21–24, 1941 (Washington: Government Printing Office, 1941).

U.S., Congress, Senate, Committee on Foreign Relations, *United Nations Charter*, Hearings, 79th Cong., 1st sess., July 9–13, 1945 (Washington: Government Printing Office, 1945).

I. Newspapers

New York Herald-Tribune, 1940–41.

New York Journal-American, July 26, 1946.

New York Times, October 3, 1940–December 10, 1941, and April 14, 1964.

New York World-Telegram, Flynn, John T., "Plain Economics," 1940–41.

J. Polls

"Gallup and Fortune Polls," *Public Opinion Quarterly* 5, no. 1 (March 1941): 148–51, 155–64; no. 2 (summer 1941): 315–16, 317–34; no. 3 (fall 1941): 472, 475–97; no. 4 (winter 1941): 666–87; and 6, no. 1 (spring 1942): 142–74.

II. Secondary Sources

A. Unpublished Manuscripts

Bartimo, Kathryn D., "American Opinion Toward the European War" (doctor's dissertation, Clark University, 1941).

Bell, Leland V., "Anatomy of a Hate Movement: The German-American Bund, 1936–41" (doctor's dissertation, West Virginia University, 1968).

Fleischer, Lowell R., "Charles A. Lindbergh and Isolationism, 1939–41" (doctor's dissertation, University of Connecticut, 1963).

Frey, Richard C., Jr., "John T. Flynn and the United States in Crisis, 1928–50" (doctor's dissertation, University of Oregon, 1969).

Stafford, Bart L., III, "The Emergence of Anti-Semitism in the America First Committee, 1940–41" (master's thesis, New School for Social Research, 1948).

Stanley, Morris B., "The America First Committee: A Study in Recent American Non-Interventionism" (master's thesis, Emory University, 1942).

B. Books

Adler, Selig, *The Isolationist Impulse* (New York: Abelard-Schuman, 1957).

Bailey, Thomas, *The Man in the Street* (New York: Macmillan Press, 1948).

Bell, Leland V., *In Hitler's Shadow* (Port Washington, N.Y.: Kennikat Press, 1973).

Burns, James M., *Roosevelt, Soldier of Freedom* (New York: Harcourt Brace Jovanovich, 1970).

Chadwin, Mark L., *The Warhawks* (Chapel Hill: University of North Carolina Press, 1968).

Chamberlin, William H., *America's Second Crusade* (Chicago: Henry Regnery, 1950).

Chomsky, Noam, *American Power and the New Mandarins* (New York: Pantheon Books, 1969).

Cole, Wayne S., *America First: The Battle Against Intervention 1940–41* (Madison: University of Wisconsin Press, 1953).

————, *An Interpretive History of American Foreign Relations* (Homewood, Ill.: Dorsey Press, 1968).

————, *Charles A. Lindbergh and the Battle Against American Intervention in World War II* (New York: Harcourt Brace Jovanovich, 1974).

Gardner, Lloyd, *Economic Aspects of New Deal Diplomacy* (Madison: University of Wisconsin Press, 1964).

Graham, Otis, *An Encore for Reform* (New York: Oxford University Press, 1967).

Johnpoll, Bernard K., *Pacifist's Progress: Norman Thomas and the Decline of American Socialism* (Chicago: Quadrangle Books, 1970).

Johnson, Walter, *The Battle Against Isolationism* (Chicago: University of Chicago Press, 1944).

Jonas, Manfred, *Isolationism* (Ithaca, N.Y.: Cornell University Press, 1966).

Kolko, Gabriel, *The Politics of War* (New York: Random House, 1968).

Langer, William, and Gleason, S. Everett, *The Undeclared War, 1940–41* (New York: Harper & Brothers, 1953).

Liddell Hart, Basil H., *A History of the Second World War* (New York: G. P. Putnam's Sons 1971).

Marquis, A. N., ed., *Who's Who in America, 1942–43* (Chicago: A. N. Marquis Co., 1943), pp. 170, 365, 1358, 1438, 1452, 2292, 2390, 2423.

Martin, James J., *American Liberalism and World Politics, 1931–41* (New York: Devin-Adair, 1964).

Russet, Bruce M., *No Clear and Present Danger: A Skeptical View of the United States Entry into WWII* (New York: Harper & Row, 1972).

Schlesinger, Arthur M., Jr., *The Imperial Presidency* (Boston: Houghton Mifflin Co., 1973).

Schroeder, Paul, *The Axis Alliance and Japanese-American Relations, 1941* (Ithaca, N.Y.: Cornell University Press, 1958).

Smith, Geoffrey, *To Save a Nation: American Countersubversives, the New Deal, and the Coming of WWII* (New York: Basic Books, 1973).

Tucker, Robert, *A New Isolationism: Threat or Promise?* (New York: Universe Books, 1972).

Who Was Who in America (Chicago: Marquis—Who's Who, Inc., 1968), IV, 1961–68, p. 319.

Williams, William A., *The Tragedy of American Diplomacy* (Cleveland: World, 1959).

C. Articles

Cole, Wayne S., "America First and the South, 1940–41," *Journal of Southern History* 44 (1956): 36–47.

———, "A Tale of Two Isolationists—Told Three Wars Later," *Newsletter, Society for Historians of American Foreign Relations,* 5, no. 1, March 1974, pp. 2–14.

Doenecke, Justus D., "Verne Marshall's Leadership of the No Foreign War Committee," *Annals of Iowa* 40 (winter 1973): 1153–72.

Polenberg, Richard, "The National Committee to Uphold Constitutional Government," *Journal of American History* 52 (1965): 582–98.

INDEX

Acheson, Dean, 29

Adams, Samuel Hopkins, 17, 51

AEF. *See* American Expeditionary Force

AFC. *See* America First Committee

AFC Bulletin, 60, 94, 114

Africa, 37, 89, 100

Aid-Allies Committee. *See* Committee to Defend America by Aiding the Allies

Aid Short of War, 17, 73, 75-76, 161

Allied Powers, 20, 90, 119, 156, 173

Allies. *See* Allied Powers

America First Committee, 9-10, 14, 26, 38, 40, 49-54, 57, 59-60, 63-64; composition and character, 15-16; principles and program, 17-23, 34; finances, 55-56, 122, 125-127, 134-135; in Lend-Lease struggle, 65-72; immediate post-Lend-Lease activities, 73-75, 79; rallies, 76, 87; public opinion polls, 78-79; in convoy struggle, 82-88; on Hitler's invasion of Russia, 90-91; on Draft Extension struggle, 93; on Atlantic Charter, 96; political involvement, 99, 110-112, 119; on shoot-on-sight order, 100-101; on Neutrality repeal, 103-104; immediate post-Neutrality repeal sentiments, 108, 110, 112; on Pearl Harbor attack and Japan, 113-116, 119; decision to disband, 99, 117-120, 140; re anti-Semitism and profascism, 121-138, 140-141, 158, 163, 165, 168; re Des Moines speech, 136-138, 150, 158; re conspiracy theory, 143, 146-147; in motion picture investigation, 149, 152; re press, 157; military service records of leaders, 174-176; historical perspective on, 116, 118, 165-166, 174, 176-178

America First Committee Papers, 11, 119

American Destiny Party. *See* Joseph McWilliams

American Expeditionary Force, 71, 75, 93, 103, 108

Anti-Defamation League, 170

Anti-Semitism, 19, 42, 150, 158-159; in AFC and NYC-AFC, 10, 11, 57-58, 120-141, 160

243

Arnold, Henry H., 175
Atlantic Charter, 96-97
Axis Powers, 66, 87, 119, 174. *See also* Germany; Italy; Japan

Barnes, Harry Elmer, 37, 54; *The Genesis of the World War,* 144
Barton, Bruce, 42, 62
Beard, Charles A., 54, 67
Benton, William, 15, 56, 72, 124, 133-134
Bliss, Robert L., 11, 26, 44, 56-58, 97, 123, 139, 175-177
Boldt, Joseph, 56-57, 63, 67, 72-73, 107-108, 123-124, 138, 174
Bone, Homer, 32
Bowles, Chester, 17, 41-42, 53-54, 60, 76, 104, 111, 118, 138, 145-146, 158
Brewster, Kingman, Jr., 16
Britain. *See* England
British. *See* England
Bromley, Dorothy Dunbar, 69, 130, 136
Bund. *See* German-American Bund
Burke-Wadsworth Act, 33, 92
Businessmen, 51, 109-110; on AFC and NYC-AFC, 14, 16, 26, 40-45; interest in war, 32-33

Carlson, John Roy, 126, 165, 168-170
CDAAA. *See* Committee to Defend America By Aiding the Allies
Chaplin, Charlie, 148, 150-151
Chase, Stuart, 54
Chicago Tribune, 61, 78
Christian Front, 122-124, 129-131, 138; *Social Justice,* 129-130
Churchill, Sir Winston, 65, 69, 96, 125, 144-145
Civil Liberties, 17, 34, 38, 48, 52, 60, 66, 88, 90-91, 116-119, 128,

159-160, 164, 168, 175, 178
Clark, Bennett Champ, 105, 149
Clark, D. Worth, 105, 149
Cole, Wayne S.: *America First: The Battle Against Interventionism, 1940-41,* 9; "America First and the South, 1940-41," 11
Committee to Defend America By Aiding the Allies, 13, 39, 83, 125-127, 131, 145, 147, 161-162
Communism, 17, 23, 49, 54, 59-60, 90-91, 122, 125-126, 130, 170, 172-173, 175
Communists. *See* Communism
Congress, 17-18, 27-28, 30, 32, 53-54, 62, 67-68, 70, 75, 82-83, 92-96, 101, 104-107, 110-112, 116-117, 149-151, 166, 168-170, 174, 179; *Congressional Record,* 11
Conservatism, 14-16, 22-23, 32-34, 41, 47, 50-51, 54, 58, 109, 125, 135, 170, 173
Conservatives. *See* Conservatism
Convoys, 71, 77-79, 81-89, 97, 105, 126, 145, 162
Coughlin, Charles. *See* Christian Front
Council for Democracy, 36
Cudahy, John, 105
Cusick, Peter, 11

Democratic Party, 14, 42, 53, 59, 95-96, 103, 106-107, 170
Democrats. *See* Democratic Party
Derounian, Avedis. *See* Carlson, John Roy
Des Moines Speech, 58, 135-141, 150, 157-158
Destroyers-for-Bases Agreement, 33, 38, 115
Dewey, John, 128-129
Dewey, Thomas E., 170-171
Dies, Martin, 170

244

247

248

111, 170-172, 174; others' views of, 22, 37; Quarantine speech, 31; Charlottesville speech, 33; re Lend-Lease, 65, 67, 69-70; March 1941 speeches, 73, 75; peace pledges, 74-75; re convoys, 81-89; May 27, 1941 speech, 87; extension of Lend-Lease aid to Russia, 81, 89, 91, 97; re Red Sea, 91-92; re Draft Extension, 93; re Atlantic Charter, 96; August 21, 1941 speech, 97; shoot-on-sight order, 99, 103; re ship sinkings, 100-103; re Neutrality repeal, 103; measures against Japan, 113-114, 117; re Pearl Harbor attack, 115-116; alleged involvement in prowar propaganda, 143-145, 147, 151, 164; re motion picture investigation, 150; re John T. Flynn, 160; cooperation with interventionist groups, 161-162; globalism, 165, 167-169, 171, 173-174; re Charles A. Lindbergh, 61-62, 85, 175-176

Roosevelt, Theodore, 48, 51

Roosevelt, Theodore, Jr., 51, 175

Russia. *See* Union of Soviet Socialist Republics

Russians. *See* Union of Soviet Socialist Republics

Sabotage! The Secret War Against America: Kahn, Albert, and Sayers, Michael, 168

Sarles, Ruth, 23, 55, 71, 78, 86, 101, 107, 116, 123-124, 133, 154, 177-178; "A Story of America First," 11

Sarnoff, David, 153

Saturday Evening Post, The, 156

Schnibbe, Harry, 39, 42, 51, 121

Scribner's Commentator, 42, 159-160

Sessa. *See* Ship Sinkings

Ship Sinkings, 99-103, 108, 119

Shoot-on-Sight order, 99, 119

Sikorsky, Igor, 90-91

Smythe, Edward James, 122, 124

Socialism, 22, 130, 132-133, 136, 146, 173. *See also* Thomas, Norman M.

Socialists. *See* Socialism

Stafford, Bart L., III: "The Emergence of Anti-Semitism in the America First Committee, 1940-41," 11

Stalin, Joseph, 54, 90-91, 108, 130, 132, 173

Stanley, Morris Burns: "The America First Committee: A Study In Recent American Non-Interventionism," 11

Steel Seafarer. See Ship Sinkings

Stephenson, William, 163-164

Stimson, Henry, 33, 59, 65-66, 85-86, 89, 93, 104, 115, 175

Strange, Michael, 96

Stuart, Robert Douglas, Jr., 11, 13-15, 17, 19, 26, 39-43, 52, 58, 70, 74, 76, 85, 90, 101, 104, 112, 117, 124-125, 137, 140, 146, 155, 158, 175-176

Subversion. *See* Profascism

Subversives. *See* Profascism

Swim, H. Dudley, 11, 42-43, 47, 50-51, 60, 108, 118, 139-141

Swim, Mrs. Katharine, 11

Swing, Raymond Gram: *Forerunners of American Fascism,* 35

Taft, Robert A., 14, 55

That Hamilton Woman. See Motion Picture Industry

The Great Dictator. See Motion Picture Industry

The Nation. See Nation, The

The New Republic. See New Republic, The

249